MASTER~~~~

D0533336

BB 029872 01

NEWBURY COLLEGE LIBRARY

This book is due for return on or before the last date shown below.

WITHDRAWN

NEWBURY COLLEGE LRC

BR 2987201 659.2

Palgrave Master Series

Accounting
Accounting Skills
Advanced English Language
Advanced Pure Mathematics
Arabic
Basic Management
Biology
British Politics
Business Communication
Business Environment
C Programming
C++ Programming
Chemistry
COBOL Programming
Communication
Computing
Counselling Skills
Counselling Theory
Customer Relations
Database Design
Delphi Programming
Desktop Publishing
e-Business
Economic and Social History
Economics
Electrical Engineering
Electronics
Employee Development
English Grammar
English Language
English Literature
Fashion Buying and Merchandising
  Management
Fashion Marketing
Fashion Styling
Financial Management
Geography
Global Information Systems
Globalization of Business

Human Resource Management
International Trade
Internet
Java
Language of Literature
Management Skills
Marketing Management
Mathematics
Microsoft Office
Microsoft Windows, Novell
  NetWare and UNIX
Modern British History
Modern European History
Modern German History
Modern United States History
Modern World History
The Novels of Jane Austen
Organisational Behaviour
Pascal and Delphi Programming
Personal Finance
Philosophy
Physics
Poetry
Practical Criticism
Psychology
Public Relations
Shakespeare
Social Welfare
Sociology
Statistics
Strategic Management
Systems Analysis and Design
Team Leadership
Theology
Twentieth-Century Russian History
Visual Basic
World Religions

www.palgravemasterseries.com

Palgrave Master Series
Series Standing Order ISBN 0–333–69343–4
(outside North America only)

You can receive future titles in this series as they are published by placing a standing order. Please contact your bookseller or, in case of difficulty, write to us at the address below with your name and address, the title of the series and the ISBN quoted above.

Customer Services Department, Macmillan Distribution Ltd
Houndmills, Basingstoke, Hampshire RG21 6XS, England

MASTERING

public relations

second edition

anthony davis

business series editor
richard pettinger

palgrave
macmillan

*BB 02987201
6592

© Anthony Davis 2004, 2007

All rights reserved. No reproduction, copy or transmission of this publication may be made without written permission.

No paragraph of this publication may be reproduced, copied or transmitted save with written permission or in accordance with the provisions of the Copyright, Designs and Patents Act 1988, or under the terms of any licence permitting limited copying issued by the Copyright Licensing Agency, 90 Tottenham Court Road, London W1T 4LP.

Any person who does any unauthorized act in relation to this publication may be liable to criminal prosecution and civil claims for damages.

The author has asserted his right to be identified as the author of this work in accordance with the Copyright, Designs and Patents Act 1988.

First edition 2004
Second edition 2007

Published by
PALGRAVE MACMILLAN
Houndmills, Basingstoke, Hampshire RG21 6XS and
175 Fifth Avenue, New York, N.Y. 10010
Companies and representatives throughout the world

PALGRAVE MACMILLAN is the global academic imprint of the Palgrave Macmillan division of St. Martin's Press, LLC and of Palgrave Publishers Ltd. Macmillan® is a registered trademark in the United States, United Kingdom and other countries. Palgrave is a registered trademark in the European Union and other countries.

ISBN-13: 978-0-230-54930-2
ISBN-10: 0-230-54930-6

The book is printed on paper suitable for recycling and made from fully managed and sustained forest sources. Logging, pulping and manufacturing processes are expected to conform to the environmental regulations of the country of origin.

A catalogue record for this book is available from the British Library.

10   9   8   7   6   5   4   3
16   15   14   13   12   11

Printed and bound in Great Britain by
CPI Antony Rowe, Chippenham, Wiltshire

to Wendy Curme
for her constructive criticism
and unfailing encouragement

contents

preface to the first edition

Why is it that everyone 'knows' about public relations? That *really* anyone can 'do it', when they have the time, that is. That public relations is just PR, and everyone knows what *that* means. As in 'a PR exercise' or 'just another PR job'. And everyone *knows* there is precious little science to it, if truth were told. Which, to mention it, is not much used, as everyone also knows, when it comes to public relations. But amidst such knowing, just how much is *really* known about public relations?

Why, in short, is the management occupation that claims guardianship of corporate reputation itself held in such universally low regard, why do its detractors expend so much effort on denigrating it and why has it become an all-pervasive and invasive enigma, referred to daily by countless millions of people around the globe? And why, most significantly, do so many young people aspire to a career in it? Why is it growing exponentially, in every walk of life?

Most books about public relations tell you, often in monotonous detail, how to do it. The rest are mainly dense academic texts, explaining public relations in terms of a multiplicity of other disciplines. *Mastering Public Relations* steers a course through the middle, with a combination of theory and practice interpretation set in a 'real world' context.

There is no hidden agenda here, whether to work out some intellectual frustration over the vapidity of much published material or a determination to distil the subject into a collection of tips and neat rules for practice made perfect. The sole aim is to provide a balanced, wide-ranging introduction to a very large subject indeed, help position it in management terms and broadly sketch its potential future development.

Books on the subject also tend to divide another way: towards euphoric endorsement of public relations in all its practice guises or relentless outright condemnation for everything done in its name. Both postures are absurd and unsustainable, but subjects that provoke such intense interest can have that effect. Here every effort is made to maintain a balanced view about the nature and purpose of public relations. That entails looking outside the loop as well as within it, at the views of its detractors and rivals, abusers and dissemblers, as well as at the observations and conclusions of its users, employers, practitioners, researchers and informed commentators.

Not that public relations practitioners are blameless in acquiring their collective reputation. Some undoubtedly have done, and continue to do, more than their bit. Perhaps the rest should have spent greater time responding, instead of being in denial or in passive acceptance of what few other occupational groups would, or could, willingly tolerate. While it is the *shallows* of practice that are exposed to the daily sunlight, because that supposedly makes 'good copy', in reality public relations also has its *depths*, wherein are found intellectual vigour and a formidable battery of communication skills. And those depths, for whoever cares to consider them, are the source of much that is most interesting and stimulating about public relations.

ANTHONY DAVIS

preface to the second edition

The practice of public relations continues to evolve, as it becomes more widely undertaken around the world, by not only professional practitioners but also many other people, whether as part of their employment, because their responsibilities include an element of public relations, or voluntarily, maybe to further a political or social cause, generate interest in an ethical or moral issue, advance a career, raise a cheer or cause a stir.

And as it evolves, public relations gathers intellectual explanations as to what *exactly* it is and *ideally* might become. From its early origins in America and Europe, public relations practice, often passing under a variety of alternative names, many chosen to reflect local social origins and customs, is busily taking root throughout all Europe, in many parts of Asia, in Russia and in South America, fanned there and beyond by the fierce winds of change driven by globalization, industrialization, democratization and, by no means least, communication and transport advances.

Communication, in all its dimensions, is central to modern life, and those who are expert at it have the possibility of playing a very substantial part in how humankind progresses from here, *provided* they can successfully weave their way through all the nuances of sociocultural and ethnic differences and fully contextualize their practice *locally*, so that it may optimize its benefits and fulfil realistic expectations.

While those who communicate for a living on behalf of organizations rightly aspire to being part of a senior management discipline, they should remain wary of discarding, in pursuit of such sobriety, their noted creative ability to enliven the mundane, divert from boredom and communicate entertainingly. That is what ensures public relations its remarkable character. Meanwhile, this second edition maintains *its* balanced approach; it develops the history narrative, includes more public relations-specific theory, now both American and European, and extends the recurrent international and ethical themes.

ANTHONY DAVIS

acknowledgements

Many thanks are due to the kind people who have so generously assisted me in sourcing material for this book and in giving their advice and comments. In connection with the case studies, I am indebted to:

Charles Todd at Carlisle Process Systems
Mark Brooks and Wendy Franklin at National Savings & Investments
Sue Hyde at Dorset County Council
Richard Anderson at Puddings & Pies
Emma Jane Taylor at Aerosystems International
Barney Holbeche at the National Farmers' Union
Clare Winterton and Emma Melville-Ross at the Prince's Trust
James Lawrence at Action for Blind People.

In addition, I also much appreciate the assistance of:

- Lindsay Mason at Lindsay Mason Public Relations, for allowing me to draw on her 2002 research into use of e-mail in public relations, undertaken for her PR masters dissertation at Stirling University
- Helen Sullivan at Shell International, for providing much information about her company's worldwide activities and UK research on sustainable development, published in 2002 ahead of the UN World Summit on Sustainable Development
- Charles Stewart-Hunt at Romeike Media Intelligence, for his overview of the current size and disposition of the European media.

Many thanks also to all those other people, too numerous to mention, who have shown such interest and support in this project to capture and distil the essence of a subject that is so huge, so relentlessly topical and of such great and widespread fascination.

introduction

Public relations is a very broad subject for study and trying to capture it succinctly can be formidable. It has several dimensions and many implications, its intellectual content being derived from a substantial number of sources and its practitioners, collectively, employing a range of skills and experience drawn from an equally wide range of occupational backgrounds.

Communication is the new mantra, and public relations is at the heart of it, but the term is susceptible to many interpretations: for instance, it may be used to describe making a telephone call, what happens in a conversation or remembering to tell everyone about a detail of work routine. Communication is a portmanteau term so widely used, and sometimes misused, as to be, ironically, the potential source of confusion. And in public relations there is much confusion also created by duplicate descriptions, over-enthusiastic creation of new language and generous one-size-fits-all adaptations to facilitate hoped-for mutual understanding.

what each chapter covers

In **Chapter 1** the *nature* of public relations is explored. Recourse is made to some of the very many definitions and to public relations culture; some widespread misconceptions are addressed and the history is traced of modern public relations from the beginning of the 20th century. There is an extended section on Lee and Bernays, the 'founding fathers' of modern practice. What public relations is *not* is covered here, but there is acknowledgement of its propagandist roots and the continuing use of *propaganda* in politics and publicity, often in the name of public relations.

In **Chapter 2** the *purpose* of public relations is investigated. Here is encountered the *corporate* direction of much public relations and how it fits into the context of the organization, whether that is a company or some other body. This raises matters of image, identity, reputation and business ethics, the latter a continuing topic throughout the book, and of creating shareholder value. These first two chapters, therefore, together provide *the basis to what follows* in the rest of the book.

Chapter 3 is the first of two that start to focus on the principal responsibilities and activities. Here concepts such as vision, mission, the learning organization and enterprise culture are discussed, together with managing change and other contemporary preoccupations of communication *within the organization.* In **Chapter 4** thought is given to how public relations communicates between the organization and its *operating environment.* There is discussion of publics and stakeholders and of risk and crisis management, and the concept of corporate social responsibility (CSR) is introduced. These two chapters together confirm that there is more to public relations than may be widely supposed.

The theory of public relations is substantially contained within **Chapter 5,** although various theories and models are discussed or alluded to throughout the book. Here, notably, communication itself, the core four models of public relations practice, the theory of public relations excellence and the contingency model make their principal appearance. Conflict resolution, consensus, diffusion and effects and the concept of the public sphere are also covered; as are the three levels of practice, the three functions model, communicative action, three types of discourse, the reflective paradigm and two-step communication.

Chapter 6 is the last in the first part of the book. Here *research, planning and evaluation* are addressed, in terms that are more managerial than technical. In particular, there is mention of power play impact on public relations roles, the implications of various influences on the formation of strategy, situational theory and segmentation and the consensus-orientated COPR planning and evaluation model. The chapter ends with a discussion of cost-benefit analysis and compensating variation.

Part 2 comprises five chapters that consider by turn *differing areas of public relations practice.* Owing to the high proportion of public relations work that is in support of marketing – one frequently quoted guesstimate suggests 70 per cent – there are not one but two chapters specifically covering Marketing Public Relations (MPR).

Chapter 7 concentrates on the *customers,* addressing how they make their decisions, the marketing approach to this all-important public and the public relations understanding of consumer relations. Dialogues with privacy and Customer Lifetime Value are also covered. In **Chapter 8** attention turns to *marketing communications,* the role of MPR, the concept of integrated marketing communication (IMC) and the practice of Cause Related Marketing (CRM). It ends with a discussion of the relationship between marketers and public relations practitioners.

Probably the one area of public relations activity that is most readily recognized, *public affairs,* is reached in **Chapter 9;** its position so relatively late in the book is not intended as any comment upon its importance. This chapter does not attempt to include much that is already, perhaps inevitably, public knowledge, but seeks instead to offer some critical perspectives relating, in particular, to government public relations and propaganda. There is also discussion of lobbying and issues management.

Community relations attract a great deal less attention than public affairs, but is often assigned higher ranking in public relations importance by corporate strategists. In **Chapter 10** this less obvious area of activity is examined, starting with corporate community involvement (CCI) and continuing with the physical environment and community action, the growing 'community sector' of self-help schemes. There is also consideration of UK companies' expenditure, public attitudes towards it and relations between the private and voluntary sectors.

The final chapter in this part, **Chapter 11**, 'last but not least' covers *the media*. Here again the emphasis is on offering some critical perspectives, addressing topics such as media values, online media news and the relationship between the media and public relations practitioners. A number of controversial issues are raised, and the chapter ends with telling private research on the use of e-mails, extracted from a dissertation for a postgraduate degree in public relations.

Part 3 of *Mastering Public Relations* comprises three chapters, starting, in **Chapter 12,** with a look at *global PR*. In addition to tracing its development across the world, there is discussion of the factors that are stimulating practice growth: globalization, industrialization, communication and transport technologies, the spread of democracy and changing political ideologies. This is followed by consideration of the critical part played by cultural differences and the communication role of NGOs. This chapter also covers international PR membership bodies, hazards to be avoided in practice, the developing countries and the European Union.

Chapter 13 turns the spotlight on the *occupation of public relations.* It considers the person specification for public relations practitioners and the image and reputation of public relations, followed by discussion of self-regulation and education and training.

With the somewhat cryptic title of 'Futures', **Chapter 14** discusses the future for public relations practice, starting with a discussion of the Internet, followed by editorial standards and globalization. Topics include the 'information poor', legal liability for Internet content and aspects of developing media law. It concludes with a consideration of key practice strands: culture, trust, relationships, ethics, crises, change and media access.

regular features of each chapter

Chapters are arranged in a format designed to ease interpretation and cross-referencing.

In addition to text and illustrations, this format includes:

- A **summary of topics** to be covered in each chapter, which appears at the beginning
- **Numbered sections,** each with a title. Some sections are further divided into **subsections,** each introduced with its own heading (not all topic descriptions are the same as the titles of sections in which they appear)
- **Emboldened main points**

- **Highlighted examples**
- A **checklist** of main points and concepts covered in each chapter
- A detailed **case study,** except in the first and last chapters, describing real life applications in a variety of contexts
- **Five questions,** which conclude each chapter and are specific to its content. These are designed to offer food-for-thought, stimulate discussion, encourage further reading and assist practice benchmarking.

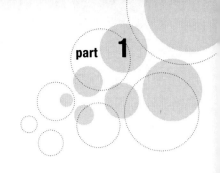

part **1**

the nature of public relations

‘Spin’ – widespread use – definitions and characteristics – persuasion – culture – nomenclature – publicity – the media – what PR is not – early development – modern origins

1.1 ‘spin’

‘Every day,’ writes Thomas Pynchon in an introduction to a recent US edition of George Orwell’s classic novel *1984*, ‘public opinion is the target of rewritten history, official amnesia and outright lying, all of which is benevolently termed “spin”, as if it were no more harmful than a ride on a merry-go-round. We know better than what they tell us, yet hope otherwise.’

This term ‘**spin**’ is ubiquitous and synonymous with deceit, trickery or, at best, exaggeration, wishful thinking or fanciful interpretation. Its use litters the daily outpourings of the Western news media, where it has become a handy tool for the lazy journalist and broadcaster, the ready means to insinuate in substitution for reporting fact. Everything, it sometimes seems, constitutes spin, and everyone knows exactly where that comes from, because spin, they are repeatedly told, is the product of public relations.

Orwell anticipated spin, his inventions in *1984* being remarkably prescient: the Ministry of Truth that busily told lies, the Ministry of Love, which dealt in torture, the Ministry of Peace that continually waged war and the Ministry of Plenty, which perpetuated starvation. And there were the contradictory doublethink party slogans, War is Peace, Freedom is Slavery and Ignorance is Strength. So much so that when the ‘real’ 1984 occurred the UK Prime Minister felt obliged to make a speech denying that *1984* had come to fruition.

Public relations, therefore, is *closely linked in the collective imagination* with politics and government, from whence emanates so much that is described publicly as spin. This in turn has led to government employees being fairly indiscriminately called ‘spin doctors’, whether or not they have any involvement with the dissemination of either governmental propaganda or public information.

But spin is not confined to politics. It is liberally used to describe communications from all manner of sources. Wherever, it seems, that the presence of public relations may be detected, or supposed, spin surely follows. Why, every journalist says so, repeatedly, so it must be so.

But should journalists, themselves not well regarded by society generally, be allowed to smear so freely, to weave their own web of selective 'postmodern irony' without challenge? Could public relations comprise rather more than they choose to represent, could it have some redeeming features, some better or higher purpose, perhaps even more honourable and serious intent than does much journalism?

1.2 pervasive and invasive

Public relations, as a recognizable activity, is widely undertaken by people in all walks of life, including:

- **Professional practitioners** employed in every corner of the public, private and not-for-profit sectors of the economy;
- **Managers** and **members of staff** whose work includes *an element* of public relations responsibility and/or activity;
- **Volunteers** who undertake public relations activities *without pay* in order to obtain and increase support for their interests and causes; and
- **Individuals** who wish to **advance private interests** on behalf of *themselves* or someone who they *represent*.

Public relations, or PR, as it is commonly called, is no longer undertaken solely on behalf of commercial interests, which is how it substantially began in the USA during the 19th century, nor by government, which in the UK a few decades earlier had laid the foundations for its later entanglement with the burgeoning public communication media.

- It is increasingly 'done' by anyone and everyone, reflecting a growing civic pluralism, whereby many voices are heard in public via 'display-for-attention-and-advantage' (Moloney, 2000), mainly generated through wanting to secure personal attention for financial gain, advance worthy causes, achieve access and influence and/or express disdain of authority in all its forms.
- It is also widely undertaken by all manner of organizations, reflecting the parallel rise in commercial pluralism, resulting from ever more competition for resources, markets and advantage, owing to globalization, finite natural resources, colossal population growth and the influence of a widely prevalent political ideology that promotes 'me first', the supremacy of self over society.

This **universality** raises interesting questions about the **exact nature** of public relations, for, if indeed, as is widely represented, it comprises an easily learned and applied set of low-cost techniques accessible to all:

- Can it be a serious management function or is it merely a popular means of self-expression?

- Is it an occupation or a hobby, a profession with barriers to entry and serious self-regulation or a trade that may be engaged in by anyone, a form of diplomacy or a euphemism for deceit and trickery?
- Does it have worthy pretensions or pretentious worthiness?
- Is it a powerful force for greater democracy or the means to brainwash the masses, central to corporate success and a significant element of an integrated approach to marketing or simply a trendy thing to do?

1.3 definitions

Probably the simplest and most straightforward definition of public relations is as the

> *management of communication between an organization and its publics*
> (Grunig and Hunt, 1984)

This contains three clues: it indicates that public relations is a **corporate** activity, comprises **communication** in some form or other and entails a degree of **specificity**, involving 'publics' rather than the general public at large. So far, so good, but is this adequate?

Most public relations people may think not, judging by the proliferation of alternatives offered. Of these, most aim to either describe the activity, what effects it seeks or how practitioners should behave. Prominent among them is the widely quoted '**Mexican Statement**' that resulted from a meeting in 1978 at Mexico City attended by practitioners representing PR associations in 31 countries. It reads:

> *Public relations practice is the art and social science of analyzing trends, predicting their consequences, counselling organizations' leaders, and implementing planned programmes of action which will serve both the organizations' and the public interest.*

This 'sits on the fence' about whether PR is an art or a science, since in practice it combines creativity and flair with incisive analysis and measurable precision. More significantly, the statement implies that there is present, firstly, a strong element of **research** and, secondly, **responsible behaviour** that is **in the public interest** as well as that of the organization.

This statement also suggests an element of **prediction**. Environmental scanning, that is to say, looking out for what is going on outside the organization and assessing the implications of what is found there, is often referred to as **issues management**, because 'one does not merely monitor change but plans to take it into continuing consideration in planning corporate strategy' (Black and Davis, 2002). It entails spotting and unravelling an issue, deciding its likely future course, following its development and seeking to influence its outcomes, most of which is more easily said than done.

The Conference Board of America has defined *an issue* as being '*a condition or pressure, either internal or external, that, if it continues, will have a significant effect on the functioning of the organization or its future interests.*' Note that here issues arise *within* **the organization** as well as outside it, and they warrant equally close attention.

The **multiplicity of terms used** to label public relations practice has been a primary cause of the many differing definitions. Back in 1988 the Public Relations Society of America (PRSA) had a committee try to unravel the confusion. It concluded that 'public relations' was indeed the correct name for this activity, within which there were various specialisms. This was similar to, for example, legal practice. 'Public relations' remains the generally prevailing 'correct' name around the world, although it is regarded by some as no more than an Anglo-American term (van Ruler and Vercic, 2004), and very many public relations posts are described differently, for instance, as being about 'corporate communications', 'communication management' or 'external relations'.

That same committee of the PRSA offered these explanations of public relations practice:

▸ *Public relations helps an organization and its publics to adapt mutually to each other*
▸ *Public relations is an organization's effort to win the co-operation of groups of people*
▸ *Public relations helps organizations effectively interact and communicate with their key publics.*

Here there is reference to **interactions** between the sender and the receiver of a communication, to **co-operation** of the receiver with the sender and, most significantly, to facilitating **mutual adaptation** to each other. In other words, this take on PR is hinting at **dialogue,** not merely communication by an organization *at* someone but communication *with* them.

The (UK) Chartered Institute of Public Relations (CIPR) had a definition, for quite a while, that read:

> *Public relations practice is the planned and sustained effort to establish and maintain goodwill and mutual understanding between an organization and its publics.*

This emphasized that public relations is an **on-going activity**, which sought, by one means or another, to **foster goodwill and mutual understanding**. This does not necessarily entail, as is often mistakenly supposed, approbation or popularity, nor does it necessitate a substantial level of exchanged communication or involvement by the receiver.

Then the Institute decided to add a bit more, a prefix about **reputation**:

> *Public relations is about reputation – the result of what you do, what you say and what others say about you. Public relations practice is the discipline which looks after reputation – with the aim of earning understanding and support, and influencing opinion and behaviour.*

This places **reputation** at the centre of public relations practice, an onerous responsibility indeed, with important implications for relationships between the public relations function and other departments and units. These definitions from the PRSA and CIPR are of interest primarily because these two bodies claim to be, respectively, the largest and second largest public relations practitioner membership bodies in the world.

Reputation certainly is a, if not the, major factor in public relations, perhaps even to the extent that 'Managing the causal linkage between reputation, perception, attitude and behaviour is what PR is all about' (Stone, 1995). Without doubt, the maintenance of behavioural standards that **minimize and manage conflict** is necessary for the fostering of **enduring, valued relationships** on which favourable reputations may thrive. About that, at least, there appears to be general agreement. 'The aim of public relations practice is to have an effect on behaviour – on the behaviour of groups of people bound into relationships. As a practice, public relations makes use of communication to affect behaviour' (White, 1991). In the management context: 'Public relations' main aim is to influence behaviour, specially the behaviour of groups one with another'.

There are many more definitions that might be preferred by individual practitioners. For instance, according to Kitchen (1997a), an 'acceptable standard of definition' among practitioners is:

> Public relations is the management function that identifies, establishes and maintains mutually beneficial relationships between an organization and the various publics on whom its success or failure depends. (Cutlip et al., 1985)

This interpretation brings us back again to interactivity, the purpose being to establish **ongoing relationships** that are **mutually beneficial.** It bears a closer relationship to the commercial purposes of marketing communications. It also serves to emphasize that, as is often argued now, **above all else public relations practice is about relationships**: image, communication and the rest are all key components, but are subordinate to this.

What these and most other definitions are saying, or implying, is that public relations practice is an activity that is *solely* engaged in by organizations. But that is not so: it is increasingly 'done' by anyone and everyone, and it is no longer, if ever it was, an exclusive corporate preserve. Why? Because, as is widely recognized, 'Mass society has made the individual voice less easily heard' (Heath, 1992), and owing to the rise of pluralism, which encourages an everwider adoption of techniques for trying to be heard and to influence others. To the extent, therefore, that they are conceived *only* in terms of organizational public relations, many definitions are at risk of being at least unsatisfactory if not defective.

Given this spread of public relations activity, perhaps a more contemporary definition might read simply:

> Public relations practice comprises purposeful communication with people who matter to the communicator, in order to gain their attention and collaboration in ways that are advantageous to the furtherance of his or her interests or those of whoever or whatever is represented.

This is about **generating and fostering relationships** to the benefit of *whoever* is making the effort, which is why such effort is made in the first place. There is no mention of mutuality, owing to the use of the word *advantageous*: no advantages are likely to accrue to the sender, or initiator, of communication unless the receiver *also* recognizes some benefits in return, that there is existing or potential **mutual benefit** to be derived from the exchange. In the absence of resulting mutual benefits that *both* parties can see and are willing to acknowledge, most relationships flounder, or never even begin to progress.

This definition also takes full account of **civic pluralism** because it applies to *whoever* is doing the communicating, whether that person is a professional practitioner or not. It also recognizes the **persuasive** nature of much public relations work. 'The heart of the new view of the practice of public relations is the mutually beneficial relationships that an organization needs to enjoy a license to operate.... [This] assumes that markets are attracted to and kept by organizations that can create mutually beneficial relationships' (Heath, 2001b). 'In a nutshell... the value of public relations comes from the relationships that communicators develop and maintain with publics... reputation is a product of relationships' (Grunig *et al.*, 2002).

In mainland Europe there has been adaptation of the original American models and theories, and the development of some home-grown ones as well. 'In Europe it seems to be more common and more convincing to think of public relations not only as an organizational activity, but also as a social phenomenon... which has societal functions and impacts on the society and its subsystems like the political system, the economic system, the cultural system or the media system' (Bentele, 2004).

Public relations research tends to be viewed in much of Europe as being part of sociology or political science, not solely as a communication science. This broader approach has resulted in the development of a social as well as commercial orientation; for instance, to there being a greater interest in the **overall social impact** of public relations, with particular regard to issues such as **social trust**, the **avoidance of distrust**, **consensus** and **conflict resolution**.

For those countries that until recently had centrally planned economies ruled by socialist hegemonies, public relations is perceived as being at the heart of *facilitating progress* towards adoption of market economies and pluralistic democracies. In this transitional period the principal feature of public relations practice is **public education** about the processes and their implications.

Thorough research into the nature of public relations practice was undertaken in 1999–2000 as part of the **European Public Relations Body of Knowledge** (EBOK) project. Public relations practitioners and scholars from 26 countries participated. 'Though concentrating on "the single one definition" may not be very useful, we do feel that it is important to continue focusing on defining the field – finding the central concepts, for instance, or the main characteristics and parameters – even if it is a multi-dimensional concept' (van Ruler and Vercic, 2004).

Respondents were asked about the role of public relations within and for an organization and 'in society at large'. Analysis of replies identified **four aspects** of public relations. 'Almost all participants agreed that these four aspects were typical of European public relations and had to be included. These aspects refer first of all to public relations as a certain concept of organisation and, second, to a professional function at a managerial, tactical, as well as an educational level'. In summary, they are:

- **Reflective**: analysis of changing social standards, values and standpoints, subsequent discussion and any resultant adjustments to organizational standards, values and views. This reflective aspect of practice is returned to in Chapter 5.
- **Managerial**: planning communication and relationships with public groups 'to gain public trust and/or mutual understanding'. This relates to not only external and internal publics but also to 'public opinion as a whole'.
- **Operational**: implementing 'for the organisation (and its members)... communication plans developed by others'.
- **Educational**: internal training 'to help all the members of the organisation become communicatively competent, in order to respond to societal demands'. This is about 'mentality' as well as behaviour.

These describe aspects of European practice and reflect the European 'social-scientific tradition', in that they extend beyond the confines of addressing individual publics to include public opinion *as a whole*, and they express an interest in broader social factors and demands. The **reflective** aspect is of particular interest; for it suggests an altogether more considered and sensitive approach than may be apparent in much practice or necessarily implied by **environmental scanning**, which is discussed in Chapter 2.

In Asia, the Chinese primarily emphasize **interpersonal communication**, and the main public relations practice activities are hospitality, known as guest relations, language translation and tour guiding. This orientation has its roots 'in part from the subtleties of *guangxi*, culture-based collectivism, and [the] low credibility of government-owned media' (Chen and Culbertson, 2003). Much time is devoted to **gaining trust**, and **personal networks** are paramount. Taylor (2001) quoted Chen and Culbertson (1996): 'They found that achievement of many professional, personal, and social goals rests on a concept of *gao guanxi*. This term means "establishing connections, creating obligations and favors among interactants, and enjoying privileges through relationships"... Public relations practitioners often perform the *gao guanxi* role'. Politics, so much a part of Western public relations, are, by contrast, outside the scope of public relations practice in China.

Japanese public relations is grounded in providing information: it is mostly called *ko-ho*, meaning **public information**. A new **self-correction model** has been proposed (Inoue, 2003) to facilitate **problem-solving** 'in an increasingly changing and complex society'. This new model 'seeks coexistence with nature and emphasizes a high sense of ethics and wisdom for resolving diverse global problems.... Its goal should include global peace that strives towards harmonious and prosperous societies in which people are respected.'

1.4 the role of persuasion

From their earliest origins people have sought to make themselves understood, and they are still having difficulties in doing so. They began with the simplest tools and gradually developed them, achieving notable landmarks along the way, such as the inception of cave drawings and paintings, the creation of the earliest handwritten documents, the laborious production of richly illuminated religious tracts and the invention of printing.

Through a simple need to be understood by others there developed (relatively) soon a desire to *enhance* understanding, in order to push the benefits of communication beyond satisfaction of simple needs towards the **achievement of power and influence**, and the resultant benefits that might be secured. Communication came to be **used to assert identity and assign qualities such as status**, for example, through the use of heraldic symbols and the design and decoration of public buildings. In the last millennium this process unfolded at a quickening pace, resulting in the modern supremacy of the **brand,** an identification that communicates various values designed to secure advantage.

Such **values** do more than simply lay claim to certain qualities, such as size and commercial or military strength. They are **persuasive,** designed to *gain willing recognition, mould perceptions, develop attitudes and influence future behaviour.*

These actions may be:

‣ *Commercial* in nature, for instance, purchases of a product or service;
‣ *Intellectual*, perhaps involving agreement with a particular argument; or
‣ *Emotional*, such as making a commitment to support a social cause.

Brands are trust marks, in which it is intended that *faith may be placed unreservedly.*

Persuasion, it is widely argued, underlies all public relations practice, and certainly much of the early activity was directed primarily if not solely at winning converts to a cause, believers in a faith or loyal followers of a recognized leader. Oratory, for instance, was widely heard, in which persuasive language was used in order to influence thought and behaviour, and this form of communication widely persists to this day in many differing cultures and for many diverse purposes.

However, by no means *all* public relations activity has persuasion as its purpose. The major exception is provided by the dissemination of that **public information** which comprises simple 'need to know' facts and figures informing the average citizen or subject about the minutiae of daily life. In so far as it plays any part in public relations, strongly denied by most practitioners, **propaganda** provides an exception, as may **mediation.**

1.5 the public relations culture

Stated simply, the **public relations culture** describes an organizational environment in which every participant both **understands the value and purposes of PR**, including the creation and maintenance of **favourable reputation**, and is committed to ensuring that his or her actions reflect that. In effect, this is translated into a *predisposition* to:

» Speak up for the organization,
» Champion its cause,
» Act towards outsiders as an ambassador,
» Strive to bear in mind the PR implications of every decision and
» Generally to daily re-affirm commitment through both attitudes and actions.

There are many organizations, both large and small, where the culture has so permeated; but the very term 'culture' is difficult to define. It may be seen as:

» A collective acceptance of a *values system*,
» A simple set of *performance criteria*,
» Informally stated *customs or conventions* by which individuals 'bond', or
» A more complex interaction of *assumptions, values,* even *philosophy*.

What *does* seem certain is that the public relations culture of an organization will *reflect* its **current overall culture**, and this is particularly observable where the **leadership values** both

» Incorporate a *commitment* to public relations and
» Are *substantially* accepted and adopted throughout.

It is probable, however, that the public relations culture will also reflect the **external environment** in which the organization functions. So, for instance, a *retailer of consumer products* may have an entirely different PR culture from that of a *hospital,* because the world that each inhabits differs according to its purposes.

The **Public Relations function** is also, potentially, a *major influence*: should its members perceive a *disparity* between the *current* public relations culture and what they *think it should become*, they may well seek to **mould the public relations culture to better meet their requirements**, *even to the extent of creating a 'counterculture'*.

Marketers have their own version of this, what they call the **marketing concept**, which emphasizes the central importance of the customer: all activities are designed with the ultimate aim of satisfying customers, because they determine present and future prosperity. This 'customer focus' unites the efforts of every unit and underscores the performance and attitudes of every participant within the organization.

There is a *fundamental difference*: marketing activity may have an interim objective that says nothing directly about sales, but its ultimate purpose is *focused very firmly* on the customer. By contrast, the public relations culture has *broader* application, although much public relations practice may be directed towards supporting marketing, in which guise it is called Marketing Public Relations, or MPR, one of five principal marketing communications tools used in promotion of products and services; more about this in Chapters 7 and 8.

1.6 'Communications' versus 'Public Relations'

The occupation of public relations is often described as being that of 'communications', on the grounds that they comprise the core activity. Not all practitioners agree, just as not all scholars perceive PR as being solely a communication science. According to Harold Burson, an American doyen of the business, interviewed in *PR Week* (19 October 2001), 'The term communications has become synonymous with PR but this does a disservice to our profession by making it tactical. ... The best term for what we do is public relations'. Long after he sold control of his consultancy, it opted for 'perception management' as a replacement for describing its services.

There is also uncertainty about whether **communication** or **communications** is preferable. The latter is widely used to refer to electronic equipment: 'I long ago adopted this form [communication without the 's'] as being more accurate and left communications to the telecommunications specialists. It's a small point but another attempt to bring clarity out of confusion.' (Jackson, 1987, quoted by van Riel, 1995).

Communication without the 's', preferred also by van Riel, better addresses the nature and range of PR-originated communications activity and appears in that form throughout this text. It is unlikely, however, to be an adequate substitute for the description 'Public Relations', whose **full practice comprises more than the act of communication alone**. Alternative descriptions, which abound, may be perceived as attempts to more accurately describe its nature and purpose and to enhance its reputation and status.

1.7 publicity

Historically, MPR was described by marketers as being *publicity in the editorial content* of the print and broadcast media, *as opposed to advertising*, or 'paid space' (Kotler, 1991), by which is meant space on the page that is purchased directly by the advertiser from the media owner. The term 'Publicity' continues to be widely and mistakenly conceived as another of many alternative *names* for Public Relations, and it is also sometimes used disparagingly to discount the PR-generated communication materials of competitors and rivals.

Publicity, however, is *a part* of public relations practice, when it usually comprises activity that is designed to draw attention and create awareness by a means that is both credible and relevant to the underlying message. Such activity is likely to comprise a contrived **event** or some other overt act that is intended **to disturb the continuity of life** for those at whom the publicity is directed. It may be interpreted, for instance, as:

▸ News,

- Comment or
- Simple distraction,
- Invitation,
- Opportunity or
- Affirmation,
- Gesture,
- Appeal or
- Wake-up call.

This purposeful publicity is undertaken in a *controlled* manner, but publicity may also occur as a result of **information becoming known** that by so doing may have either a beneficial or harmful consequence. The act of making known may have been purposefully controlled or *unintended*, and thereafter found to be *uncontrollable*. Nor is all publicity necessarily 'good', in the sense that it is calculated to appear by its nature favourable, and some publicity is deliberately 'bad', because, ironically, it is expected to provide good results, as where commercial fame benefits from notoriety.

1.8 the media

The relentless **growth in the scale and influence of the mass media** continues around the world, creating an ever-greater demand for material to fill the pages of print and the airwaves. As technology advances continue to streamline the processes used to gather and disseminate material of all kinds, notably news and its accompanying commentaries, *the demands of the media on public relations intensify.*

Public relations uses the media in order to communicate with its publics and it benefits from whatever **added credibility** the chosen medium of communication may attach to its messages. Whether people choose to believe whatever they read or see in the public media is, ultimately, for them alone to decide. That applies whether what draws their attention appears in a newspaper, magazine or Internet website, or on television, radio or the 'big screen'.

Those who are relatively new to receiving the outpourings of the mass media are likely to be more trusting, credulous perhaps, and believing of any item that appears, simply because it *does*. Although this faith in the veracity of the media tends to decline over time, with experience, and people the world over are becoming increasingly more aware, nonetheless marketing messages routed through the media, *as editorial matter or in programmes*, continue to **generate higher levels of credibility** than those that go via, for instance, advertising or direct mail.

The downside to media intervention is that most if not all messages have to acquire certain immediacy, a '**news angle**', and great may be the effort to assign one that can meet journalistic requirements. To this end public relations practitioners and journalists frequently collaborate closely in order to contrive a 'peg' that may warrant publication to their mutual satisfaction.

There are many more detailed aspects of what is known as **media relations**, the interactions by which public relations communication is filtered through the scrutiny of the media intermediaries, notably the editors, subeditors, reporters, specialist writers, photographers, producers, directors, presenters, scriptwriters and film crews. This *mediated* communication illustrates the value of **endorsement by opinion formers**, people whose very involvement, say in reading the news, may provide some added interest and relevance to a communication.

For their part, the media need public relations inputs to provide **subsidized or free, to them, material and ideas** with which to supply their customers. They have much space and airtime to fill and seemingly always too little real time in which to do it. They value 'copy' that is reliably sourced and ready for use, and accept that in using these outside, or secondary, offerings they *abdicate some of their control over the news agenda*, by which they, *and they alone*, determine what is and what is not news. The media benefit from any **growth in customers** that may result from using such material, for instance in readers attracted by competitions funded by retailers or in viewers who enjoy programmes that discuss and test products supplied for that purpose by manufacturers.

The consequences of this *mutuality of interest* do not escape criticism. Journalists 'are being colonized by it [public relations]. There is a PR-isation of the media happening in the UK. This is a growing identity in the attitudes, behaviours and personnel of journalism and PR. It implies a growing dependency of journalists on PR, leading to the disablement of their critical faculties' (Moloney, 2000). This growth of dependence by journalists upon public relations sources, which is occurring wherever public relations practice is becoming well established, is seldom acknowledged publicly. Many display ambivalence, privately recognizing their reliance while publicly disparaging public relations.

Just how cosy this conspiracy is between public relations and journalism to 'manufacture news' and other content greatly depends upon the perspective from which it is viewed. Significantly, public relations practitioners now have to hand, in the **Internet**, a powerful means to **communicate direct** without mediation by journalists and broadcasters, and they are also using and developing *other direct links* with publics such as shareholders, or stockholders, employees, pressure-group members, local civil administrators and neighbouring community leaders. The benefits derived from **media endorsement** of filtered messages are being weighed *routinely* by practitioners against those of direct communication of more closely targeted *unmediated* messages.

1.9 what public relations is not

Just as public relations can be misunderstood to be publicity by another name, so too it may appear to be synonymous with journalism, particularly when they are closely entwined, even though the two sets of activities are distinct. Nor do the confusions end there; public relations is often mistaken elsewhere:

marketing

Although much public relations activity is directed at support of marketing, to the extent that it *may in some instances* amount to the principal promotional tool used by marketers, it has its **broader remit,** that perceives customers as being but one public, or several disaggregated publics, *among many.* This is not to diminish the importance of customers, but rather to recognize also and allocate time to addressing the powerful claims of others, notably shareholders, employees, suppliers and the media.

advertising

Most advertising seeks to achieve **optimum persuasiveness** with a view to **achieving sales,** although much is now *less directly* persuasive, designed instead to achieve *interim effects* that in turn will assist in generating sales. Such purposes include: to remind or reinforce, bring brands to 'front-of-mind' or calm post-purchase doubts. And some advertising is not at all about sales, directly or indirectly; here the purpose may be, for example, buying supplies, recruitment of personnel, announcing trading results or communicating public information.

For Public Relations, however, achieving sales, or helping others to achieve sales, is *by no means* its *principal* purpose. Practice may be directed, at any given time, for instance, to inform, educate, create better understanding, gain credit, encourage loyalty or provoke discussion.

In theory, at least, publication of editorial content *cannot be purchased directly,* unlike advertising, but has to **earn its inclusion on its merit** as judged by the media (although this is far from universally so internationally). Accordingly, the advertiser's **level of control** over what appears is relatively absolute and exceeds that of the public relations practitioner's over non-advertising mediated communication.

Further, *traditionally* advertising agencies' remuneration has been through commission **paid by the media** in which their advertisements appear and/or **payment of fees by clients for creative work,** unconnected with its later appearance in the media. Public relations practice has been paid for by employers through **wages and salaries** and by purchasers of public relations services via **consultancy fees.** This difference, however, has been lessened lately, to some extent, with the introduction of **payment by results** in certain circumstances: paying advertising agencies 'a performance fee based on the overall sales achieved by the business unit' (Doyle, 2000) and public relations consultancies an additional fee for being 'on the winning side'.

sales promotion

Sales promotion is directed at gaining short-term results, usually measured over weeks or months, whereas public relations can be, and usually is, assessed over longer periods, ranging from a few months to several years, perhaps even a decade or more: successive short campaigns are individually evaluated in the context of their contribution to long(er)-term objectives. This difference arises because sales promotion seeks to **affect a market quickly** and thereby achieve changes, whether in competitive attack or defence, whereas public relations sets its sights on securing **results** that by their nature are **likely to take time to achieve**. Indeed, 'The major return from public relations may occur only once every 10 to 20 years, and that return may represent a problem that public relations prevented from happening – such as a strike, a crisis, litigation, a boycott, or regulation.' (Grunig *et al.*, 2002).

Some types of public relations activities may be confused for sales promotion, owing to their having close similarities to some promotional tactics, and this in turn can give rise to the false impression that public relations practice constitutes 'free' sales promotion. Both sales promotion and public relations do share, however, the ability to *communicate directly* with *individuals* and *relatively small groups* of people.

propaganda

It has been argued (Grunig and Hunt, 1984) that in publicity there is propaganda. 'Practitioners spread the faith of the organization involved, often through incomplete, distorted, or half-true information.' Certainly publicity often relies upon an element of self-praise and in telling rather than listening, features shared with propaganda, but in most uses of publicity those further characteristics of propaganda, such as belligerence, dogmatism and demand of unquestioning agreement and obedience, are absent. Typically, publicity is more likely to be associated with *celebrity* and *celebration* than with seeking uncritical following through arousing emotions and evoking spiritual responses.

It might be contended more convincingly that propaganda persists elsewhere in some nooks and corners of modern public relations, as where, for example, communication is intended to mould public opinion about a political, economic or social matter. But these are **increasingly questioning times**. Public relations people aim to communicate with convincing argument and presentation, and take great care in nurturing and defending reputations that they value.

1.10 early development

Public relations practice has deep historic roots. Just how deep they go is open to interpretation. Kunczik (2003), for instance, cites Alexander the Great (356—323 BC) as an early ruler who used PR techniques. These included propagandistic reports written for the Macedonian court, and his employment of an historian whose job it was to promote Alexander's image, claiming him to be the son of Zeus, the supreme god of those times.

Coming much closer to our age, Kunczik mentions two German rulers. The first of these was Emperor Maximilian I (1493–1519), thought to be the very first leader to use the newspapers to influence public opinion (the printing press having just been invented). These were '"new newspapers" (newe zeytungen)' which were 'predecessors of the modern newspaper'. He also used 'biased war reports', both at home and abroad: 'he tried to incite ... to insurrection' the people of Venice against their rulers.

The second was Rudolf II. Upon election as emperor of the Holy Roman Empire in 1576, he launched into various activities designed to rally support against the Turks, who had declared war on the Germans. This included the production of leaflets, coins and medals, newspaper stories of Turkish atrocities, organizing of festivals and 'political acts of symbolic value' and the use of art and architecture, such as the construction of triumphal arches.

Then the French adopted similar techniques. Cardinal Richelieu (1585–1642), the 'Great Cardinal' who was Louis XIII's prime minister, had a press office and a Minister for Information and Propaganda. He used leaflets, the weekly *Gazette* and 'pamphlets to fight France's foreign opponents', especially the Hapsburgs. He founded the Académie Française to protect and promote the language 'and influence long-term public opinion'. He was, for Kunczik, 'a master in public relations' for whom reputation 'was the political keyword'.

Next up was Louis XIV (1638–1715), the 'Sun King', 'a master of image construction' and 'impression management' who ruled for over half a century, until 1715. He too used print media, grand architecture, public celebrations, multiple statues and portraits, court entertainments, and so on. Kunczik quotes Burke (1992): 'Long before the cinema, the theatre affected perceptions of politics. For his contemporaries the sun-king was a star'. The keyword had been *gloire*, or glory. Nor was this a passing phenomenon: 'The brilliance of the first years of the 'great reign' [1661–1672] continues to capture the imagination', but for all that 'Opinions about Louis XIV have varied a great deal from one century to another ... [It] is well known that Louis was detested in Germany and Holland, and that the English historical school, normally elegant and measured in its judgments, has not been kind to him' (Goubert, 1991).

Then the Americans adapted such techniques and developed them for their own purpose: to secure independence from Britain. On the 200th anniversary of the American Revolution in 1976, Cutlip wrote in *Public Relations Review* (Grunig and Hunt, 1984) that 'several propagandists' had incited the war against the British, among them Samuel Adams, who had used techniques familiar to public relations people today. These comprised:

- *Formal organization,* using an appealing name, the Sons of Liberty ('because the revolution was not a popular uprising')
- *Use of media,* mainly newspapers, sermons in places of worship, speeches at public meetings, pamphlets and letter writing by dedicated 'committees'
- *Use of a symbol,* The Liberty Tree
- *Use of a slogan,* 'Taxation without representation'
- *Creation of events,* or 'pseudo-events', to make news, including the 'Boston Tea Party', when tea was thrown into Boston harbour
- *Partisan presentation,* to promote favourable interpretation of events such as the 'Boston Massacre', when British soldiers attacked their civilian tormentors, and

- **Sustained campaigning,** in this case through all available media *over 20 years.*

It worked, and these public relations-like activities continued to be used by proponents of the creation of a federal government for the whole continent, who needed nine of the then 13 states to sign up for the constitution. The successful outcome, which included the **negotiated** addition of a Bill of Rights, served to emphasize the value of such techniques. According to Black (1989), the actual term 'public relations' was not used by an American president, however, until 1807, when Thomas Jefferson amended his Seventh Address to Congress, or speech to parliament, by substituting 'public relations' for the phrase 'state of thought'.

1.11 'For as long as the newspapers [are] important'

Meanwhile, in Europe, from George III onwards – he reigned during the last sixteen years of the American independence campaign – British monarchs became increasingly interested in what *their* subjects were saying and writing about current political, economic and social issues. In 1809 the British government joined in when the Treasury assumed the role of **press spokesman on overseas policy**. In December it sent a message to the Department of War and Foreign Affairs and to the Admiralty, the latter at that time, significantly, accounting for about 20 per cent of British public spending, saying: 'as long as the newspapers shall continue to be considered as important as they now are, some person in each of the three departments ought to read the principal newspapers every morning, and send to the Treasury ... either a correct statement of the facts, if facts are to be stated, or a hint of the line which it is wished should be taken' (Black and Davis, 2002).

In France, meanwhile, another major **image-building** exercise was well under way. 'Just as the memory of Napoleon lives on, so his legend is not dead. Launched by his own initiative and the skilled pens of his close companions during the Italian campaign, the legend ran through all the bulletins of the Grande Armee' (Goubert, 1991). This involved use of images, songs and

> popular literature and lithography, imitated and reproduced countless times... Even as late at 1930 many humble French homes contained tarnished images celebrating the grand Napoleonic gestures... this heroic tale... carried nationalism or patriotism to a frenzy... the legend has profoundly transformed the reality – which was of course its function – and transfigured Bonaparte the man... from the time of his exile [1815], his great stature dominated more than half a century of French history, and for almost as long haunted the peoples and kings of Europe.

Throughout the 19th century the techniques used by the American revolutionaries came to be adopted with greater frequency on both sides of the Atlantic. These notably included:

- Use of the term **public relations**

- **Publicity stunts,** often using arresting claims
- **Staged events,** often to inaugurate or commemorate
- Publication of **magazines and journals** by companies or their employees
- Publication of **annual reports.**

In America, in 1829, there appeared a newspaper editor employed in the White House, Amos Kendall, later to become regarded as 'the first presidential public relations man.' He worked for Andrew Jackson, the first 'commoner' president, a man said to be barely literate, largely unschooled and much in need of communication assistance. Possibly Jackson's reputation as one of the 'great' US presidents owes more than a little to Amos (Grunig and Hunt, 1984).

In the Netherlands, the 18th century Enlightenment view that science and knowledge should be accessible to everyone led to the development during the 1800s of *voorlichting*, or 'enlightening', the dissemination of public information and education by *voorlichters*, who travelled the country, instructing and advising on a wide range of practical matters. This had parallel governmental purposes: 'many people were afraid of enlightening ordinary people, which is why *voorlichting* is also used to show people how to behave as good citizens and to control them' (van Ruler, 2003). This combination of information and emancipation and of education and persuasion was pursued 'under the ("Dutch uncle") dogma of knowing what is good. In all theories of *voorlichting*, the rather pedantic premise is that it is given for the benefit of the person or group to be enlightened, even when the people involved do not want to be enlightened at all or at least not in this way.' As the country industrialized, this led directly to the development of modern public relations practice, which is orientated around **public information** and well-intended 'but patronizing' **education.**

In Austria, business, trade unions and various special interest groups were the early adopters of public relations, or *Offentlichkeitsarbeit*, meaning 'public sphere work.' The first trade union funded newspaper appeared in 1867, and the constitution adopted that year, which asserted the right of every citizen to 'have access to all offices', prompted the development of **lobbying**, which is now the principal area of practice. Indeed, in 2002, a German magazine referred to Austria as 'the land of lobbying.'

In Germany, the first government press office, the Prussian 'governmental bureau of newspapers', started in 1841; the first such 'literary bureau' or 'press bureau' in the private sector was begun in 1870 by steel maker Alfred Krupp, who had decided four years earlier to employ a 'literate', the contemporary German term for a public relations specialist.

The advent of the 20th century quickly led to the development elsewhere in Europe of public relations in the service of government. Finland had a small and thinly scattered population, and it was *this* that prompted the start in 1900 of disseminating public information by advertising, or *reklaami*. The Lutheran church established its information centre in 1917, and the first film promoting Finland appeared in 1922. **Public information** remains a strong component of Finnish public relations practice.

In the UK, too, much of the development of public relations rested with government, which led to the recruitment, in 1912, of lecturers tasked to explain the new National Insurance law to employers and employees throughout the country. This marked the beginning of the dissemination of public information as an integral part of British government and public administration. It was soon followed by the formation of both the War Propaganda Bureau and the Home Office Information Bureau, to generate propaganda during World War I, directed at friendly foreign countries and at the homeland. In 1917 they were combined to form the Department of Information, which was dismantled following victory, and only gradually over the following years did the British government appoint press officers in each department. This is significant. In 1918 it was considered that the need for propaganda had ceased, and what emerged later was regarded instead as public relations.

The advent of World War II in 1939 prompted a new Department of Information, whose role included not only **propaganda** but also dissemination of **unadulterated public information** to a civilian population that was enduring war at first hand. This included:

- **Practical advice** about living through a war,
- **Training** in how to cope with food rationing and other privations,
- Heavy use of radio to disseminate **information** and **evoke support** for the war effort and
- Production of cinema films that combined patriotism with **entertainment**.

This produced a **substantial pool of skilled communicators**, many of whom, following the war, embarked upon careers in public relations and advertising, often on the same premises, with advertising agencies alongside public relations consultancies.

The two great wars also served to hasten the development of public relations practice in the USA. In 1916, on entering the war, the president appointed a journalist friend to form a Committee of Public Information to generate domestic support for the war effort. This provided the impetus to a surge in the development of public relations, led by a group of young men newly experienced in propaganda that included press agent Edward Bernays, a nephew of the psychologist Sigmund Freud: Bernays's mother was Freud's sister and his father's sister was Freud's wife. Bernays's earlier publicity clients had included the world-renowned singer Enrico Caruso.

Thereafter the growth in public relations practice began to gather pace elsewhere, both in government and among larger companies; the steady increase between the wars soon accelerated after the second war, once national economies were well advanced towards recovery.

1.12 the founding fathers of modern public relations

In exchange for a box of cigars that Bernays sent to his uncle in Vienna, while he was attending the Versailles peace conference near Paris in the winter of 1918–

19, Freud sent his nephew a copy of his latest work, *A General Introduction to Psychoanalysis,* which expounded the proposition that there lay within people hidden irrational forces. This convinced Bernays that people might be persuaded not only to support a war effort but also to adopt new ways of thinking in other directions and to adapt their 'organized habits and opinions'.

On returning from Europe in 1919 Bernays went into business in New York with his wife, Doris Fleischman, as **'public relations counsel'**, a term he devised, by his own later account, *in substitution for 'propaganda'.* In 1923 he developed and delivered the **first course in public relations**, at Cornell University, where he taught using his own book, *Crystallizing Public Opinion,* published that year, the **first text** on the subject. Quickly the firm acquired as clients many large companies and well-known personalities.

Bernays (1892–1995) is regarded today as one of the two founding fathers of modern public relations. In addition to his distinguished uncle, several others inspired him, notably Walter Lippmann, whose *Public Opinion* appeared in 1922. Lippmann viewed propaganda as part of government and he conceived of pseudo facts, the pseudo environment and of stereotypes as 'the mental phenomena used by people in the formation of public opinion... The PR counsellor creates news to strengthen, weaken or amend stereotypes' (Moloney, 2000).

Ivy Ledbetter Lee (1877–1934), acknowledged as PR's other founding father, also influenced Bernays. Having dropped out of Harvard law school 'when his money ran out' (Pearson, 1992), Lee became a reporter in the 1890s, writing successively for three New York newspapers, including *The New York Times.* At that time a group of journalists, who came to be called 'muckrakers', were busily exposing employers for their concentration on profit with scant regard for the health and safety of their employees. Lee came to specialize in writing about banking and business, through which he encountered a wide range of managers in major corporations. 'As a reporter, Lee apparently lacked the cynicism of many of his fellow journalists. He identified with the powerful businessmen he wrote about and generally thought they were good people, although misunderstood.' (Pearson, 1992).

In 1902 he set up as a publicity writer, his first client being a political reform group, which led him to consider whether there might be a market for **publicity on behalf of business** that was designed to counter the prevailing hostile publicity. With George Parker, a political publicist, Lee established a **public relations consultancy** in 1904, the third to be started, the first being in Boston (1900) and the second in Washington (1902). These first firms appear to have been solely concerned with conventional publicity, as it was then understood, though they were relatively short-lived. Lee, who had other ideas, soon parted company with Parker and continued alone, eventually establishing Lee, Harris and Lee (1916).

In his noted 1966 biography of Lee, *Courtier to the Crowd,* Hiebert's interpretation of Lee's motives for moving from law to journalism 'suggests that if Lee could not serve justice and democracy as a lawyer, he would have to find another way. Indeed, he would have to invent one'. Pearson continues: 'Hiebert, as much as Lee, is keenly interested in truth, justice, and democracy as ideals that inform the idea of public relations'. Hiebert had reported in glowing terms of approval Lee's famous 1906 **Declaration of Principles**, which was one of two key documents that Lee devised to initiate his policy of '**the public be informed**' while working for the Pennsylvania Railroad company.

Lee circulated a **statement to editors**, offering to assist them by supplying *whatever information they required*, itself a significant innovation. To this he appended a copy of his **Declaration of Principles**, which began: 'This is not a secret press bureau. All our work is done in the open. We aim to supply news. This is not an advertising agency; if you think any of our matter properly ought to go to your business office [advertisement department], do not use it.' The declaration asserted that all 'matter' was accurate – he had by then begun issuing press releases, or handouts, that, for the first time, *stated their source and interest* – and that further details relating to each item or information about the clients on whose behalf he worked would be supplied promptly upon request: '... any editor will be assisted most cheerfully in verifying directly any statement of fact.' Every effort was being made, he claimed, to be frank and open.

This was revolutionary indeed, and arguably Lee's greatest legacy. He also introduced the '**facility visit**'. On the basis that publicity meant making public, he began to organize opportunities for reporters to visit the scenes of rail crashes, hitherto closely guarded secrets, where they might **investigate and report freely on what they found**, *provided* that they gave a *balanced and fair account* that included the organization's version of events as well. This practice soon began to spread to visiting other sites, including factories, or facilities.

In 1914 Lee was engaged by the Rockefellers, at that time reputedly the wealthiest family in the USA. 'The Rockefellers hired Lee to provide public relations counsel during the aftermath of the Ludlow Massacre', according to Hansen-Horn (2001), who goes on to quote Cutlip in *The Unseen Power* (1994):

> Father and son 'were under heavy verbal assault from the nation's press and public for their brutal strike-breaking tactics in their Colorado Fuel and Iron Co. (CF&I) strike'. The Rockefeller mining company had authorized troopers and mine guards to assault miners and their families through the use of firearms. Both women and children were killed. The Rockefellers turned to Lee, whose public relations counsel was successful in 'skilfully muffling... the criticism of the Rockefellers in the wake of [the Ludlow Massacre]'.

Part of Lee's response was to persuade John D. Rockefeller Jr to visit and tour the mines, itself remarkable at the time. Later John D. Rockefeller Sr began to reveal publicly his charitable activities, in order to counter allegations about his business practices. Yet again, this was a first in building a sustained favourable reputation by *speaking openly* about matters that hitherto had been seen as strictly private.

He picked up similar business later from the West Virginia coalmine owners, the purpose being, according to Cutlip, quoted by Hansen-Horn, 'to counter the ugly publicity that had flowed from their use of a large armed force to crush a miners' march against union organizers'. To the modern mind, such brutality was bound to result in negative publicity, and, perhaps not surprisingly, Lee has been identified as one of several early US public relations counsel whose real role in life was to fight on behalf of 'big business' against trade unions in the ongoing 'them and us' conflicts that so characterized industrial relations at that time and long after.

Lee's career had a sad ending. In the 1920s he embarked upon a 'personal crusade' to win US recognition of the recently created Soviet Union, in the belief that openness and frankness between nations might bring **greater international understanding**. And recognition by the USA was achieved in 1933. But by then he had been engaged by a Nazi-controlled German industry association to advise it on international relations. He had pushed his experiment too far, found himself publicly vilified in the press and came under official investigation for Un-American Activities. He died prematurely in disgrace.

Lee's novel techniques were so successful that it could be argued they served to mask the moral issues that were central to his consultancy work. For his part, Lee took the high ground in explaining his purpose. For instance, Hiebert, quoted by Pearson, reports Lee as having spoken in 1921 at Columbia University's School of Journalism in these ringing tones: 'We live in a great democracy, and the safety of a democracy will in the long run depend upon whether the judgments of the people are sound. If the judgments are to be sound, they will be so because they have the largest amount of information on which to base those judgments'. Critically, Lee made clear that it was the job of public relations to assist in supplying this information on which democracy depended.

In their fascinating account of Lee's career, Grunig and Hunt (1984) concluded that Lee worked purely on **an intuitive sense of public opinion**, what good sense indicated. In other words, what might be expected and appropriate to the given circumstances. Bernays, they reported, once remarked that his work was based on science, whereas Lee's was based on art. Lee had never conducted an opinion survey: 'Lee's work was typical of contemporary practitioners of the public-information model. They advise management on public opinion – and often understand public opinion quite well – but they rarely do any scientific research to measure that opinion'. That is a debatable assertion likely to be refuted by many current practitioners.

1.13 'Order out of chaos'

Bernays is probably a rather more controversial figure even than Lee. Perhaps significantly, his *Crystallizing Public Opinion* was a 'how-to' book, designed to fill a gap, left, in his view, by Lippman's failure to explain practicalities. By the early 1920s Bernays had 'begun to recognize the growing force of public opinion, and the fact that organizations were becoming increasingly dependent on public reaction and support', according to White and Mazur (1995), who quoted from an interview that Bernays gave on the eve of his 100th birthday in 1991.

In this Bernays revealed how much he owed to his uncle: 'What I learned from reading psychology when it came in the late 1920s/early 1930s was that the proverb – actions speak louder than words – was so true. Before you ever use words you have to find out what people respond to. I found out that there are only four ways of affecting people. One is authority. The second is reason. The third is persuasion and the fourth is tradition.'

Bernays had a fondness for propaganda, which never left him. In his second book, *Propaganda*, published in 1928, he wrote of the 'conscious and intelligent manipulation of the organized habits and opinions of the masses' as being 'an important element in democratic society'. He continued menacingly: 'Those who manipulate this unseen mechanism of society constitute an invisible government which is the ruling power of our country'. Later he wrote 'Propaganda will never die out. Intelligent men must realize that propaganda is the modern instrument by which they can fight for productive ends to bring order out of chaos' (Moloney, 2000).

His later title, *The Engineering of Consent* (1955), persisted in the view of public relations as being a means to manipulate and control opinion, using the mass media and visual symbols, a one-way, rather than a two-way, process of communication. Decades later, throughout another interview in his 99th year, a four-hour-long conversation, Bernays 'conveyed his hallucination of democracy: A highly educated class of opinion-moulding tacticians is continuously at work, analyzing the social terrain and adjusting the mental scenery from which the public mind, with its limited intellect, derives its opinions' (Ewen, 1996).

In advance of the interview Bernays had forwarded a copy of a *Life* magazine special issue, in which he was named among the 100 most influential Americans of the 20th century. During the encounter he maintained an 'unabashedly hierarchical view of society', referring to 'an intelligent few' with responsibility for contemplating and influencing the tide of history, a comment echoed in modern preoccupations with legacy issues. 'Bernays', wrote Ewen, 'perceived me as one of these "few", so he was willing to share his outlook with me in straightforward terms... [He] sketched a picture of the public relations expert as a member of the "intelligent few" who advises clients on how to "deal with the masses ... just by applying psychology". The PR person was an applied social scientist who also understood sociology, psychology, social psychology and economics in order to influence and direct public attitudes.

After his death at the age of 103, Bernays's attitudes were summarized by his daughter, Ann Bernays:

> Democracy to my father was a wonderful concept, but I don't think he thought that all those publics out there had reliable judgement and that they very easily might vote for the wrong man or want the wrong thing, so that they had to be *guided* from above. It's enlightened despotism in a sense. You appeal to their desires and their own recognized longings, that

sort of thing, but you can tap into their deepest desires or their deepest fears and use that for your own purposes. (*The Century of the Self*, RDF Television/BBC, 2002)

Reflecting upon Bernays's effect upon the people around him, she added 'You make other people feel stupid, the people who worked for him are stupid, and children were stupid. If people did things in ways he wouldn't have done then they were stupid. It was a word that he used over and over and over, dope and stupid.' And the masses? 'They were stupid.' Referring to her father's use of the Soviet Union's first H-bomb in 1953 to manipulate public fears in the USA as a weapon in the 'Cold War', she explained 'Groups are malleable and you can tap in to the deepest desires or fears and use it for your own purposes.'

So as founding fathers go Bernays too has left this life somewhat ingloriously, provoking comments varying from the downright unflattering to the mildly distancing: 'There is an unspoken but palpable feeling that Bernays, particularly because of his literary legacy, is an embarrassment' (Moloney, 2000). 'In any event, Bernays was the first PR academic and his influence continued throughout his long life (he died in 1995)' (Fawkes, 2001).

There appears to be little doubt that the very substantial development of public relations practice since World War II has not been impeded by its propagandist origins, however much they may still discomfort current public relations practitioners. But equally there is little doubt that contemporary political propaganda, the source of much alleged 'spin', with which we began, is very damaging to the reputation of public relations practice.

To the modern mind propaganda has entirely negative connotations, associated with the many dictators and repressive regimes that have strutted the globe in the last 80 years, and disassociating public relations from propaganda has been a concern of many PR people in recent decades, but they are unlikely to succeed until propagandists cease to claim the mantle of public relations, which is improbable, since they find it too congenial to abandon. In his interview with Ewen, Bernays at one point retorted, on mention of commercial imagery, 'Of course, you know, we don't deal in images ... We deal in reality.' Perhaps at the time he had in mind his remark in a foreword he wrote some three years before: 'The phrase "public relations" is today in the public domain and anybody can use it to mean almost anything. Words today have the stability and permanence of soap bubbles' (Black, 1989).

CHECKLIST

☐ Public relations activities are undertaken widely throughout society for a variety of purposes relating to the furtherance of corporate and private interests.

☐ Practice is variously defined, including: the management of communication, an art and science, the promotion and defence of reputation, creating mutually beneficial relationships and the furtherance of self-interest through gaining attention and collaboration.

☐ Four aspects of European practice have been identified: reflective, managerial, operational and educational.

- Much public relations practice is designed to be persuasive.
- A public relations culture exists where everyone within an organization understands and fully supports the value and purposes of PR.
- Communication, not communications, better describes the nature and range of public relations communications activities.
- Publicity is a type of purposeful public relations activity, not a substitute name for PR. It may also occur when information becomes known unintentionally.
- Communication through the media adds credibility but messages are filtered and have to satisfy media priorities.
- The media benefit from public relations sourcing but thereby may relinquish some editorial control.
- Messages may be unmediated as well as mediated, going direct to publics and influential third parties direct, without journalistic intervention or interpretation.
- Much public relations activity is in support of marketing, when it is known as Marketing Public Relations (MPR), but an estimated half as much again is about communication outside marketing.
- Public relations differs significantly from advertising, in that it has a greater range of purposes, media space for publication of its messages cannot (usually) be purchased and it exercises less control over mediated messages.
- Although propaganda is still used in politics and publicity, most public relations activities rely instead on convincing argument and presentation.
- The origins of modern public relations practice have been traced to the seeding of the American Revolution against Britain in the two decades or so before 1776, the interest of King George III of Britain (1760–1820) in public opinion and the formal monitoring of the daily press by the British government from 1810.
- The acknowledged 'founding fathers' of public relations are two Americans: Ivy Ledbetter Lee (1877–1934), best remembered for his credo 'The public be informed' and for the 'facility visit', and Edward Bernays (1892–1995), who devised the term 'public relations counsel', established the first university course on PR and wrote the first book on the subject, *Crystallizing Public Opinion* (1923).

QUESTIONS

1 In what ways might public relations be both pervasive and invasive?
2 How could its PR culture impact upon an organization?
3 Why could publicity be seen as a 'two-edged sword'?
4 Is the 'PR-ization of the media' a benefit or a threat to press freedom, and why?
5 Why in public relations might advocacy be mistaken for propaganda?

the purpose of public relations

Corporate communication – communication and leadership – creating shareholder value – systems theory – environmental scanning – image, identity and reputation – business ethics and values

2.1 corporate communication

The Confédération Européenne des Relations Publique is in no doubt about the scale of responsibility of the public relations function: 'When someone refers to "PR", he is making reference to a profession which uses its own proper methodologies and techniques to manage Corporate Communications, the total communication needs of a Company or an Organization' (CERP website, 5 October 2002). But what does 'total communication needs' mean in practice?

Corporate communication may be divided into three categories (van Riel, 1995):

▶ *Management* communication, primarily by all managers within the organization but also externally, when chairmen and chief executive officers, or managing directors, perform their 'symbolic' role in representing their organizations.
▶ *Marketing* communication, all those activities that come under promotion within marketing, including MPR, advertising, direct sales, direct marketing and sales promotion.
▶ *Organization* communication, 'a general term' to describe 'all forms of communication used by the organization, other than marketing communication'. This includes the non-marketing elements of PR and internal communication both between employees and to the outside world.

Although in this analysis public relations appears to be mainly found in the third category, in reality it permeates all three:

▶ Modern management communication internally is primarily about optimizing efficiency and effectiveness; the external ambassadorial role of senior managers is recognized as being the public relations element of their jobs.

- The support of marketing forms the majority of PR practice in the UK and many other countries; as economies grow the weight of practice gradually moves towards MPR.
- Organization communication is primarily about public relations vis-à-vis, for example, finance, human resources, public affairs and environmental issues; expenditure may be lower than with MPR.

CORPORATE

| Management |
| Marketing |
| Organization |

COMMUNICATION

figure **2.1** **corporate communication**

There is much scope for the public relations function to be involved in addressing the *total* communication needs of an organization, but where does such a broad remit fit into the organizational structure and how may it realistically expect to 'manage' all corporate communication? Might not some non-PR managers contest the claims of the public relations function, particularly in technical correspondence and instruction?

2.2 communication and leadership

A successful leader, in any environment, has to be **an effective communicator** in order to arouse confidence, sustain credibility and generate excitement. He or she has many tasks to fulfil through communication, particularly:

- The creation of trust in management's competencies and decision-making skills,
- The delineation of a credible and inspiring vision for the future, and
- The demonstration of a willingness and ability to anticipate, initiate and implement change.

Within the organization these challenging purposes are designed in order to motivate and empower. *Outside,* they tell onlookers about the nature of the organization in ways that do much to create its corporate image. Powerful attributes may be assigned to an organization on the basis of **perceptions** created through *observing* and *hearing* the chairman or chief executive.

This external communication by the figurehead is not confined to announcing annual results or shaking hands; the style of presentation and the content of the messages form a **composite picture** that investors and others carry with them in their overall impression of the organization. Those in turn inform the attitudes and behaviours of external publics towards the organization and accordingly they establish **the parameters** within which the managers may **develop the organization,** for instance, in raising capital, securing credit, generating commercial opportunities, accessing grant funding and fostering joint ventures.

Few senior managers are likely to go forth to communicate beyond the confines of the workplace without *first* recognizing the *serious* public relations implications. Some still trust in their innate skills, but most take good care and many of them allocate considerable attention beforehand, working to a plan that accords with the organizational and public relations objectives. This attention to detail is necessary because the leader's *primary* communication motive is **to secure attention from others**. 'Organizations participate [in the attention market] when they want to attract attention from their customers, business partners, investors, or employees.' And 'as the amount of information increases, the demand for attention increases' (Davenport and Beck, 2001).

Among *these* attentive and attention-maximizing managers there is likely to be more recognition of the *potential value* of public relations in the **development of corporate strategy** and its implementation. That may mean that the most senior PR person is both a director and part of the inner cabal of senior managers who in effect run the show, who is located physically close to hand, readily available to address a broad range of communication matters as they arise at this level, perhaps even specializing in management communication throughout the organization. Some prominent leaders acquire popular fame, a bit like entertainers; not a few of them rather like it.

2.3 creating shareholder value

In addition to communicating the corporate values, it is necessary to spell out and explain the values of products and services in terms that are understood and appreciated by both existing and potential customers. It is here that MPR and all other *marketing communications* contribute to the creation of **shareholder value**. This is based on the principle that 'a business should be run to maximize the return on the shareholders' investment... Creating shareholder value is ... essentially about building a sustainable competitive advantage – a reason why customers should consistently prefer to buy from one company rather than others' (Doyle, 2000).

The *traditional* approach to placing a value on a company is to assess its ability to produce optimum returns for investors. This encourages emphasis on short-term profits and takes little if any account of intangible assets, such as the ability of particular brands to generate sales and the quality of relationships between the company and its customers and suppliers. *Shareholder value* analysis, by contrast, looks *also* at **the strategies that are going to generate cash in the future**, to assess their prospects for obtaining greater returns than the same money would have earned for the investors elsewhere in circumstances bearing similar risks.

This more penetrating analysis of a company's future prospects has been prompted by **the growing competition for capital, as well as customers**, with which to build businesses. For investors around the world what matters most is the *quality* of prospective return on their investments, and to that end the ability of the intangible assets to stimulate future profits is a major factor. Implicit here is the important role of marketing communication. To judge MPR within this as no more than a minor player, in terms of relative expenditures, below 5 per cent in the UK when compared with advertising and the other alternatives, would be seriously mistaken, for its *potential impact customarily far exceeds its cost*. Furthermore, it is not only product and service brands but also *corporate* brands that may constitute valuable assets for future growth. Public relations can, and often does, contribute much to their development.

2.4 where is home?

Given the proximity of the public relations function to senior management implicit in its role within management communication and the extent of its involvement in marketing communication, the initial likelihood that the probable home for public relations is in organization communication now seems doubtful. This is the category that covers the routine of daily exchange, surely just the place for a function with pretensions to manage all corporate communication? *Or is it?*

Systems theory provides the clue. There are three models that offer explanations of how humans organize themselves:

- A *mechanism,* comprising interacting elements that maintain equilibrium within a closed system that exists in isolation from its environment
- An *organism,* in which each component performs a specific part that contributes to the functioning of the whole and to the maintenance of equilibrium within an open system, where there is constant interaction with its environment
- A *social system,* in which each member freely accesses and interprets information to satisfy individual needs through socially responsible, co-operative actions that resolve conflicts and produce social harmony and unity.

The first two of these are considered to be 'traditional', having been developed in the 19th century, whereas the third was proposed in the late 1960s, and 'addressed issues such as conflict, deviance and social control, which traditional models are unable to deal with' (Pieczka, 1996).

During the 1950s a general systems theory evolved, in which a system was defined as being a group of related elements organized for a purpose. When this was applied to looking at how organizations operate, particularly larger ones, three types of system were identified:

- *Mechanistic* systems, with highly controlled and engineered processes
- *Probabilistic* systems, where there is rather less control and more uncertainty
- *Adaptive* systems, highly flexible and readily responsive to change.

In an increasingly competitive and complex world, the managerial struggle for control of processes has intensified while many of the old certainties have been lost. During the 1970s it became clear that organizations had to:

- Endeavour to master their environments by contesting more vigorously what they found there
- Develop an ability to engage more robustly within their world and evolve cultures that would seek to master changes around them and exploit them successfully.

While *closed* systems may be preferred for the degree of certainty that they may provide, because they fulfil their vision and mission without support or disturbance from outside, *most* organizations have *open* systems, **interdependent on their external environments and influenced by them**. Boundaries may be created, but essentially the system depends upon *a continuing flow of contacts, in and out*. Usually, the more the organization thrives upon this *the greater its likelihood of achieving enhanced performance and results.*

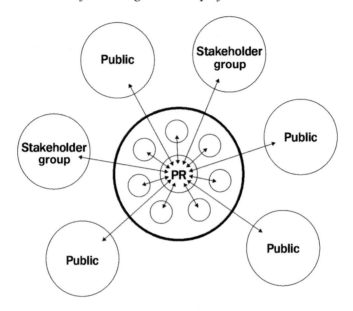

figure **2.2 boundary spanning**

Within the system there are a number of **subsystems** which may be variously described as divisions, departments, sections and units, all parts of the whole. So every organization may be viewed as **a collection of subsystems** that together work in **dynamic equilibrium** or 'steady state' of continual response and adjustment to influences, forces and pressures for change that arise from both within the organization and outside it in the social system comprising a variety of publics.

The public relations department is a subsystem, formed to undertake the communication work that existing managers are having difficulty in doing, or doing adequately, owing to their lack of sufficient relevant skills and available time. These first began to appear late in the 19th century in American companies. 'Typically, organizations develop a formal communication subsystem when the organization or its publics behave in a way that has *consequences* upon the other. Those consequences upon one another create a *public relations problem*' (Grunig and Hunt, 1984).

The role of the department is to **communicate both with other subsystems within the organization and with the external publics**, but there is also reciprocal communication occurring between *subsystems and publics*, both of which can have **consequences on the other**. In other words, communication outwards is not solely the job of the PR people; individual subsystems are busy doing it too, and that may, and often does, require the assistance of the public relations department.

So the public relations practitioners find themselves working *both inside and outside the organization,* located therefore somewhere along the perimeter boundary but also *crossing the internal boundaries* between each subsystem. This **boundary spanning** is a fundamental characteristic of the function.

Most organizations have similar subsystems, and these may be described as:

- *Management* subsystems that lead, co-ordinate and control the others, sorting out conflicts between them, assigning resources and balancing their needs one with another and with the demands laid upon the organization from outside it.
- *Production* subsystems, the 'powerhouse' of the operation, where what comes in is converted before it is exported out. These subsystems often comprise manufacturing and engineering but they embrace any process by which products and services are created.
- *Disposal* subsystems, charged with the task of making sure that products and services are marketed and distributed.
- *Adaptive* subsystems, tasked to keep on top of change, so that the organization may adapt and thereby enhance its position. These are likely to be involved in planning, research and development.
- *Maintenance* subsystems that provide cohesion of effort and efficiency of operation of the whole organization. These include personnel, training and development, and facilities.

So where exactly *is* the PR function among these?

1 Most often it is located within the group of *management* subsystems, where it may be close to the centre, because much of its work is concentrated on advising senior management, or further out, reflecting a broader or more evenly spread workload.
2 Alternatively, it is likely to be found in the *disposal* subsystems, standalone (preferably) or as part of marketing.
3 It may be located in the *adaptive* group, emphasizing its external environmental scanning and issues management.
4 Or it may be among the *maintenance* subsystems, reflecting an emphasis on internal communication.

2.5 the 'organizational eyes and ears'

The elitism of Bernays, Lippmann and others of their generation pre-dated the advent of the Internet, the dramatic spread of education, the creation of mass tourism, 'frivolous flying' and much else; in short, the *mass circulation of knowledge* about other people and places, perceptions and attitudes, beliefs and behaviours, tastes and languages, norms and values.

Then information was still expensive and in short supply for most people most of the time, not cheap, accessible and constantly on tap. Now the world is different, and any organization, unless it is a closed system, needs to be sensitized to what is going on within the environment in which it operates, if it knows what is good for it. This is called **environmental scanning**, gaining information about the macroenvironment that can be turned into useful intelligence.

PR people consider issues and trends. Their aim is to gain insights about the social environment that may be interpreted correctly and used by the **dominant coalition**, 'groups [of managers] with the power to set organizational structures and strategies over a sustained period of time' (White and Dozier, 1992). These groups have 'the power to make and enforce decisions about the direction of the organization, its tasks, its objectives, and functions'.

Such groups may comprise a small proportion of senior managers, typically three or four people, or the whole of a large senior management team. Good sense suggests that public relations should be represented there, but failing that it should most certainly be permitted to contribute what it knows before decisions are taken. Public relations is prominent among the boundary spanners within the organization, and its strategic inputs contribute to the definition and redefinition of organizational purpose and direction.

At the heart of this research and analysis lies the hunt to **identify and locate** the **critical forces** that are **impacting on the organization**, whether helpfully or otherwise, and to ascertain *how each relates to the other*. The techniques are common to all planners, arguably the most popular being the PEST categorization, in which the environment is examined under four headings: Political, Economic, Social and cultural and Technological. Owing to the growing complexities encountered, some have adapted this framework to include Legal and Environmental, when it is referred to as PESTLE; others, also adding Information, use the acronym EPISTLE. There are several more versions, but the point is made; this work has to be *thorough.*

In addition to environmental scanning, public relations practitioners gather **information about their publics and stakeholders**. They need to be *fully aware* of and *understand* their attitudes and behaviour towards the organization and current issues, and *how these may alter over time,* and *with what likely consequences.* They also need to know how one public or stakeholder group might *relate to another and interact.*

To this end, in addition to using secondary research methods, practitioners:

- Engage with all their numerous external contacts and
- Consult widely with other boundary spanners within the organization;
- Also undertake **primary research** into opinions and attitudes, continually probing to assess the potential power and influence of stakeholders, their needs and wants, their expectations of the organization, *their inclination and capacity to act* and *under what circumstances they might do so.*

In this the public relations function acts as **the eyes and ears of the**

organization. Because it connects widely outside, it develops useful contacts, observes and hears what might well pass by or evade someone *less externally active and contextually sensitized*. Public relations practice provides well-attuned **corporate antennae that can pick up distant signals** as well, providing early indications of how operating conditions may change over time, facilitating future scenario planning, trying to answer the *'what if?'* questions thrown up by the scanning. This may well affect markets, but it is just as likely to have *wider* implications or possibilities.

2.6 image, identity and reputation

So if, as Bernays asserted, images differ from reality, just *what is* **image**, a term that has entered universal usage and is widely applied with ease by people generally. An image is a **composite mental or sensual interpretation**, a perception, of someone or something; a *construct arrived at by deduction* based upon all the available evidence, **both real and imagined**, and *conditioned* by *existing* impressions, beliefs, ideas and emotions. Perceptions can be, often are, *intuitive*, relating to, for instance, aesthetic qualities, fundamental truths, absolute 'givens', basic understandings.

Images may be cultivated that are *factually accurate reflections of reality or essentially ephemeral and insubstantial*. They may be relatively honest or downright deceitful, randomly communicated or carefully contrived.

EXAMPLE

In 1927 American women were introduced to the concept of the image and were told that their appearance determined their images, the way in which other people perceived their personalities. They were advised to *acquire appearances designed to give them favourable images* that would be materially or socially advantageous to them. It was the spark that ignited consumerism; to have the 'right sort' of image necessitated attention to the detail of dress, make-up and much more besides, creating wants as well as needs.

This interest in images grew rapidly, so that by the 1960s the humorous novelist J. B. Priestley conceived of 'Social Imagistics' in his satire *The Image Men*. His underlying theme was that images are bogus. 'They're part of the unreality that's swindling us,' declares one of the principal characters, reflecting the widespread view that 'The average person sees image as the opposite of reality' (Grunig and White, 1992).

For an organization, its *current* image is of keen interest, particularly if it differs from the *wish* image, how it would *like* to be perceived. **Corporate image** can be as important as the image of the organization's product and service brands, for it translates the organization into a *personality, with qualities and values* that provide **foundations to expectations of its behaviours**.

There is much controversy about image. Practitioners are criticized for using the term too freely, when referring to many differing concepts, including 'reputation, perception, attitude, message, attributes, evaluation, cognition, credibility, support, belief, communication, or relationship' (Grunig and White, 1992). Images are typically described as being vapid, imprecise, superficial, figments of reality, but 'however unpalatable ... [image] remains a popular focus of interest. Even companies that prefer to adopt a low profile are assessing their corporate image' (Oliver, 2001). And it is not only companies; **all manner of organizations** are interested.

This scepticism is acknowledged by those who nevertheless champion the development of corporate images that 'build-up goodwill and confidence in the firm, create identity and publicize the firm's strengths' (Lancaster and Massingham, 1988). The value of a carefully constructed corporate image turns upon its **credibility** in the *varying interpretations* placed upon it, and this can have a **cumulative effect**, as these mental pictures are *shared*, often informally. Both the *rational and irrational* sets of meanings ascribed to the organization can become confused and *result in loss of definition*, so that the values that it is *intended to convey* have been submerged in contradiction or incomprehension.

Corporate identity

Corporate image differs from **corporate identity**, which 'denotes the sum total of all forms of expression that [an organization] uses to offer insight into its nature' (van Riel, 1995). Corporate *identity* is 'the strategically planned and operationally applied self-presentation of the organization (the corporate self) on the basis of a desired image.' It 'raises employee motivation, inspires confidence among the organisation's key external groups, acknowledges the vital role of customers [and of] key financial groups' (Varey, 1997a). In other words, it is **how the organization presents itself, warts and all**, which, if done artfully, may bring it benefits leading to tangible rewards.

Corporate identity is primarily thought of in the context of symbols and logos, once very popular mechanisms for distinguishing one outfit from another, although now less so, because corporate identity in the last decade has acquired a *broader interpretation.* These branding tools are now joined by other considerations, including:

▸ *Presentation,* in all its manifest details, including not only the design of all materials and the corporate colours and patterns but also such finer points as staff livery, the appearance of premises, what the vehicles look like and so on, right down to such minutiae as distinctively shaped internal door windows, choice of canteen cutlery and all the other applications of the 'corporate look' that stake out the territory, assert the corporate distinctiveness and preferences
▸ *Personality,* the organization's values, its mission in life, its vision and purpose, as these are manifested
▸ *Behaviour,* how that personality comes across in the way people within the organization behave, 'live the values' or otherwise, particularly when they are in contact with publics such as customers and shareholders

- *Communication,* in whatever form: organizations communicate with their environments all the time, by omission as well as commission
- *Connections,* the company that the organization keeps, such as various charities and political parties, the causes and interests that they sponsor and the types of celebrities and public personalities they employ or attract.

In essence, this recognizes that people **consider** *in the round* and they **connect up the bits** of information they gather about the organization: so, for instance, what they consider to be poor handling of their enquiry, whether or not that is warranted, affects what they think about the organization when next they see its logo or livery.

This broad interpretation of corporate identity can be bruising. It means that in effect **the organization is never 'off duty'**, *it cannot relax if it is serious about a holistic approach to communication.* Even dirty delivery vans in bad weather, for example, can do damage if what they carry is food, no matter that the products are unaffected. And dangerous driving by the van drivers can speak reams about process standards and work attitudes.

EXAMPLE ▬▬▬▬▬▬▬▬▬▬▬▬▬▬▬▬▬▬▬▬▬▬▬▬▬▬▬▬▬▬

'Companies pour millions of pounds [and other currencies] into creating strong brand identities that, once released into the world, become potent but difficult forces to control' (*The Observer*, 13 August 2000). Printed corporate names in public places are often altered in attempts to subvert their carefully constructed meanings, an activity described as 'political jujitsu' by Naomi Klein in *No Logo*. 'Jujitsu is a martial art that aims to take the energy of an attacker and redirect it against his or herself.' These guerrilla tactics, or social commentaries, represent a desire to make clear to the organization that the identity presented *does not accord with perceived reality.*

'The [visual presentation] programmes that seem to be most effective are those where identity schemes are part of a total and cohesive process of change that affects everything the company does. Not only does it mean operations and communications are working together, but it tends to encourage the involvement of employees. Whatever the scope of the programme, involvement should be a core objective' (Ind, 1995). This should *anchor the result closer to reality,* and avoid the persistent tendency for some identities to be 'slapped on' the organization, as if applying a cosmetic.

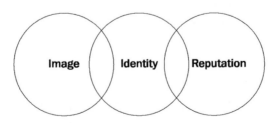

figure **2.3** **image, identity and reputation**

Image and **reputation** are also often mistaken for being one and the same. However, *there is a key difference.* The reputation of an organization is based upon *experience* of it, which is *not* a prerequisite of deciding about its image. Experience may be:

- *direct,* as where a product is purchased and or a service is received, or
- *indirect,* when the direct experiences of others are recounted.

Those 'others' are people whose

1 judgement may be trusted, or whose credibility is plausible, and
2 whose circumstances are recognizable and sufficiently similar to be relevant.

The *quality* of the experience is assessed by reference to the behaviours of the people with whom there have been contacts, at whatever level within the hierarchy.

The most common circumstances in which reputation is established are sale and purchase transactions, hence the emphasis placed upon **customer care** and **customer relations**, but there are *many more opportunities* for the organization to alter its reputation, both with individuals and generally, through the aggregation of individual experiences, as people advise one another. The fostering of reputation is also subject to the vagaries of *rumour*, whether or not malicious, and the *quality of interpretation* of the messages received; **too much weight may be attached to gossip and innuendo and too little given to reasoned assessment of the experience.**

Image, identity and reputation are closely linked. The identity contributes to the image and both condition the reputation. It is a popular adage that **positive reputations take a long time to create but may be destroyed very quickly**, the implication being that *attention to detail* in all reputation-making situations is highly advisable.

Clearly, this has a direct bearing on the *size* of the organization, for as the numbers of contacts increase so too do the *opportunities to get it right or get it wrong*, as continues to be vividly demonstrated in the UK National Health Service, which employs some 1.2 million people and is said to be the largest organization in Europe. Deficiencies of reputation, which is based on experience, may *jeopardize well-deserved and long cultivated* favourable image and identity.

EXAMPLE

Boots is a UK international retailer, trading in pharmaceuticals, toiletries and related products. It is long established and has both an image and reputation as a caring employer. An internal document, 'leaked' to the press in spring 2003, revealed that a year before the formal announcement was made the company had decided to close a factory in Scotland and transfer the work to its facilities in England, France and Germany. This would cause the loss of 1000 jobs locally.

The document implied that the closure, codenamed Project Tuscan, would occur regardless of the outcome to a prior review of manufacturing options: 'We debated two possible approaches: i) announcement of Airdrie closure, ii) announcement of a manufacturing review. On balance it was agreed that approach ii) was preferable ... This would give us a much more positive, media-friendly story to tell.' When the announcement of closure was made it was disclosed that at the end of 2002 the company had refused the offer of government funds to secure the future of the plant, because it did 'not need support'.

The document listed four audiences to be managed if the closure was not to damage the brand – employees, the media, politicians and business partners – and rated the probability of various reactions and their impact. It listed actions to control media impact and to 'limit government interference', including a suggestion that the closure announcement be timed to coincide with 'key political events'. When the company was informed of the leak it replied: 'The documents that have been leaked do not properly represent the extent of the total review process undertaken by the company. Our review was full, thorough and undertaken in keeping with our obligations' (*The Guardian*, 10 March 2003). Boots has since sold all of its manufacturing interests.

2.7 business ethics and values

Widespread and growing distrust has implications for public relations practice. The *Concise Oxford Dictionary* defines **trust** as being:

> *firm belief in reliability, honesty, veracity, justice, strength, etc., of person or thing.*

Interestingly, to be trust*ful* is defined as being *full of trust, unsuspicious, confiding,* that is to say, believing confidently in the veracity of another person. Trust*worthy* is to be *worthy of trust.* When these terms are applied to organizations, rather than individuals, they strike a deeper resonance. For instance, *how many* organizations provoke *confidences* worthy of the name and how many may be accurately described as being *trustworthy*? Are not these values cornerstones of communication, and why do they appear to be in short supply?

It is widely agreed that trust is a precious commodity that every organization needs. The arguments in favour are familiar:

- That trust in the workplace improves efficiency and creates greater enjoyment in the work
- That it creates the foundation for meaningful relationships with customers and other publics
- That it facilitates decision-taking and engenders confidence.

Trust is a product of *moral awareness of the ethical dimensions,* the rules of moral behaviour, encountered both within the organization and in its contacts with its external environment.

- But are ethical considerations to be discarded, as competition intensifies and communication becomes more complex, hurried and demanding of patience and expertise?
- Or might the widely acknowledged flight from trust be reversed, to advantage, applying some age-old truths to some very modern problems?

utilitarianism

Probably the most commonly cited ethical principle is '*do what is likely to create the greatest happiness for the greatest number of people*', first propounded in 1725 by Francis Hutcheson, thinking about politicians and nation states. This is the simplest form of **utilitarianism**, in which the ends justify the means. It is the most widely used in routine 'common-sense' decision-making. It was used, for example, by the British Prime Minister in March 2003 when seeking parliamentary support for the military invasion of Iraq.

Jeremy Bentham (1748–1832) added to this, with his Principle of Utility, by which each action should be judged according to the *results* achieved by it, on how it *benefits everyone*, not just the performer. Also, he asserted that *everyone should be treated equally*; one form of happiness was not more important than any other. Then John Stuart Mill (1806–73) added that the *effects* of observing rules should be considered where their observance would *benefit society as a whole*, and universally respected when they are framed for the benefit of everyone. He disagreed with Bentham about happiness, saying that there are higher and lower pleasures.

Utilitarianism is among the **teleological** ethical principles and systems that emphasize the **importance of the outcome** rather than the actions taken by which it is reached. Some forms of teleology are *restricted* to the likely consequences for a single person, company, organization or social group, such as a family, rather than to people generally. There is, for instance, a theory, widely applied, that the *preferences of the individual* should be taken into account, unless those of others outweigh them. That is to say, the people concerned should be allowed to say what *for them* constitutes pleasure or pain, and there should be appropriate *equal consideration* of interests.

Utilitarianism has its *practical limitations*, owing to conflicts of interest and divergence of views. If such teleological approaches to ethics are applied *universally*, the final decision has to be in the interests of the majority, not the minority or the individual, and that may not square readily with respecting individual preferences where that is intended. Nor does utilitarianism:

- Adequately allow for *motive*, which is important when thinking about morality
- Explain why some moral rules should not be broken, *despite the consequences*
- Allow fully for handling *complex moral issues*.

Furthermore: 'Critics of teleology note that knowing the consequences of actions before the fact can be difficult, that not all things can be assigned a numerical value (e.g., human life), and that looking only at short-term consequences can be shortsighted' (Curtin and Boynton, 2001). The central practical issue here is the *difficulty in predicting consequences*. 'Since you cannot be sure, ahead of time, what that good will be, or even, at times, where the greatest number will lie, you need to speculate as best you can on the consequences, or end, of your action' (Kidder and Bloom, 2001).

categorical imperative

The second commonly cited approach is the **categorical imperative**, the view of morality that is based on knowing what *ought* to be done, having **a sense of duty**, *regardless of the consequences*. This belongs to the **deontological** category of ethical principles and systems, where actions themselves are always right or wrong, some acts have to be done regardless of their consequences and satisfactory outcomes do not necessarily guarantee good actions. It is **absolute and unconditional**, very much suited to the person who prefers to act by the rulebook.

Immanuel Kant (1724–1804) is most closely associated with this; in 1785 he asserted that a person should only do that which he or she would be prepared for everyone else to be able to do as well. A main theme is that **actions should be consistent with treating people as the *ends* and not as the means**. Kant was not troubled by consequences, preferring to concentrate on motive and the particular act. Expected results, he thought, could not be used to demonstrate conclusively that a proposed action was right or wrong; there would never be enough evidence and agreement about interpretation. Action should be out of *a sense of personal moral conviction*. The moral certainties of the categorical imperative may appeal, but prove difficult to follow, involving strict adherence to duty, justice and recognition of rights.

This perceiving of what is right or wrong based on duty may be anchored to formal rules ('rule deontology'), such as a professional code, of which there are many in public relations, promulgated by various trade bodies and practitioner associations. These codes have several advantages: they give practitioners a useful point-of-reference and steer them towards what is thought by their peers to be ethical – this is relatively objective, in the sense that it is not subjective; they establish the grounds for what conduct may be expected of them, by their employers, clients and others; and they provide a 'rulebook' basis for disciplining members who are found to transgress. But 'following the rulebook' in all circumstances can have unexpected and undesirable outcomes, maybe even disastrous results. And: 'This approach is inherently difficult to apply... and often results... in ethical relativism, where each situation is approached individually and no consistent guidelines are applied' (Kidder and Bloom, 2001).

situational ethics

As the name implies, here everything turns on the particular circumstances, taking into account all ethical responsibilities encountered in each specific situation. This may involve balancing both teleological and deontological principles, starting from such basic precepts as the deontological 'do unto others as you would they do unto you' that is found in all the great religions and addresses a *universal truth* about human nature. 'Withholding requested information from the press when disclosure of that information would be harmful to one's client is an example of ethical decision-making in this style' (Day *et al.*, 2001).

A 'more extreme approach', **subjectivism**, or individual relativism, is based on doing whatever seems to be 'right' **regardless of any objective principles**. This may be situational, or more general. 'Of the four approaches to ethics, this approach usually is seen as the least ethical.' Curtin and Boynton say situational ethics is often 'misused as a synonym for ethical relativism.' Further ethical theories include the **justice theory**, which holds that loss of liberty nullifies any gains, and **virtue theory**, that the individual should act virtuously, beyond 'mere' duty and self-interest.

stages in moral reasoning

Kohlberg (1981, 1984), reported by Curtin and Boynton (2001), developed a **six-stage typology of moral reasoning** that they consider relevant to public relations practice. This may be summarized briefly as:

Preconventional: 'a restricted teleological stance focusing on self-interest.'

    Stage one: Obey orders, fear reprisal, use emotion over reason, concentrate on personal goals and situational consequences.

    Stage two: Exploit situations for personal gain, manipulate and deceive to achieve, focus on the short term.

Conventional: 'conformity to commonly accepted expectations or standards.'

    Stage three: Promote the interests of one's culture, peer group or organization – reasoning is based on principles held by the group or result in actions beneficial to the group.

    Stage four: Obey the law and fulfil duties to benefit the group, keep the rules.

Postconventional: 'personal autonomy and critical reflection.'

    Stage five: Base decisions on universal social well-being.

    Stage six: Weigh every decision 'on its benefit to society in terms of universal principles such as equity, justice and fairness.' People are ends, not means. Principles are good for everyone to live by.

Perhaps not surprisingly, most adults mainly use the middle level of reasoning, and although people might rely on one type of reasoning more than any other, in practice they may use a *combination*. Kohlberg thought 'true' stage six was purely theoretical, because 'he believed that most people could not achieve the rigor of thought necessary to employ it with any consistency'. None of the models in this are said to be 'a better form of practice'.

This can be seen to align with the **four types of public relations practice**, discussed in Chapter 5: stage two with press agentry, or publicity, 'the propaganda model'; stage four 'roughly' with the public information and two-way asymmetric models; stages five and six 'roughly' with the two-way symmetric model. With these four types, the last is definitely rated to be a better form of practice compared with the others.

game theory

Game theory also has relevance to public relations ethics. Developed in the 1950s, game theory is about competitive situations that can give rise to co-operation or conflict, in which the consequences of possible actions are assigned mathematical values. This is a form of cost-benefit analysis that, it is argued, can facilitate decisions that take into account the best possible outcomes for *all* 'players' in the 'game'.

The theory identifies **four types of games**: probably the best known is *zero-sum*, or *win-lose*: one person wins all the points while the other loses all the points. The sum of the win and the loss equals zero. To the players, winning is all. This is highly adversarial, and not what public relations practitioners are likely to seek or welcome. In the remaining types, however, there is the possibility that every 'player' may win some points, and everything depends upon three key elements:

‣ Co-operation: in *non-zero-games* every participant rates co-operation above simple winning or losing
‣ Bargaining: in *bargaining games* everyone bargains with the aim of achieving an outcome that best satisfies everyone under all circumstances
‣ Timing: in *timing games* the emphasis is on calculating the optimum moment for making a move.

Practitioners are familiar with these types: trying to obtain co-operation, maybe between an organization and one of its publics; seeking to bargain satisfactory outcomes for all concerned; calculating finely just when is the most propitious moment to act, say in releasing information. Game theory facilitates *structured thinking* in moments of uncertainty, possibly confusion, maybe even crisis. It is a teleological approach that, by concentrating on all possible consequences to all players, asking the 'what if?' questions, provides a practitioner with not only an ethical framework but an enhanced practical way of trying to better understand how other players are likely to behave and coalesce; in other words, it is also a potentially powerful strategic planning tool.

There are problems in applying game theory. These include the familiar diffi-culty of *achieving accuracy* in identifying consequences *beforehand*. Assigning *specific values* to each possible action and its likely consequence can prove to be less than scientific. And there is the question of just *how ethical the means might have to be* in order to achieve the most satisfactory result. Furthermore, intended outcomes based on this cost-benefit analysis may be thwarted by harsh realities, as when *consequent costs* are considered more important than 'intangibles such as public faith and goodwill'. Nor may *human nature* be much help in using game theory: it requires 'players' to be truly empowered to play, and they have to be prepared to fully co-operate and forego 'gamesmanship' for the duration.

three practice value systems

Sullivan is credited with having developed in the 1960s 'the most complete theory on ethical public relations practice', according to Pearson (1989), reported by Day *et al.* (2001). Sullivan 'proposed that public relations as a profession deals with images of reality just as medicine as a profession deals with the human body'. He 'insisted that public relations professionals must strive to provide true information to the public... [He] also proposed that public relations was influenced by and must address three value systems: technical, partisan, and mutual'. In summary, these are:

- *Technical values*: efficiency and pride in the job
- *Partisan values*: 'loyalties such as commitment, trust, and obedience'
- *Mutual values*: 'the rights and well-being of others'.

Most importantly, as it later turned out, Sullivan, by identifying mutual values as early as 1965, had anticipated **dialogue** as a component of practice, which later was to be developed strongly by others, as the central means to recognizing and respecting other people's rights and interests and to fostering mutually beneficial relationships.

CHECKLIST

- ☐ Corporate communication may be divided into three categories: management communication, by managers both internally and externally; marketing communication; and organization communication, being all other forms of communication by an organization.
- ☐ Public relations practice occurs in all three categories, but primarily in the third.
- ☐ By their communication skills senior managers motivate and empower others internally and establish the external parameters within which they may develop their organizations.
- ☐ Those senior managers that recognize the public relations implications of their communication responsibilities acknowledge the relevance of PR to the development of their corporate strategy.
- ☐ MPR contributes to the creation of shareholder value and investment returns.
- ☐ The PR department is a formal subsystem, usually established when the activities of an organization or its publics, both internal and external, affect the other.
- ☐ The function is usually located among the management subsystems, but may be found in the disposal, adaptive or maintenance subsystems, depending upon workload weighting.
- ☐ The function spans boundaries, both internally between subsystems and between the organization and components of its external environment.
- ☐ Environmental scanning enables the PR function to ascertain, understand and record attitudes

and behaviours towards the organization, evolving issues of potential consequence to the organization and the interactions of its publics and stakeholder groups.

□ Image is a composite mental or sensual interpretation of someone or something that is based upon all the available evidence, both real and imagined, and conditioned by existing impressions, beliefs, ideas and emotions.

□ Corporate identity describes how the organization presents itself in the round.

□ Reputation is based upon experience gained, whether through direct contact or indirectly via information received from third parties who have had contact.

□ Widespread and growing distrust has implications for PR practice, in which ethical dilemmas are commonplace and arise frequently.

CASE STUDY

A TALE OF TWO DOT COMS

Upmystreet.com is one of the UK's largest Internet businesses, originally a pitch promoting a consultancy, Aztec Internet, which was transformed, using £12.5 million external financing, into *the* site for all manner of local information, such as statistics on crime, the identity of elected representatives and, perhaps most importantly, given the British obsession with property, current house prices. In January 2003 alone it attracted 665,000 visitors: the same month the company went into administration, beset with severe cash flow problems. In the following April it was put up for sale, one of its founders posting the plea 'Buy my baby please'.

The company had been devising new products, including its praised 'world first in social software', a discussion board for conversation among neighbours, and had targeted services at the public sector and at business, to counter a downturn in advertising revenue, on which it is substantially dependent. But there are likely to be limits to how much local information and chat with neighbours is individually needed or wanted, and winning commercial contracts is costly and time-consuming.

This brand has been built with hardly any advertising expenditure, ironically, given the dependence upon it for income. It is rich in goodwill, intangible assets and intellectual property. And it has professional management that is positive about its future and its business model (*The Guardian*, 14 April 2003).

Friends Reunited is another major UK Web-based business, founded by a married couple and their friend in a modest suburban house in 2000 to 'put people in touch with their old classmates'. Thousands of e-mails poured in daily, each one being answered individually, and soon relatives and friends, appropriately, were enlisted to help, a charge for the service being introduced in April 2001. In March 2003, still operating partly from the original tiny bedroom, the founders made known publicly that they were open to offers for the site, with its eight million registered users in the UK. Reported offers of up to £30 million came in, from companies thought to include AOL and Yahoo.

This company too has been adding to what it offers. It has GenesConnected, for people wanting to trace their family history, which also proved very successful, and is involved in online dating services that introduce strangers to one another socially. It is developing an international reach, notably into Italy, Spain, the Netherlands, Australia and New Zealand.

But Friends Reunited's owners decided at that time not to accept an offer for the company, preferring instead to 'have other people managing it... We don't really see ourselves as businessmen... We describe it as an old-fashioned cottage industry'. It has reached this point with virtually no marketing or advertising. 'Basically there has been nothing spent on marketing so far, everything has been PR driven, which has been fantastic, but there is a point at which you need marketing to go further', according to the company's new chief executive (*The Times*, 13 March 2003). Subsequently Friends Reunited was bought for £120m in 2005 by UK television broadcaster ITV.

QUESTIONS

1 What might be the 'total communication needs' of an organization, and why?
2 How may public relations contribute to shareholder value?
3 What might be meant by 'image is in the eye of the beholder'?
4 Why may reputations be made slowly and destroyed quickly?
5 How accountable is public relations for the quality of business ethics, and why?

within the organization

Vision and mission – the learning organization – enterprise culture – motivation – organizational structure and environment – communication channels – managing change – organizational body language

3.1 vision and mission

The vision and mission of an organization provide the framework for all of the formal internal communication and are therefore wholly relevant to public relations. **Vision** addresses the 'big picture', **what the organization aims to be and look like within a stated period**, typically several years ahead. It conveys a clear indication of ultimate direction for everyone engaged within the organization or connected with it in some way: *what the dominant coalition that steers the enterprise envisages being the organization's future.*

In a complex and uncertain environment, where there is **constant change**, it can be very reassuring to have a precise, clearly stated overall view of a credible, if distant, aim. That has universal application, and public relations practitioners, among others, are preoccupied with change, in all its dimensions, because, as the proverb says, if you do not know where you are going any road will take you there. So the purpose of **vision statements** is to *set out clearly* the intended destination.

Mission, by contrast, is concerned with **how the organization performs at present**, specifically concerning standards of behaviour. **Mission statements** abound: some even are displayed in entrance halls and boardrooms to tell visitors, as well, about the character of their organization. When framing these statements there is an understandable temptation to *embroider reality*. Where that occurs it is the public relations task to provide employees with **valid interpretations** that they may recognize and accept as *having some bearing on their individual experience and perceptions*. This may be no easy task, but unless the mission statement has credibility it is likely to be rejected as mere irrelevant gibberish, meaningless verbiage, and this in turn can *foster doubts about other aspects of their employment.*

The *potency* of mission statements is, therefore, in proportion to their credibility and the degree to which they reflect values that the organization *has in common with* its members.

- Research and corporate experience confirms that people *will* their employing organizations to demonstrate that they uphold their personal values.

Employees want to know that what they think is right or wrong in their private lives *coincides* with what goes on when they get to work. When asked for their perceptions of their employment, typical of the approving responses are comments such as 'They know how to treat people' and 'We are all a happy family'. Where these and similar sentiments are expressed in house newspapers and other internal media, as often they are, they **must accord with employees' experience** if they are to be accepted.

This desire to see **shared values** in the workplace that foster accord and confidence goes *well beyond* the satisfaction of what seems right and proper, important though that is:

- Employees often seek reassurance that their organization *outperforms others owing to its superior behaviours*. These 'others' may be competitors, rivals or *all* organizations that are outwardly similar, including those in entirely different fields of activity.
- There is a need to know that *their* organization is superior, simply 'the best', and this has *implications* for performance and competitive advantage.

There are four **elements of mission** (Campbell *et al.*, 1990): *organizational purpose*, *strategy*, *behaviours* and *values*, which both reflect and reinforce each other; and there are *three categories of company* where purpose is stated :

- The first is primarily concerned to maximize *shareholder value*
- The second exists primarily to satisfy *all* of its *stakeholders*
- The third prioritizes some *higher ideal* that all stakeholders may be proud to support and to which they contribute.

These categories may be adapted to other types of organization. Clearly they have important implications for the structuring of internal communication, which needs to be *framed within the context of vision and mission*. The constant threat of confusion about mission and how it relates to vision compels eternal public relations vigilance, particularly since on occasion vision and mission coincide. This can occur in conditions of rapid change, where the mission may be more concerned to address desirable future rather than current behaviours.

The case for developing and maintaining meaningful mission statements is compellingly simple.

> A management team capable of defining a clear mission will have advantages over a team that has defined only its strategy. The mission team will have values as well as strategic concepts to guide it through important decisions; the strategy team will have commercial logic only. Business decisions and people decisions are often hard to take, particularly on a consistent basis... In these two areas ... senior managers need as much

support as possible. A clearly defined set of values reinforcing the strategy gives this extra support.

Vision and mission are integral to **corporate culture**, the character of the organization, what it *feels* like to an 'insider'. 'Organizational culture consists of value and judgments unique to each organization', according to Heath (1992), who quotes Deetz (1982): 'An organizational culture consists of whatever a member must know or believe in order to operate in a manner understandable and acceptable to other members and the means by which this knowledge is produced and transmitted.' Public relations practitioners are active contributors to the creation and maintenance of the culture, through communications via a variety of media.

Through this and also their boundary spanning, public relations practitioners are highly aware of and sensitive to the corporate culture *at all levels of the hierarchy*. In developing both vision and mission statements they can have a strong contribution to make and an equally strong interest in the outcome. *And* they are better placed than anyone else to have at their fingertips the raw data of *external* attitudes and perceptions across all publics and stakeholders. *And* they have a ringside seat in seeing how other people within the organization interrelate with parts of the outside environment. All of which makes them a *key source* of input.

Furthermore, what emerges is *fundamental* to public relations strategic planning. The vision and mission statements are building blocks used for the foundations, without which any PR practice is at serious risk of being constructed on insecure premises and to being seriously hindered in its effectiveness. For public relations, therefore, the organization's current vision and mission is not simply 'nice to know' but absolutely '*need* to know'.

3.2 the learning organization

Internal communication is primarily about securing universal *motivation* and *commitment*, because **organizations are rated on their scope for leveraging assets**, obtaining more from what they have, and the human asset is potentially the richest source of enhanced performance.

- Managers in knowledge-based and in service-driven environments understand that they have to optimize the *organizational value of each person.*
- That in turn requires everyone to have his or her very own *personal development plan*, a career signposting that has less to do with jobs and more with self-fulfilment. They are the outward manifestation of a *mutually advantageous deal* between employer and employee, and where this pact works well the internal communication can assume some *very stimulating and worthwhile* dimensions.

It is this drive to enhance performance and competitive advantage through people skills that has brought about the concept of the **learning organization**.

Learning may be defined as:

> the process of acquiring, through experience, knowledge that leads to changed behaviour.

Expressed like that, not surprisingly many organizations want to become learning ones, in which their members routinely acquire knowledge that they can readily apply in the workplace. To qualify for the accolade involves everyone becoming and remaining *demonstrably at the cutting edge of knowledge acquisition.*

The learning organization addresses this at several levels. First and foremost, it has a *vision*, one *that is shared.* Knowing where the organization is aiming for and being wholly committed to that creates a powerful combined determination to 'pull weight'. This may foster a relatively informal workplace, because, in perception if not in reality, the structure becomes *flatter*, as each person exercises power through **an ability to acquire knowledge and share information in a common cause**. The emphasis is on the 'learning curve', securing *up-to-date intelligence that can be used to advantage*, and on facilitation and collaboration to this end. **Creativity,** in ideas and implementation, is highly valued.

Communication has a significant role to play in enhancing this environment, for it serves information and ideas, supports and supplements coaching and mentoring and provides both advice and reassurance. 'How people listen depends on the organization's culture... Culture 'refracts' communication... The central skill in managing today's organization has gone from 'telling the troops' to fostering and facilitating communication. The aim ... should be to align attitudes, share knowledge, and manage information' (Quirke, 1995).

It is observable that *an intensity of commitment* to learning often tends to be found within *smaller* organizations and units, perhaps owing to:

- The immediacy of competitive pressures,
- Readier identification with core values and
- The necessity to adopt flexible work attitudes.

Small businesses in computer-related occupations or new media products offer typical examples.

3.3 enterprise culture

Grunig and Grunig (1992) reported **four types of organizational culture** that had been identified by reference to the interaction of *two dimensions of attitude and behaviour*: authoritarian versus democratic and reactive versus proactive:

> *Systematized* cultures are authoritarian and reactive.
> *Entrepreneurial* cultures are authoritarian and proactive.
> *Interactive* cultures are democratic and reactive.
> *Integrated* cultures are democratic and proactive.

Subsequent research had indicated that nine out of ten in the sample were either *integrated* or *entrepreneurial.*

The idea of the individual taking initiative, unassisted by anyone, is widespread, as is a tradition of *enterprise born of initiative*. The term **enterprise culture** is used to describe a **disposition towards bold, outward-going dynamic action** that is based upon a set of **supportive values** that has been widely described as a philosophy of 'free enterprise'. Talk of creating an enterprise culture is intended to encourage and exploit people's adventurous ambitions, as a means to achieve economic growth and wealth generation more widely.

Within the enterprise culture there abides the *entrepreneur*, who may be defined as anyone who undertakes a business activity with the chance of making a profit or loss. Entrepreneurs are noted for their ability to:

- *Focus*, to the extent of seldom being 'off the job',
- Analyse what they know and believe,
- Demonstrate self-reliance and resourcefulness,
- Exercise judgement,
- Provide leadership and
- Think flexibly.

They keep *asking the tough questions* and *try to avoid set thinking*, a kind of corporate hardening of the arteries. Often they concentrate till it hurts and they are always looking for ways around obstacles. In *What They Don't Teach You At Harvard Business School* (1984) the entrepreneur Mark McCormack counselled that 'Running a company is a constant process of breaking out of systems and challenging conditioned reflexes, of rubbing against the grain'. This calls for lateral thinking.

> The trouble is that there is no logical reason for looking for alternatives unless we are dissatisfied with what we have. And yet in creativity it is vital to be looking for alternatives no matter how satisfied we may be. There therefore has to be a deliberate intention or exercise of will to seek alternatives... Curiously we do not have a verb to describe the need to look for alternatives. That is why it was necessary to create the term 'lateral thinking' (de Bono, 1978).

Creativity is the very life-blood of public relations practice, which is closely identified with the enterprise culture. Practitioners are required to demonstrate their ability to be creative and think laterally. *Organizations in search of a more entrepreneurial bias in their cultures look to their public relations departments to communicate some of that outlook and 'can do' approach* which character- izes their work. Public relations is expected to provide an inexhaustible flow of creative solutions that are distinctive, and practitioners are generally noted for their seemingly relentless energy and enthusiasm.

3.4 motivation

The house magazine may have a long history, but it has not been a particularly glorious one. Too often these popular components of the 'created media' have included a varied collection of management opinion and assertion, propaganda, cloying supposed entertainment and inconsequentialities. Front pages and covers invariably featured the chairman with a drink in his hand or the managing director gripping a public speaker's lectern. Inside there would be a few more photographs, mostly involving the chairman and the managing director again, the finance director too if he or she were lucky.

Sometimes merely to *glimpse* such organs seemed an unwarranted intrusion upon the private lives of the senior management. Seldom did the employees *learn anything much* of substance *about management's thinking, conclusions, decisions and purposes.* Instead they probably had to be content with a concoction of instructions and heavily contrived news, *mostly filleted of facts worth having*, interwoven with a few well-placed entertainment items of the utmost banality.

All this *should* be past, for the motivational role of communication within the organization has never been clearer. Whatever the primary purpose, such as greater efficiency or customer focus, managers *need the positive collaboration* of employees in coming forward with their feedback, ideas and suggestions, so that those **whose experience tells them** where **changes** might be usefully made **inform those who have the authority to make them**.

Now the emphasis is on *involving everyone*, bringing them into the thinking, getting them wanting to come forward, creating believable futures and so on. Content standards have improved. The purpose is to stimulate a *united sense of motivation and loyalty* through a more collegiate approach that takes greater account of readers' knowledge and perceptions.

Entertainment and information remain components of the communication mix, as do persuasion, but the thrust is on **engagement, dialogue, trying to have conversations that will benefit the organization**. In *Up The Organization* (1970) Robert Townsend, former chairman of Avis, observed that people 'don't have to be forced or threatened [to work]... But they'll commit themselves only to the extent they can see ways of satisfying their ego and development needs'.

The idea that simply making people *feel good* about their employment is *no longer adequate within an unstable operating environment*, where the organization must be quick on its toes, responding to external changes and striving to change itself advantageously. People have needs, which managers must recognize and address if they are to establish and maintain mutually beneficial relationships. Those needs include recognition and tangible appreciation. And managers have to understand what emotional and psychological hurdles may have to be jumped before upward communication becomes possible.

3.5 organizational structure and environment

The organizational **structure and environment** and its **management style** are also fundamentally important to the planning and conduct of public relations, because they *determine the approach to developing communication systems and media.* There are four management theories, or groups of theories, that provide the framework to thinking about this.

In the early part of the last century a group of theories, collectively described as **machine theory**, perceived of the organization and its people as being a *machine*. All of these theories saw humans as *cogs in the machine*, there to labour at their narrow specialisms with minimal autonomy within rigidly structured hierarchies. Communication in these structures runs:

1 **Vertically**, from superiors to subordinates and vice versa,
2 **Horizontally**, from colleagues to colleagues within a unit or between units at the same level and
3 **Diagonally**, between units at differing levels.

However, the *main* flow is **downwards**, usually with instructions and exhortations to work harder, quicker.

In response to the deficiencies of machine theory there emerged **human relations theory**, which focused on *people* and how they might be *motivated* to achieve greater efficiency.

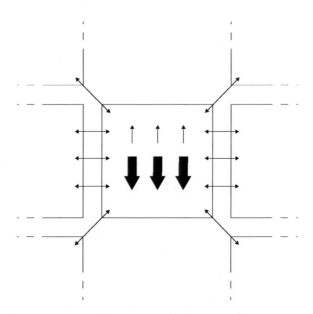

figure **3.1** **communication flows within the 'machine'**

The industrial psychologist, Elton Mayo, argued that *relationships* were the most important factor, and in consequence *teamwork* was the key. He and two colleagues from Harvard University conducted research at the Western Electric Company's plant at Cicero, near Chicago, which became known as the 'Hawthorne Studies'. The team concluded that:

▸ People should be viewed not in isolation but *as part of a group*
▸ *Informal groups exert powerful influence*
▸ Managers need to *allow for the social needs* of employees to secure commitment.

They had found that *through information, explanation and willingness to listen*, the researchers had inadvertently induced the women to **form a self-governing team** that **co-operated wholeheartedly** with management.

Another contributor to human relations theory was industrialist Chester Barnard, who recognized **communication as the first priority in management** but thought it should be 'expressive', not 'instrumental'. He favoured the machine concept but in addition to giving instructions he saw value in 'feel-good' messages that made it all seem somehow better for the workers. Here again, *horizontal contacts were discouraged* for fear that inaccurate information, rumours and 'the wrong news' might circulate. Communication up the line was limited by conditions and was often motivated solely by a *desire for recognition and approval*.

These machine and human relations theories underpin the management approach in more structured organizations:

- Instructions come from the centre,
- The emphasis is on close adherence to performance targets and
- The contributions of employees are lauded.

This is because 'More competition requires more co-operation' (Peters, 1987). Large and numerous awards may be given to honour acts of co-operation: 'The chief issue is attitude, but such awards can help change attitudes, over time.'

Out of human relations theory there developed **human resources theory**:

- Maslow argued in 1943 that **people have a 'hierarchy of needs'** that start with fundamental requirements of food and shelter and ascend, progressively, through safety to society and affection to self-esteem and finally fulfilment. Each level is dominant until satisfied and *only then* is the next a motivating factor; self-actualization, the top tier, *cannot be satisfied*.

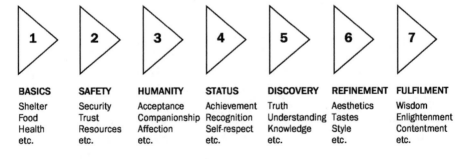

BASICS	SAFETY	HUMANITY	STATUS	DISCOVERY	REFINEMENT	FULFILMENT
Shelter	Security	Acceptance	Achievement	Truth	Aesthetics	Wisdom
Food	Trust	Companionship	Recognition	Understanding	Tastes	Enlightenment
Health	Resources	Affection	Self-respect	Knowledge	Style	Contentment
etc.	etc.	etc.	etc.	etc.	etc.	etc.

figure **3.2 hierarchy of human needs, after Maslow**

- Many models have been based on this, usually depicted as a triangle. Cartwright, however, decided to create an extra layer, so creating a blank summit. The model 'cuts off the top of self-actualization to reflect the fact that there are things that will never be totally achieved. Part of human motivation is to strive for the unreachable' (Cartwright, 2001).

- Herzberg's **motivation-hygiene** theory identified **what causes dissatisfaction and satisfaction at work**. He called these *hygiene*, because they are essentially preventative, or *maintenance* factors. He thought people felt a need to *avoid unpleasantness*, which could be satisfied by hygiene factors, which were short-lived and repeatedly in demand, and for *personal growth*, which could be met by motivator factors. And he specified three typical ways by which work might be altered in order to motivate: *job enrichment, job enlargement* and *job rotation.*
- In examining how managers handle people, McGregor identified two **extreme sets of assumptions, which determined the styles adopted.** Theory X stated that the average person has an inherent dislike of work and will try to avoid it. There is little ambition and no want of responsibility, but preference for being given direction and a craving of security.
- According to his **Theory Y**, however, the expenditure of physical and mental effort in work is as natural as play or rest. There is no inherent dislike of work; for it may be the source of satisfaction or punishment. There is self-direction and control when there is commitment. McGregor intentionally polarized his theories, knowing that in practice managers' assumptions may fall somewhere between the two extremes.
- Blake and Mouton produced a 'management grid' in 1964, known as **Blake's grid**, based on **two dimensions of managers' behaviour in ensuring efficiency and effectiveness**: concern for *the job* in hand and concern for *the people* doing it. They identified five styles:
  - *Impoverished* (not much bothered about targets or people),
  - *Country club* (satisfying relationships is the priority),
  - *Task management* (achieving results is the priority),
  - *Middle of the road,* or *the dampened pendulum* (aiming for a balance between productivity and morale) and
  - *Team* (high work accomplishment through leadership of committed people who identify with the organizational aims).
- Ouchi in 1981 combined Japanese and Western management techniques in his **Theory Z**, which asserted that **ability to gain the co-operation of people, not technology, increased productivity**. He based his thinking on the concept of *wa*, or harmony, and *nenko*, or lifelong employment.
- Handy's **motivation calculus** was based on **expectancy theory**, by which **people decide** on their **effort** based on what they **think is in it for them** and **how likely that result is**. He argued that there was *more than Effort alone required,* including Energy, Excitement, Enthusiasm, Emotion and Expenditure, his **E-factors**. In the workplace:
  - The *intended results* had to be made clear, so that the person could work out how much 'E' was required, and
  - there had to be *feedback* on performance, for confidence, prevention of hostility and so on.
  - People committed when *the goals were specific,* particularly if they had helped identify them; however,

if they were rewarded for performance tied to specific standards people might then *set themselves lower standards*, when the likelihood of success and reward was greater and required less 'E' to be exerted.

Human resources theory perceives **engagement and involvement of employees** as being **central to motivation that will result in co-operation**. This is achieved through *more flexible structures* and *greater autonomy for the individual* based upon a degree of **open communication between managers and staff**, open in the sense that the substantive background decisions and their circumstances are explained and discussed. The environment is less about managers giving orders and more about *managers and staff collectively 'taking orders' from their shared situation*.

In this environment:

▸ *Communication is encouraged,* vertically, horizontally and diagonally, and
▸ There is *less inhibition*;
▸ Ideally, messages flow backwards and forwards *without regard for status* of senders, encouraged in a dynamic atmosphere of collaboration and mutual respect.

But this much looser approach does not have universal appeal. It often works very well in *smaller settings*, with *fewer people involved*, typically where everyone has readily *recognizable symbols of comparable status*, but where one subsystem differs from another in its approach it may not be so practicable. And people have *variable levels of willingness* to participate in these less formal structures; hence much emphasis is placed on **team building**.

Finally, there is **systems theory**, which, instead of specifying any one approach, advocates 'horses for courses': **what suits best in the given circumstances, the organization's environment and technologies**. This applies not only to the whole system but also to each and every one subsystem.

So the design of communication systems has to take into account the variables. Here it may serve a more structured environment, there it may reflect a less structured one; content may be orientated here more around instruction, encouragement and happy families, there more around ideas, opportunities and objective, timely tips. Less specialized people tend to prefer 'keeping it simple' whereas the more specialized may well want more 'bite' and objectivity.

3.6 communication channels

Owing to the historic emphasis on printed media, such as the 'house journal', there is still a *substantial use of hard copy publications*, but a growing proportion of internal communication uses *other tools*, notably electronic media, and benefits from continuing innovations. These media include:

▸ *Magazines,* to tell the human story, explain a complex issue, convey organizational qualities and status
▸ *Newspapers,* tabloid size, with timely news, hard facts, friendly tips, bonding messages

- *Newsletters* that provide facts and comment, decisions and deadlines, calls for action, often electronically instead of or as well as hard copy
- *Bulletins*, often daily, with a digest of what matters most there and then
- *Presentations*, using audiovisual equipment, to treat a larger subject in detail
- *Video tapes*, for advice and instruction simultaneously at multiple sites or individual viewing by scattered staff
- *Audiotapes*, for much the same but where vision is not needed, to be heard by staff individually off site or at home
- *Closed-circuit television*, for immediacy across sites in a very popular format
- *Displays and exhibitions*, for complex messages, three-dimensional interpretations, opportunities to linger and ready access to answers
- *Telephone 'hot lines'*, for enquiries and contributions
- *E-mails*, for short messages and generating immediate interest
- *Letters*, particularly for contractual and other messages that require personal attention and may involve consultation with others
- *Brochures and booklets*, for information that may be needed routinely in the future or to address a major current issue involving many people/everyone
- *Books*, fictional or non-fictional, for education about the organization, its sector, history, connections, interests
- *Notice boards*, for fast rotation of information in arresting displays
- *Pay-packet notices*, for short messages guaranteed to be read
- *Annual reports*, to share the corporate whole and emphasize involvement – these may be the original version or a specially produced adaptation
- *Recruitment literature*, to demonstrate how the organization recruits and to encourage recruitment.

This is not a definitive list. For instance, mobile (cell) telephones, with their facility for sending and receiving text messages, may be used for short calls to action or exchange of information among scattered staff. Technology advances are likely to produce many more such developments; in each instance the public relations practitioner balances the *intended content and purpose* of the communication against the *suitability* of each medium to convey it.

3.7 managing change

The increase of knowledge and flattening of hierarchies within organizations, resulting in less formality and greater involvement of people in the workplace, is increasing the need to engage everyone in the *processes* of **change** that have become a commonplace feature of corporate life. This again is of keen relevance to public relations practice.

Two initial points about this:

1 The term 'marketing change' has gained currency, but this implies that employees are customers. They are *not* customers, but members of an organization in which they are investing their time and labour, and the

planned approach to communicating change and implementing it should fully respect this.

2 Particular emphasis is likely to be given to relatively less structured consultation and to explaining the benefits for both the organization and the individual in terms that are meaningful.

Not everyone is against change, as 'marketing change' implies; far from it. After all, change can be quite comfortable *when it is predictable, more of the same.*

> Thirty years ago most people thought that change would mean more of the same, only better. That was incremental change and to be welcomed. Today we know that in many areas of life we cannot guarantee more of the same ... Change is now more chancy, but also more exciting if we want to see it that way. Change has, of course, always been what we choose to make it, good or bad, trivial or crucial. (Handy, 1989)

Among those who positively welcome change, not only for the variety that it brings but also its new possibilities, are the *'corporate entrepreneurs'*, people who 'do not start businesses; they improve them. They push the creation of new products, lead the development of new production technology, or experiment with new, more humanly responsive work practices' (Moss Kanter, 1984). These people are categorized as:

▸ System builders,
▸ Loss cutters,
▸ Socially conscious pioneers, or
▸ Sensitive readers of cues about the need for strategy shifts.

Sometimes they become public 'heroes' for their involvement in a successful innovation.

The communication effort has to *harness all the available commitment and goodwill,* and this is unlikely to be achieved within a vacuum, where hitherto the system has not encouraged participation or has 'paid lip service' only to what people say, hearing but not listening.

▸ Explaining change and managing it through participative dialogue with everyone concerned is a delicate skill that takes time to acquire.
▸ When the challenge comes, managers need *the right kind of form* in the eyes of their employees, credible track records of having engaged in meaningful dialogue in the past.

Then there should be no need to 'sell' anything but ample scope to *share everything.*

3.8 organizational body language

The term 'organizational body language' was conceived by Cartwright and Green in *In Charge of Customer Satisfaction* (1997) and developed in relation to enhancement of customer relations. They argued that organizations, as well as individuals, exhibit a form of body language that *sends out messages* about the organization (Cartwright, 2001). 'OBL relates to the whole atmosphere that an organization creates.' This may be said to equally apply *internally* as well as externally, because for the communication loop to work there needs to be feedback, and that can prove much more difficult to provide for someone inside the organization who is taking a living from it than for a customer on the outside.

Commitment, it is often said, only really comes from *a sense of ownership*; that is to say, when people feel that it is really *their* organization, no-one else's. They reach that conclusion slowly, often hesitatingly, only when they are *sure* that it is *safe* to invest the necessary *emotional capital*. So they look for *call signs*, wanting to know:

‣ If it is dangerous to say anything
‣ Whether there is any risk of retribution should they speak up
‣ What the managers do with the suggestions after they have them
‣ Whether their eyes glaze over when they are supposed to be concentrating on people's concerns.

People are doing within the organization *what they do anyway elsewhere*, so they are well practised at it. They are **studying the body language**. In the corporate sense, that has many dimensions. Messages go out to the internal publics (there can be more than one) through many channels.

EXAMPLE

Staffers may not *say* anything but they may *think* plenty, about, for instance, non-action, silence, slow response, all talk and no do, a sense of foreboding, empty senior management floors, endless management meetings behind closed doors, and so on.

Employees are *close to the action*: they are **uniquely placed among publics** to climb the ladder through awareness, understanding, support and involvement, but *then* comes the final rung, *commitment*. That is the moment of truth. Is the corporate body language *right*?

The **7S model** that management consultants McKinsey and Co. designed in the 1980s for **understanding ineffective organizations and managing change**, provides a perspective on this. The seven elements are:

Strategy, Shared values, Skills, Staff, Systems, Style and Structure

Effectiveness is achieved when the *strategy fits the values* and both are *fully supported* by the other elements. **Mission** can be defined using this model: strategy, shared values and policies and behaviour standards, including all the other 'S' factors, interconnect and reinforce each other (Campbell *et al.*, 1990). **Right in there is *style***, or 'the way we do things around here'. Communication has to take this factor fully into account for the body language to pass penetrating scrutiny.

Even when all these building blocks are in place, the *quality and nature* of the **feedback** is dependent upon *what exactly* people are paying attention to in the *detail* of their daily experience, whether out of choice or necessity, because they think it's what is *expected* of them or *best fits* their interpretation of the culture. And 'If they're paying attention to the wrong things (as judged by the leader), the organization will be unlikely to move in the direction the leader desires' (Davenport and Beck, 2001).

CHECKLIST

- Corporate vision and mission differ: vision indicates what the organization aims to be and look like within a stated period, the future; mission describes current organizational behavioural standards, which should accord with individual members' experience and perceptions.
- In addition to describing current behaviours, mission statements also address organizational purpose, strategy and values; they are a key communication.
- The learning organization communicates and fosters the enhancement of individual skills through the acquisition, via experience, of knowledge that leads to changed behaviours.
- Creativity and lateral thinking are fundamental internally as well as externally to public relations practice, which is closely identified with enterprise culture.
- Internal communication tools have a strong motivational purpose.
- The internal communication system should accurately reflect and benefit from the nuances of the organizational structure and culture that it serves.
- Each communication method is chosen for its specific suitability to transmit the intended message and the purpose of that communication.
- The communication effort has to harness all the available commitment and goodwill in order to effect beneficial organizational change.
- People look for call signs that assure them it is safe for them to invest their emotional capital in adopting a sense of ownership in their organization.

CASE STUDY

CARLISLE ALIVE AND KICKING

When market leader Carlisle Process Systems embarked upon complete re-structuring, which also included a name change under new ownership, this 77-year-old multinational initiated its 'Alive and Kicking' communication programme to explain the transformation to employees and customers; both publics had to be convinced of the need for and the benefit of the changes. Internal communication was built around monthly face-to-face leadership contact sessions, which created great interest and generated many *ad hoc* discussions with individuals and small groups.

Carlisle designs, engineers, fabricates and installs a range of plant required by hygienic liquid processors located in Europe, North America and elsewhere in the temperate climate zones. These industrial products include pasteurizers, separators, homogenizers and cleaning-in-place (CIP) machinery designed to ensure hygiene maintenance to match the requirements of further customers in the supply chain, such as Marks & Spencer, Nestlé and Waitrose.

The UK company was started by the Gate family, of later Cow & Gate fame, which went on to become Unigate. Two mergers later, it is now part of Carlisle Process Systems Inc., part of Carlisle Companies Inc, with 10 subsidiaries that include the three pre-eminent names in the sector: Carlisle in the UK, Damrow in Denmark and Scherping in the USA.

The purpose of 'Alive and Kicking' was to win employees' acceptance and understanding for the restructuring and to gain improved commitment, productivity and sales. The programme name embodied the intention to demonstrate positively to the world the dynamic and resolve of the newly revitalized company.

Hitherto the company had been known as Wincanton Engineering, and it was decided to make optimum use of the residual strength of the brand by applying it to all products. This would ensure continuity of positive perceptions about the company and would, in turn, support and strengthen the new Carlisle corporate brand. The Wincanton name meant much to employees, who found its retention and extended use reassuring, particularly given the potential for disorientation and divided loyalties brought about by the changes.

From a business hierarchically based on functions, Carlisle had adopted a flatter structure comprising three distinct customer-focused groups: Cheese; Dairy, Food and Beverage; and Manufacturing. This restructuring marked a return to the company's core strengths and was accompanied by demanding new profit targets. The focus now was on the 'bottom line', not on 'sales at any price'.

The benefits of this radical re-thinking needed to be fully appreciated and grasped by everyone, if the concept of 'selling solutions to process problems' was to be turned into a reality. Staff had lived through a period of turmoil and uncertainty, in which their company had lost some credibility in the market. Now they needed to engage with the idea that through their efforts customers really were enabled to add more value to what they, in turn, sold on to their customers.

'Alive and Kicking' had several specific objectives. These included:

- recognition of the major changes as creating both corporate and personal growth opportunities
- acceptance that core values, relationships and corporate status survived intact
- commitment to 'making it work' by accepting new responsibilities, demonstrating greater flexibility in problem-solving and taking 'ownership' of the outcomes.

Communication centred on the message 'It's *your* business, they're *your* customers.'

Monthly financial indicators on sales and profit were published: actual versus budget, linking every person and every act every day to the results, with the message 'Everyone helps the sales process, it is not just down to the salesman. We all have to be right on customer service, quality, delivery and price, and we have to be right first time!'

The proportion of profit over budget was advised every month; 'it can go up or down, we can add or destroy value.' Whatever was in the 'pool' at the year-end was divided equally, on the basis that 'if the business fails we are all equally out of a job, so we should equally share in the reward.' Monthly indicators were also provided to show current size of the 'pool' and relate this to each person's personal cash take, which proved to be a powerful communication tool.

The programme ran throughout 2002 and produced remarkable results. Within months Carlisle Process Systems moved out of loss and into profit. This was achieved on lower turnover and higher margins. No staff quit and lost customers began to return. Employees demonstrated a new drive and purpose, resulting in major new orders obtained internationally.

Interest remains 'Alive and Kicking', as evidenced by a continuing strong flow of informal communication. The employee profit share scheme has been maintained, with internal profit centres making monthly presentations, and taking quarterly presentations from general manager Charles Todd, whose ambition is 'to have all employees knowing instinctively the things that make or lose profit and therefore guiding their everyday actions. This is the only way that the business will have its own natural momentum to take it into a long-term future.'

QUESTIONS

1 Why might it be necessary to disentangle confusion over vision and mission?
2 What factors drive creativity, energy and enthusiasm in PR practice, and why?
3 What are the civil liberties implications of motivational workplace communication?
4 Why might employees misconstrue organizational body language?
5 Should the 'grapevine' be encouraged or suppressed, and why?

outside the organization

The operating environment – turbulent times – publics and stakeholders –
corporate social responsibility – risk and crisis management

4.1 the operating environment

Internal publics may expect to find out about their organization from within,
but, except in the unlikely event that it is a closed system, they *also learn about
it from the world outside.*

'It often happens that a message – the content of a communication – reaches
the internal public subsequently from the outside world, from an indirect
source, rather than directly delivered to the internal public as first addressee.
Opinions and judgements of the internal publics interact with those of the
external publics, and the combination of the two identifies the frame of the
enterprise's communication' (CERP website, 5 November 2002).

In other words, *internal publics also have a life outside* in the organization's
operating environment, where their members may *belong to one or more other
publics*, providing ample opportunity for cross-fertilization of attitudes and
perceptions, facts and rumours, news and innuendo. **Internal and external
publics are therefore closely interrelated.**

micro and macro environments

The environment in which an organization operates may be broadly divided
into:

- The *micro* environment actors, the external publics that affect the
  organization's ability to operate successfully, particularly the investors,
  customers, suppliers, distributors, regulators, competitors, opinion
  formers, pressure groups and relevant media, and
- The *macro* environment forces, the political, legal, economic, social,
  cultural, technological and environmental factors that set the broad context.

From a *marketing* perspective the environment is primarily of interest for its effect upon *profitability*. A marketing intelligence system is used to identify and follow trends and important developments that are assessed and graded as *opportunities* or *threats*. 'One of the major purposes of environmental scanning is to discern new opportunities' (Kotler, 1991). 'We define a company marketing opportunity as ... an attractive arena for company marketing action in which the company would enjoy a competitive advantage. These opportunities should be classified according to their *attractiveness* and the *success probability* that the company would have with each opportunity.'

Given that the majority of public relations activity is connected with marketing, this emphasis on commercial prospects is likely to be at the forefront of many practitioner's thinking. However, *the environment is of great interest in public relations for further reasons*, not least because some organizations are not companies seeking to make a profit and not everyone engaged in PR-driven environmental scanning is doing it for an organization. What are the critical forces 'out there' that are, or may, affect us, and why? What do we know about them? How might they develop from here? How might they interact one with another? These forces are as likely to be social as commercial. The opportunities and threats identified are therefore likely to have *broader* implications, which may or may not relate to profitability, either directly or indirectly.

static and dynamic environments

Organizational environments as a whole differ one from another thus:

- **The more *static* provide a stability that favours routine and prediction** based on extrapolation of past experience. Unfortunately they can also breed complacency, leading to inadequate scanning and insufficient attention to detail. This skimping can in turn impair performance and render the organization vulnerable.
- **The more dynamic are invariably**, but not necessarily, **complex and experiencing frequent change**, probably powered by rapid advances in *knowledge, technology applications* and *demand* for products and services. They rely on the closest possible scrutiny of their environments and there is no scope for any let-up on the job.

Grunig found six characteristics that separate static from dynamic environments. These included variable levels of:

- *Technology* change and *mechanization*,
- *Demand* for the organization's products and services,
- *Competition* within its markets,
- *Social and political support* that it enjoys and
- Rate of growth in its use of *knowledge*.

Grunig and Hunt (1984) report the conclusions of Howard Aldrich in *Organizations & Environments* (1979), who identified six characteristics, which may be summarized briefly as:

- *Resources* – the richer the resources in the environment, the greater the opportunities for the organization, and the greater the competition
- *Differences* – the more pronounced these are, whether between organizations or within the environment, the greater the need for flexibility and innovation
- *Stability* – the more frequent the changes, the greater the need to forsake routine
- *Spread* – the wider the geographical spread of resources and key systems, the greater the difficulty of establishing routines relating to them
- *Concord* – the more disagreement between the organization and its publics, the greater the need for flexibility in addressing them
- *Turbulence* – the closer the connections to unpredictably changing inter-penetrating systems, the greater the need to change, to cope with the chaos.

It is not, however, 'the public relations department's responsibility to deal with all of these elements of a complex, dynamic environment. Nevertheless, [it] must deal with key interpenetrating publics and organizations and help other subsystems improve their communication'.

environmental cultures

The environment may be said to have a number of ingredients comprising a '**cultural web**' (Johnson and Scholes, 1999). This concept helps explain the culture of organizations for the purpose of developing corporate strategy, but it may also be applied externally. The organizational environment has within it, for example, various **power structures that need to be accurately identified and understood,** because they are *primary* influences and relate directly to the *relative amount of turbulence.* All these factors are equally deserving of investigation and evaluation.

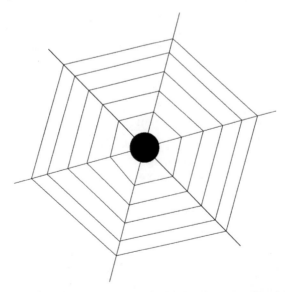

figure **4.1   the web of cultural factors in the organizational environment, after Johnson and Scholes**

Three techniques for scrutinizing the environment were mentioned in Chapter 2, where reference was made to there being several more such tools. Among these is SPECTACLES analysis, designed to assist in **coping with the more complex environment** (Cartwright, 2001). This embraces: Social analysis, Political, Economic, Cultural, Technological and Aesthetic factors, Customers, and Legal, Environmental and Sectoral features, the last covering both competitors and collaborators, or partners. This analysis emphasizes the multiplicity of possible interactions between each of these ten elements, their potential complexity and their variable importance to the organization.

4.2 turbulent times

In the last quarter century the **incidence of turbulence** has greatly increased. In addressing this development, Drucker (1980) observed that all those *many social tasks that used to be undertaken within the family unit had been assumed by institutions* 'organized for perpetuity and dependent on leadership and direction given by managers in a formal structure'. The most 'visible' of these institutions were companies, civil services, universities and bureaucrats generally. This process was worldwide and completed in the developed countries. Meanwhile, he asserted, central government had become increasingly impotent the larger it had become.

In this 'society of institutions', Drucker argued:

> The special-purpose institutions have progressively become carriers of social purpose, social values, social effectiveness. Therefore they have become politicized. They cannot justify themselves any longer in terms of their own contribution areas alone; all of them have to justify themselves now in terms of the impacts they have on society overall. All of them have outside 'constituencies' they have to satisfy, where formerly they had only restraints that created 'problems' for them when disregarded.

These new obligations represented a very major change, for hitherto each institution had been expected to dedicate itself to a single service in order to serve one public, or constituency: 'It was ... expected to look upon other social concerns as restraints.' To Drucker, a public, or constituency, was a group 'that can impede an institution and can veto its decisions. It cannot, as a rule, get an institution to act, but it can stymie and block it. Its support may not be necessary to the institution; but its opposition is a genuine threat to the institution's capacity to perform and to its very survival.'

The phenomenon to a large extent expressed 'the pluralistic character of a society in which no one institution is by itself charged with the responsibility for the welfare of the whole. Each institution pursues its own specific goal. But who then takes care of the common weal? This particular problem, which has been central to pluralism at any time, underlies the new demand "to be socially responsible"'. The implications of this turbulent environment for organizations were, in summary, that

- Organizations had to make sure that they were not rejected or opposed by groups that could veto or obstruct their activities
- Managers had to be realistic about what extra they undertook, not imperil their primary functions, and always think through the impacts of their decisions
- Their tasks and responsibilities had to be more broad and inclusive, and they had to make time to learn at first hand and provide leadership
- They had to be the integrating force, spokesmen for the interests of society in producing, performing and achieving
- Corporate policies had to be in the general interest and provide social cohesion before there was a problem or issue
- Managers had to create the issues, 'to identify both the social concern and the solution to it', and speak for the producer interest in society as a whole, not just for 'business'.

The process that Drucker described has continued, to the point that it is now probably present in most countries of the world. He set out very clearly **the gathering role of managers as leaders and integrators** as well as people who manage their organizations for optimum performance.

For Ehling *et al.* (1992) he had provided the 'rationale for the existence of a public relations function in an organization that cannot be matched by any that are set forth in college-level public relations textbooks. [He had] provided a clear justification for the establishment and departmentalization of the public relations function and for separating public relations management from marketing management'. Public relations people had been 'mandated' to deal with what Drucker called political problems that were not about marketing. If they did not, they would be rendered ineffectual and, a ringing phrase, the 'losers in the politics of confrontation'.

Drucker's explanation for the growing turbulence was plain. There was an increasing move from the creation of consent, finding the common denominator, seeking compromise, to creating confrontation and adversarial behaviours, identifying the least and most uncommon single cause, favouring 'trial by combat'. The intervening years have proved him correct and provided a compelling explanation for the growth of public relations practice during that period.

Competition is also a primary cause of turbulence. 'The intensity of competition in an industry is neither a matter of coincidence nor bad luck. Rather, competition in an industry is rooted in its underlying economic structure and goes well beyond the behaviour of current competitors' (Porter, 1980). In addition to the rivalry between companies supplying a given market, there were four further sources of competition: *buyers* and *suppliers*, both of whom exert bargaining pressure; *potential entrants* to the market; and *potential substitute new products and services*, both of which threaten the existing market.

These **five forces** are key features wherever there is competition, in all three main sectors of the economy, and the turbulence of recent years suggests that this model may be refined by the addition of *five significant additional forces* or pressures:

- *Existing players*: scope for rationalization (acquisition, merger, closure, departure or re-entry)
- *Customers*: the information available to them (how much or how little they know)
- *Suppliers*: the globalization of sources of supply (how practical or impractical)
- *New entrants*: the barriers to entry (how expensive or cheap to get in)
- *Substitutes*: the depletion of finite resources (how accessible or inaccessible).

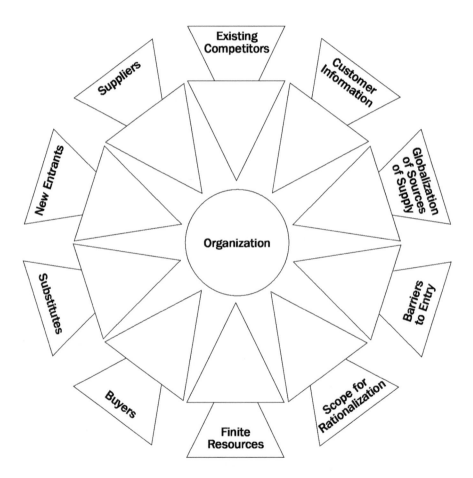

figure **4.2   ten competitive forces, after Porter**

These additions to the original model have grown in importance owing to the intensification of competition; for instance, **organizations that diversify represent a threat wherever they may be minded to enter**, but so too do the barriers that prevent entry, because if they are invitingly low they may be *positively encouraging entry* and thus heightened competition.

Of particular pertinence to public relations practitioners, among these ten forces, is the question of **information supply that empowers customers**. They have to assess continually the likely implications and consequences of information flows with all these competitive factors in mind.

4.3 publics and stakeholders

The repeated reference to publics has been accompanied by occasional mention of stakeholders. But what is the difference? A **stakeholder** has a 'stake' in the organization, an interest that may be direct or indirect, active or passive, known or unknown, recognized or unrecognized, immediate or removed.

EXAMPLE

An individual person may have an interest in the activities of a company that is establishing a new plant some distance from his or her home, yet the factory will be close enough for this person to be affected by air pollutants that will be discharged from it. Little if anything is known of this development or its implications. Then again, that same individual may work for the company and be well informed of the development. In the first instance, the interest is feint, perhaps as yet non-existent, and when interest is aroused perceptions are likely to be negative. In the second, the interest is already strong, and perceptions are likely to be on balance positive: the source provides employment as well as future air pollution.

This stake, however, may be held the other way around: 'An organization has a relationship with stakeholders when the behaviour of the organization or of a stakeholder has a consequence on the other' (Grunig and Repper, 1992). Stakeholders may comprise *large groups*, even masses, and the language commonly used in describing them is *typically generalized*. There is mention, for example, of whole communities of interest being stakeholders. The concept was developed in the 1960s but did not enter wider usage until the 1990s, in response to rising pluralism, when it presented something of a problem for public relations practitioners, who had been ascribing similar characteristics to publics since the 1940s. Could there be any difference, or was an established term simply being 'made over'?

The contribution of public relations to organizational effectiveness substantially depends upon its ability to identify and understand **publics**, which may be elevated to the ranks of 'strategic constituencies' depending upon their relative importance to the organization, that is to say, **the degree to which the organization depends upon them for** *survival*.

Put that way, publics sound more important than stakeholders, and they are probably more closely identifiable. Particularly if they form 'when stakeholders recognize one or more of the consequences as a problem and organize to do something about it or them'. However, pressure and cause-related groups *do not necessarily* form out of, or emerge from, stakeholder mass – they might skip the stakeholder stage – and it is self-evident that *by no means all publics are active.* Nor are they all necessarily *adversarial*, an assumption that fails to take into account the latent goodwill that is often present in publics without any attempt to foster it. Most times a public is benign until it is aroused, either in support or opposition.

It is more likely that the practical differences between a public and a stakeholder are those of *relevance and specificity*; that:

- *Publics* have importance attached to them because of their **more specific interest and power, current and potential**, while
- for *stakeholders* the levels of **interest and influence are relatively lower and more generalized**.

This is itself a generalization, but it may help to disentangle the frequent use of the two terms interchangeably.

'a licence to operate'

The role of the stakeholder gained accelerated currency when in 1993 the Royal Society of Arts in London (in full: The Royal Society for the encouragement of Arts, Manufactures and Commerce, founded 1754) initiated an inquiry, *Tomorrow's Company*, in which 25 senior managers from leading UK companies participated. The team 'developed, tested and refined a shared vision of Tomorrow's Company, and of its inclusive approach'. It concluded that:

> The companies which will sustain competitive success in the future are those which focus less exclusively on financial measures of success – and instead include all their stakeholder relationships, and a broader range of measurements, in the way they think and talk about their purpose and performance.

The inquiry acknowledged 'companies' growing need to maintain public confidence in their operations and business conduct; in other words, to maintain a strong *licence to operate*'. It identified the external influences that grant this **licence to operate**:

- Law and regulation
- Industry and market standards
- Industry reputation
- Political opinion
- Public opinion and levels of confidence
- Pressure groups
- The media
- Individual attitudes of customers, suppliers, consumers, employees, investors and the community.

This represented a significant advance in thinking about **the environmental conditions in which not only companies but also organizations generally operate**. Much of this was not new but it provided a succinct and well-argued case, following extensive research and consultation across a swathe of British commerce, for what it called **the inclusive approach**, by which all external and internal interests are recognized and their mutual relationships are strengthened. Of particular interest to public relations was the *recognition accorded to reputation, opinion and confidence.* Significantly, 'the community' was included among the major publics whose attitudes counted for licensing purposes.

Publics and stakeholders not only have relationships with the organization but *between themselves* and there may be *extensive multiple membership of differing publics or stakeholder groups.* 'There is increasing recognition of the complexity of the web of influence ... an organization is but part of the web of stakeholders' (Varey, 1997b).

This serves to further emphasize the *potential scale and complexity* of stakeholder relationships; accurate interpretation and adaptation to meet the circumstances identified in the organizational environment are *fundamental* to the development of public relations strategy.

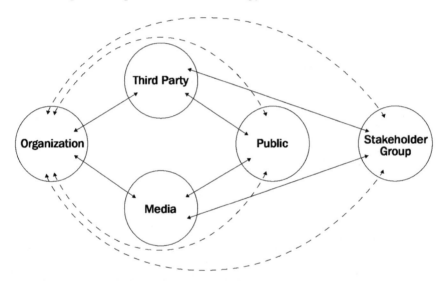

figure **4.3   communication between organizations, publics and stakeholders**

four types of linkages in the environment

The contacts that any organization may have with its environment can be depicted as:
- *Enabling* – with those outside upon whose authority and resources the organization's very existence depends (shareholders, senior managers, government, local authorities and opinion leaders)
- *Functional* – with those that input to the organization (employees, suppliers, utilities) and those that consume its outputs (customers, consumers, end-users and graduate employers)
- *Normative* – with organizations that have similar problems or share similar values (trade and professional associations and bodies, political parties, cultural and similar groups and societies)

- *Diffused* – with those who have an interest in the organization but no formal links with it (the media and other publics, including minorities, pressure groups and local communities).

These last, the *diffused* linkages, are with publics:

- That *cannot be readily identified* through formal memberships,
- which are **affected by the organization** in some way, or
- consider that **it has transgressed current expectations of appropriate standards of conduct**, a familiar enough contemporary theme.

'Organizations have developed such public relations programs as environmental relations and minority relations to deal with diffused linkages. Although consumer relations and community relations also can be explained by other categories of linkages, the publics served through these two programs also can be described as diffused' (Grunig and Hunt, 1984). The mass media may perform a role here too, in *alerting diffused publics* about the organization's *consequences for them.*

4.4 corporate social responsibility

If indeed central government has become increasingly impotent the larger it has become, to the cynic this might explain official enthusiasm for the transfer of its **social responsibilities** to organizations, with resultant contraction in the scale of government, presumably leaving it better able to pursue other activities. The UK government certainly champions this process vigorously. It claims 'real business benefits from being socially responsible' (DTI website, 9 March 2003) and reports evidence of rising levels of interest from businesses both large and small in reporting their (physical) 'environmental performance' and communitarian activities. It is busily supporting this **corporate social responsibility (CSR)**, with various tax incentives, co-funding, brokering of new partnerships, encouraging consensus on UK and international codes of practice, promoting 'effective frameworks for reporting and product labelling', advice on resources and helping to 'promote the business case and celebrate business achievements'.

The corporate benefits of CSR have been identified in *Winning with Integrity* (2000) by campaign organization Business in the Community (BITC), as:

- '**Reputation** – affected by the costs and benefits of a company's goods and services, how it treats its employees and the environment, its record on human rights, its investment in local communities, and even its prompt payment of bills;
- **Competitiveness** – the advantages of good supplier and customer relationships, workforce diversity and work/life balance, as well as efficient management of environmental issues;
- **Risk management** – better control of risks – financial, regulatory, environmental, or from consumer attitudes.'

The report quoted research in support of these conclusions. Surveys had indicated varying levels of favourability relating to perceptions of CSR involvement by companies, translated in terms of levels of loyalty to employers and willingness to purchase products by reference to the ethical policies and practices of suppliers or their associations with 'good causes', such as charitable donations.

In 1999 a poll of 25,000 citizens across 23 countries on six continents showed that perceptions of companies around the world are more strongly linked with corporate citizenship (56 per cent) than either brand quality (40 per cent) or the perception of the business management (34 per cent). Although it has been variously demonstrated that respondents can be hypocritical, feeling that they *have* to respond by claiming to support CSR because of social pressures, these findings nevertheless have *significant implications* for companies and *all other* types of organization.

BITC has an annual awards scheme to 'recognize the impact of companies integrating responsible business practices into their mainstream operations – on the environment, marketplace, workplace and community.' To this it has added its Corporate Responsibility Index (CRI) is to 'enable large companies to report on and compare their performance on the environment, the workplace, the marketplace, the community and human rights.' There is growing political interest in this throughout Europe; both within the EU and among member states, for instance, French listed companies (whose shares may be purchased and sold in public stock exchanges) are required to report extensively on their environmental and social impact.

Expectations about CSR are rising. Research indicates, for example, that the vast majority of UK adults consider that industry and commerce **do not pay enough attention to the communities in which they operate**. 'Surprisingly, almost two out of three business journalists think not enough attention is paid to social responsibility, while nearly two out of every five investors and industry leaders think the same' (*The Guardian*, 25 November 2002). That so many people claim '**an ethical dimension**' to their *purchasing decisions* is of considerable relevance to marketing public relations; the majority of customers are said to be influenced by what they perceive to be disreputable practices by companies, such as environmental harm, unacceptable working conditions, poor human rights records, bribery and corruption and workplace discrimination.

Only a small percentage of people are thought to *actively boycott* products on ethical grounds, and relatively few place ethical considerations *at the top* of their list of factors affecting purchasing decisions. Nonetheless, an estimated one in three people claim to have bought a product because of its **association with a charity** and the vast majority say they think companies should tell them about their social and environmental programmes. For their part, many managers regard CSR as mere 'window dressing', although the vast majority say they want more. This raises the question: If organizations are *not* reaping recognition for their 'good works' are they likely to dismiss CSR as an *optional extra*, a desirable add-on only provided it does not impair earnings, and a 'good thing' only when it enhances profits?

In 2005 the UK government decided against requiring publicly quoted British companies to publish information about their 'impact on society' in an annual Operating and Financial Review. Instead, UK company directors are to acquire legal duties to report on 'environmental issues, employee welfare and the community' in an annual business review. The majority of companies will be required also to report on their dealings with their suppliers. Some of these new requirements will apply only to publicly quoted companies (*The Guardian*, 6 November 2006):

> CorporateRegister.com reports that 85 of the FTSE 100 companies
> produced non-financial reports by March this year. Another three reported
> via a parent company or a subsidiary, and the remaining 12 included a short
> section in their annual report or on their website. Consultants Context,
> which analyses corporate responsibility reports from around the world,
> found that 90 of the top 100 European companies now publish them,
> compared with 61 in the rest of the world, and 59 of the US top 100.

Socially responsible investment (SRI) is gradually gathering momentum; 'mainstream' investors and analysts are taking more account of social and environmental criteria in their assessments of companies. 'The key thing is not to draw too wide a distinction between what is an SRI issue and what is a financial issue', a specialist analyst says. 'There are grey areas such as EU directives, black empowerment in South Africa and pharmaceuticals prices. This uncharted territory is where the interesting ideas will come from' (*Financial Times*, 28 February 2003).

4.5 risk and crisis management

Upon returning from a mid-winter conference jaunt to the Caribbean, the then British Prime Minister encountered reporters at the airport who were demanding to know what he was going to do about the crisis, to which he memorably replied 'Crisis, what crisis?'. This did incalculable damage and soon after the electorate removed him from power. Didn't he *know*, asked Mr and Mrs Sensible-Citizen, wasn't *someone* keeping him informed? How could he go swanning off at our expense and not know what was going on back home? And so on. In reality, the 'crisis' had blown up very quickly and, we were assured, unexpectedly; but then crises have a way of doing that.

Corporate life, just like real life, is **full of risks and potential crises**. That is *why* public relations keeps scanning the horizon, trying to identify and anticipate trouble **before it happens**. There are two distinct kinds of crises (Black, 1989):

- **Known unknowns** – these are mishaps and worse that occur *owing to the nature of the activity that the organization undertakes,* or, for that matter, the individual.
  - In most organizations there is risk present that may create crises and each element has to be assessed in order to determine the likelihood of trouble occurring under varying circumstances.
  - The probability rating accorded to each is influenced by any number of external environmental features and 'it is *known* that a catastrophe may occur but it is *unknown* if or when it will take place'.
- **Unknown unknowns** – which are 'sudden calamitous events that cannot be foreseen by anybody'. These are often the result of:
  - Inconceivable coincidence,
  - Some combination of events or circumstances that combine to create a crisis, or
  - Aberrant behaviour such as inadvertent pollution and criminal tampering.

'Much of our work as public relations practitioners is predictable and can be planned ahead in an orderly manner. Crisis public relations is a rare requirement and may never affect most of us, but if we are in a field [industry or sector] where disasters may occur it is essential to have a plan to meet sudden emergencies'.

This is probably too complacent. What began as a practice more associated with potentially dangerous occupations, such as oil extraction and nuclear fuel production, has lately gained much greater currency, particularly within more dynamic environments, and prudence suggests that it should be part of *all* public relations practice. But recognizing a crisis may prove demanding. Physical attack, overnight destruction by fire, failure of computer systems, grounding of transport by bad weather; these are all fairly readily recognizable, because the drama visually unfolds, but what of the many more subtle situations that can occur? For instance:

- What if a pressure group is busily spreading malicious rumours and deceit about some aspect of the organization's operations without its knowledge?
- What if some small adjustment that the organization has made to its processes has inflamed opposition and hostility that is destroying demand without a murmur?
- What if something the chairman said at a recent conference has been completely misconstrued by key opinion leaders and damagingly relayed to others?

Much has been the advice offered on how to recognize and accurately evaluate risk, anticipate crises and handle them competently with minimum damage to image and reputation. However, the reality is seldom as anticipated.

EXAMPLES

Bomb explosions are proven sources of crises that are very difficult to anticipate. When oil company Kerr-McGee planned for crises it thought along fairly conventional lines, with small-scale crisis plans for North Sea oil rigs and installation fires. In 1995 it was not expecting a disaffected youth to blow up a government building two blocks from its Oklahoma City headquarters. Then managers realized in the ensuing crisis that they had far too few telephone lines and for hours overlooked where they had plenty in another building, and that they did not have the home telephone numbers of staff, so that they could reach them to discuss arrangements (Dozier, 2002). Invariably 'the devil is in the detail'.

Similarly, Royal Dutch/Shell suddenly found itself at the centre of a serious storm over its decision to sink a redundant North Sea oil platform in a deep part of the Atlantic Ocean. Greenpeace protestors boarded the platform, boycotts of Shell petrol were called, sales across Western Europe briefly plummeted and a German petrol station was fire bombed. The *Brent Spa* had to go another way: dismantled and recycled, in part as elements of a new roll-on, roll-off ship quay in Norway. And when, also in 1995, the Nigerian government executed nine political protestors, Shell 'was accused of different levels of complicity and collusion, or simply failing to use its position in the country to prevent the executions. Whatever the arguments, it left many observers in the West blaming Shell for the executions' (Henderson and Williams, 2002).

It can be very tempting to take the view that it will not, or even cannot, happen to us, as if there is some immunity granted. And seldom is the cost involved in achieving and maintaining favourable images and reputations *fully and adequately linked with the cost of making proper allowance for risks and crisis management.* **Some very valuable relationships can be disrupted,** so why the reluctance to audit the risks, develop contingency plans, learn from past crises (there are bound to have been some), create a positive attitude among managers to thinking about this and prepare a blow-by-blow scheme for handling the *next* crisis under a range of 'what if?' scenarios?

crisis management planning factors

Five factors have been identified about this (Regester and Larkin, 1997):

- Risk is perceived differently by different people
- Fundamental attitudes are hard to change
- People expect risk, evaluate risk against benefit and choose accordingly
- Not all sources of information about risk are perceived as trustworthy
- Emotional symbols can be more believable than hard scientific fact.

> All too often, when bad news does break, the resulting corporate image is full of negative factors. This may frequently result from a misinterpretation of events by the media ... If a company at the centre of a crisis is seen to be unresponsive, uncaring, inconsistent, confused, inept, reluctant or unable to provide reliable information the damage inflicted on its reputation will be lasting – and measurable against the financial bottom-line.

Some further points to note:

- The *media are often blamed,* but reporters and their editors are as likely to be driven by human instincts and calculations as anyone else; if they do not *know* they are just as prone to making *suppositions*, however reluctantly.

▸ For 'company' here read 'organization': it can happen *to all types* of outfit.

▸ And for 'bottom line' read *'financial consequences'*: those who live by grant aid, for instance, are not immune.

▸ And as for being unresponsive and uncaring, that can be a hard one, because the lawyers will never agree to there being any apologies or gestures that offer the merest *hint* of potential liability. The public relations practitioner has to be concerned and humane while not admitting anything.

CHECKLIST

☐ Static external environments may be distinguished from dynamic ones by reference to: technology and mechanization; demand for products and services; market competition; social and political support; and organizational knowledge.

☐ Within a complex, dynamic environment, the PR function concentrates on improved communication with the key interpenetrating publics and how these relate one with another.

☐ The rise of pluralism has fostered turbulence and the need for PR to address non-marketing 'political problems' founded upon demands for social responsibility.

☐ The growth in competition has also engendered turbulence, with correspondingly greater implications for the direction and control of information flows.

☐ Stakeholders have an interest, that may be active or passive, direct or indirect, known or unknown, recognized or unrecognized, immediate or removed.

☐ Publics may have a more specific interest and power, current or potential.

☐ Strategic constituencies are relatively more important publics upon which the very survival of the organization depends to a greater or lesser extent.

☐ Corporate social responsibility (CSR) programmes by companies primarily benefit their reputations, competitiveness and risk management.

☐ The principal relevance of CSR to PR is the growth in consumer claims to there being an ethical dimension to their purchasing decisions, which has a direct bearing on image and reputation.

☐ Crises arise in consequence of the 'known unknowns' resulting from current operations or the 'unknown unknowns' that cannot have been foreseen.

CASE STUDY

TRANSFORMATION FROM PUBLIC TO PRIVATE SECTOR

When National Savings & Investments (NS&I), a UK government agency with 30 million customers, sought to communicate its new name and corporate identity, designed to reflect its three-year business transformation programme, the £2 million cost equated to just eight pence per customer. This represented a substantial economy for the taxpayer, when compared to the more usual levels of expenditure for similar corporate identity changes undertaken by large companies.

Two factors made this possible. Firstly, the name change was a simple, straightforward extension, from National Savings to National Savings &

Investments, so making the most of an established name rather than adopting a complete change. The new name had a ring of familiarity about it and sought to capitalize on the 'heritage factor' benefits of residual understanding and goodwill even as it embodied the agency's new, more commercial, character. A complete change of name, by contrast, would have necessitated a lot more explaining and consequent expenditure.

Secondly, the communication of the change was viewed as a long-term project, to be implemented gradually by informing the customers in the course of routine mailings. This avoided the cost of media advertising, notably on television, where many such changes are heavily advertised, and conformed with the central purpose of building in the future on the foundations of the past.

The UK media has been very critical of what it perceives to be 'money wasted' on renaming, or re-branding, companies and organizations at substantial expense. There have been some spectacular failures, typically where a completely new name has not been understood or appreciated. The economical emergence of NS&I provoked favourable media comment, especially because it is a government agency, and it continues to escape inclusion in the frequently published critical reminders that castigate the alleged corporate identity 'makeover money wasters'.

The NS&I name change was prompted by research among customers and the media that indicated perceptions of the organization as being old-fashioned. It was seen as an antiquated part of government concerned to persuade people to save through a form of bonds conceived following the Second World War that paid not interest but cash prizes determined by periodic chance selection.

In fact, NS&I's constitution had been radically altered in 1996, with empowerment to compete against other providers of savings and investments products in the private sector, and perceptions had not caught up with reality. In effect, the agency is in the private sector, where it occupies a unique and distinct part of the financial services industry.

The key aim of the UK government in turning this department into an agency and giving it a commercial remit was to reduce the cost to the taxpayer of government borrowing. To achieve this, National Savings & Investments set out to become 'a distinct and valued part of people's savings and investments' and 'an integral and valued component of national debt management'. This called for major changes, including a complete culture change, from a traditional preoccupation with sales and procedures to a marketing orientation focused on customers.

The PR objectives were, firstly, to communicate these changes visibly through the new name; secondly, to counter prevailing negative media coverage; and, thirdly, to secure routine favourable coverage for both the agency, its products and services. The key messages included:

- total security for investors: the agency is part of the UK government's Treasury
- large-scale operation, with £62 billion of investor funds
- economic importance, financing about 20 per cent of the UK's national debt
- weight of influence, given that the agency holds around 10 per cent of the cash-based UK deposit market.

Public relations targets reflected the long-term nature of the exercise. One year on, the new name was being used by an estimated 90 per cent of journalists and media coverage had greatly improved. In the previous year (2000–01) the agency scored overall positive on its total media coverage, including television and radio and online, in only two of the 12 months. In the first year following the new identity launch (2001–02) coverage had been more positive than negative in 11 of the 12 months.

The only negative month arose through some criticism of the new logo, which incorporates a chestnut, or 'conker', to represent renewal, security and growth, and a crown, to emphasize security through government backing. 'Conkers' are a familiar feature of English culture.

The first-year coverage included 2141 press mentions, compared with 1516 in the preceding year. Four major and positive news items had significantly assisted in this. They included: the appointment of a new chief executive, introduction of a website with an online channel, a new product launch and reinvigorated sales of the traditional Premium Bonds product.

This appears to confirm that, however well conceived and executed a new corporate identity and its thorough application, the media relations element of the PR follow-through has to include several truly newsworthy pieces and cannot rely solely on the identity itself or pseudo events. The new identity and the subsequent communication have to be complementary and consistent, and this applies to all publics to which such communication is directed.

QUESTIONS

1 What relevance does chaos theory have to public relations?
2 What are the likely ethical implications of managers creating the issues, in order to identify social concerns and their solutions?
3 Why might research showing support for CSR and demand for more be misleading?
4 What weight should investors attach to non-financial reporting and why?
5 When might risk and issues management be thought irrelevant and why?

chapter **5**

Communication

Communication theory – four types of public relations practice – excellence – three levels and functions of public relations practice – conflict resolution – consensus – the public sphere – the reflective paradigm – diffusion and effects – two-step communication

5.1 communication theory

Given that the 'strategic role of public relations is to define and manage stakeholder relationships' (Oliver, 2001), it is fundamentally necessary for the PR practitioner to understand **the processes of communication** upon which such management so heavily depends. For *effective* communication, itself a term open to a variety of interpretations, is not a natural gift, as often supposed, characterized by expressions such as 'the gift of the gab', but a skill based on understanding, observation and practice.

The communication process is described as being circular, linking the sender of the message with its receiver, backwards and forwards between the two. Shannon and Weaver identified the basic structure in 1948 and Schramm refined it in 1953; this is the model commonly referred to as the *communication loop*.

The key components here are:

- The *sender*, who is seeking to communicate information, ideas, attitudes and desires, and
- The *receiver*, who is trying to understand the message, its meaning and its purpose, and *what to do about it.*

The model seeks to answer five questions: (1) who (2) says what (3) in what channel (4) to whom (5) with what effect? The sender starts the process by identifying to whom the message is to be sent and then crafting it as he or she considers most appropriate to fit the requirements of the communication. This all-important initiating phase involves thinking, hard, about the proposed recipient; for instance:

- How is the message likely to be received?
- Will it be understandable?
- Will it be understood?
- What interpretation may be put upon it, and *why*?

In other words, how is the message likely to be ***decoded, or deciphered,***what will it *look* and *sound* like to the receiver?

With the ***message*** content decided, the next stage is to ***encode*** it so as to make as easy as possible the accurate decoding of it at the other end. This entails deciding how best to *express* the information.

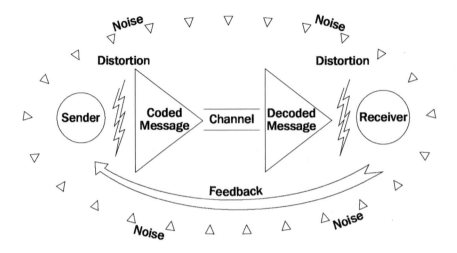

figure **5.1** the communication process, after Shannon and Weaver and Schramm

- There may not be a 'shared vocabulary', whether in the choice of language or symbols,
- Or the sender and receiver may *believe* that they are using the same language and common usages when *in fact* there are dialectical or other differences that may affect meaning and understanding,
- Or there is *technical* jargon that is either not shared by sender and receiver or is open to differing interpretations,
- Or each may use *differing* jargon, technical or otherwise.

In addition to encoding, the sender has to decide about what ***channel*** to use in order to convey the message, and this in turn may influence the encoding. **The choice of means by which a message is received can greatly influence the outcome.** For instance, face-to-face conversation may be most appropriate in some circumstances, an e-mail message in others; generally, the amount of time taken by the sender in making the communication can be perceived by the receiver as indicative of its relative importance.

The next stage in the loop is the receiver's ***decoding*** of the message. This is the critical intellectual exercise that may take seconds or weeks.

- *Has* the message been understood?
- *How* has it been understood?
- Does it change anything?
- Does it require a reply? If so, in what form, and when?
- What consequences flow from it?
- What other actions are required, when and how?

The processes of encoding and decoding are further complicated by **distortion**, barriers relating to the perceptions of both senders and receivers. This distortion may arise in many differing ways; for instance, owing to:

- Differences in social, racial, educational and/or religious backgrounds
- Ageism
- Mutual distrust
- Divided loyalties
- Partial or excess information supplied
- Contradictory signals, such as visual gestures at variance with speech
- Differing priorities or perspectives in a given situation.

The *credibility* of the sender, in the eyes of the receiver, can be a major distorting factor, and social conditions influence credibility. In Saudi Arabia, for instance, the identity of the sender is more important than the message itself.

Selectivity is also a key factor. 'The target audience [receiver] may not receive the intended message for any of three reasons. The first is *selective attention* in that they will not notice all of the stimuli. The second is *selective distortion* in that they will twist the message to hear what they want to hear. The third is *selective recall* in that they will retain in permanent memory only a small fraction of the messages that reach them' (Kotler, 1991).

This arises in consequence of the **noise** that envelops the communication process. This is the source of many problems, for it is unplanned static or distortion that serves to compound the effects of distortion already present between the sender and receiver. Noise can be literally noise, so that verbal messages are not heard, but the term is more generally used to describe the 'cacophony of sound', all those messages, usually several hundred, with which most people are assailed from the moment they awake until they lose consciousness again.

Receivers have **variable predispositions to receiving messages**, depending upon their perceptions of the sources, including:

- What is potentially in it for them,
- Whether it offers or implies reward or portends punishment, and
- Linkages with established memory and memory creation.

The distortion occurs when messages are reconstructed to accord with the receiver's beliefs, a key point in relation to branding. To achieve this congruence the receiver may **add to, or embroider, the message or choose not to notice parts of it**, processes that Kotler describes as amplification and levelling.

Up to this point the flow has been in one direction only, from sender to receiver, but the model indicates *a loop*, in which *messages flow in both directions*. For that to occur there needs to be **feedback**, that is to say, *that part* of the receiver's response that is communicated back. Great indeed is the effort that is exerted by most senders to generate feedback, and, what is more, feedback that can be converted into useful intelligence in order to consider the development of a further message, and the creation of dialogue.

Feedback, however, can be negative as well as positive, useless as well as useful; it can be in a fleeting facial expression or a long memorandum; in action, such as picking up the spade as instructed; or an omission, because in some circumstances even *non-reply* can constitute a response for what it tells the sender.

So the communication model envisages **a circular flow of messages** that is subjected to a welter of hazards that can break the circuit. It has been modified over time to recognize changing conditions, and to allow for the role of the media, but it remains a reliable foundation for trying to understand communication in a world that is burdened with communication failure.

5.2 four types of public relations practice

Within this framework public relations practitioners set out to communicate effectively, and in the course of time they have developed clearly distinguishable methodologies designed to best serve their various communication purposes. Grunig and Hunt (1984) postulated **four distinct types of practice**, based upon their analysis of the historic development of PR in the USA. These four types have been generally accepted as accurate, although not without criticism. They may be summarized as:

one: press agentry, or publicity

This originated in the 1830s, when legends and heroes, such as Daniel Boone, were created. The purpose is described as propaganda, there being little respect for truth. Noted among these agents was Phineas T. Barnum, founder of the Barnum & Bailey Circus, who 'said he didn't care if the newspapers attacked him as long as they spelled his name right'. The credo of these agents was 'There's no such thing as bad publicity', an attitude that has proved remarkably enduring; 'Barnum's famous statement, "There's a sucker born every minute", lives on.'

In a neat turn of phrase, 'Eric Goldman, in a little book on the emergence of the public relations counsel written in 1948, called the era of press agentry the era of "The Public be Fooled". Publicity, then, is identified as being a **one-way form of communication**, the feedback probably being 'bums on seats' for entertainment and sport or sales of promoted products. For added effect, publicity may be sought through the involvement of hired 'celebrities', people who are publicly recognized, probably because they make a living of being so, and are likely to attract attention. **Research may well be minimal.**

two: public information

This strain of public relations practice was traced back in the USA to around 1900, when the first laws were passed in order to contain the excesses of American big business, which had resulted in one per cent of US citizens owning 54 per cent of their country's wealth. This was the era of 'muck raking', the formation of labour unions and the advent of Lee's 'Tell the Truth' dictum. By then the dissemination of public information had already begun in earnest in Europe: in Austria, Britain, France, Finland, Germany, the Netherlands and doubtless elsewhere. The purpose of public information is to disseminate truthful facts, figures and advice on behalf of organizations in all three main sectors of the economy. It is a **one-way process and research may be minimal**. This is the knowledge dissemination that is often characterized as being 'useful to know', particularly in relation to social issues, public administration and so on.

three: two-way asymmetric

This is 'scientific persuasion' developed following the US propaganda effort of World War I by Bernays, Carl Byoir, Rex Harlow and other early public relations counsel. The two-way asymmetric approach involves **messages going in both directions** but **there is an imbalance in favour of the sender**, who is intent upon securing advantage from the exchange without recognizing much conditional need of reciprocity. Grunig and Hunt quote one of the early practitioners, John W. Hill, founder of Hill & Knowlton in 1927: he wrote about dissemination of non-controversial information, 'But when controversy exists, public relations may become the advocate before the bar of public opinion, seeking to win support through interpretation of facts and the power of persuasion.'

This rather grandiose interpretation likens public relations to legal advocacy and uses the, then novel, concept of **public opinion. Research may well be substantial**, for the purpose is to persuade and change 'organized habits and opinions'. In the late 1920s surveying of public opinion was initiated, and heavily developed in the 1940s and 1950s, to give 'an organization the ability to learn what the public wants and will accept, thus indicating the direction a public relations program should take'.

four: two-way symmetric

This is 'mutual understanding' and respect, where **both parties to the dialogue are relatively equal and mutually respectful**, both being able to influence the other and thereby effect change. Cutlip and Center are thought, by Grunig and Hunt, to have first introduced this concept, in 1952, when they wrote about the **two-way flow** of communication, ideas and opinions 'to bring the two into harmonious adjustment'. However, they concentrated most of their attention on the other three models.

In this two-way symmetry, the evaluation of outcomes concentrates not on attitudes but on **levels of understanding** and is therefore most likely to be initiated by regulatory bodies and businesses that are heavily regulated, where there is *greater incentive to develop dialogue*: 'symmetrical public relations refers more to a process than to an outcome' (Grunig, 2001). 'Symmetry means that communicators keep their eyes on a broader professional perspective of balancing private and public interests. ... They must listen as well as argue ... they must consistently remind themselves and management that they might not be right and, indeed, that their organizations might be better off if they listen to others'. Grunig says he might have chosen to describe this type of public relations alternatively, since 'Mixed motives, collaborative advocacy, and cooperative antagonism all have the same meaning as does symmetry'.

These four types of public relations practice have been found to *generally fit well with reality*, as experienced by practitioners and observed by scholars. Grunig and Hunt, writing in 1984, calculated that publicity accounted for about 15 per cent of US practice, public information 50 per cent, two-way asymmetric 20 per cent and two-way symmetric 15 per cent. Generally:

▸ Where public relations practice is *less* prevalent, its public information role is more pronounced, and might even account for the vast majority of activity
▸ Where it is *more* prevalent, the other types of practice are more evident.

Critics have argued that the two-way symmetrical model is seldom practised and effectively it is an *ideal*. Certainly empirical observation suggests that not many organizations readily embrace dialogue that risks (in their interpretation) leading to any more than cosmetic adjustment to their positions. The two-way nature of *the third model* is for purposes of feedback; among companies it *is likely to be the most commonly followed type of public relations practice*.

5.3 excellence

Grunig and Grunig (1992) suggested that the **most effective** public relations practice, which they described as **excellent PR**, would occur in *the two-way symmetrical* model. They and others had found correlations between the two-way asymmetrical and symmetrical models, which led them to suggest that *'professional' public relations* embraces both, with **excellence including asymmetrical components**, to take account of *'mixed motives'* such as persuasion and 'managerial bias'.

The excellence theory emerged as part of a 15-year-long project by a team of public relations scholars (mostly) and practitioners that sought to answer how, why and to what extent communication affects the achievement of organizational objectives. The research was conducted in three countries: the USA, the UK and Canada. The course of the project may be traced through three books: the literature review that appeared in 1992; a short account for practitioners summarizing the results of the quantitative and qualitative studies; and a concluding, expanded summary (Grunig *et al.*, 2002). 'The Excellence study has provided a comprehensive picture of how we think the communication profession should be practiced. It shows that public relations is an important profession for society. It can make organizations more responsible. It can give publics a voice in management decisions that affect them. It can enhance relationships and manage conflict.'

The excellence theory has become very widely accepted, and used as a benchmark by which to consider public relations beyond the 'Anglo-Saxon' mould. But it is not without its critics. The theory identifies and explains 14 characteristics of 'excellent' public relations practice that, in aggregate, 'make organizations more effective'. These are grouped. At the 'program level' there is but one characteristic: that practice is managed strategically. This implies that much practice is not, and about that the authors have written at length. The remaining features of best practice are divided into those found at departmental and at organizational levels. In addition, there are three effects of excellence identified: objectives are being fully met; costs of regulation, dealing with pressures and with litigation are reduced; and there is high job satisfaction among employees.

It is unlikely that seasoned practitioners will find fault with the majority of the characteristics, which are probably seen by them through training and experience to be 'commonsense' that has now been confirmed by copious research. The characteristics relate, for instance, to such matters as there being a discrete public relations function, with a direct reporting relationship to senior management, senior practitioners occupying positions in the organizational management and equal opportunities for both men and women (women widely predominate in much practice). A fifteenth characteristic, relating to ethical practice, has been added subsequently. It is the fifth item, the two-way symmetrical model, which attracts most controversy.

'For many reasons, the models of public relations and the two-way symmetrical model, in particular, have become popular theories and topics of research in public relations.... The models have stimulated many studies of public relations in both developed and developing countries of the world' (Grunig, 2001). However: 'Whenever a theory becomes as ubiquitous as the models of public relations have become, it also becomes the target of criticism by scholars who want to defend or develop competing theories. Therefore, it is not surprising that the models have become the target of several critics.' Much of this criticism has centred on the two-way symmetrical model: just how much *is* it the normative ideal? Many practitioners too may have their doubts. It all depends on circumstances, they might argue. And some scholars consider that one or more of the other models are 'superior', perhaps because they are working in a differing culture.

In a spirited response to his academic critics, Grunig discerned a basic difference in stance by them, between those who consider persuasion to be perfectly ethical and appropriate in practice within a commercial context, and those who object to all partisanship in public relations, asserting that it renders public relations 'undemocratic': 'to them, the symmetrical model represents a utopian attempt to make an inherently evil practice look good ... [that it] is overly idealistic and is based on assumptions that seldom exist in reality'. He describes as naïve various arguments about the high-minded purposes and morality of practice, and asserts that

> symmetrical public relations does not take place in an ideal situation where competing interests come together with goodwill to resolve their differences because they share a goal of social equilibrium and harmony. Rather, it takes place in situations where groups come together to protect and enhance their self-interests. Argumentation, debate, and persuasion take place. But dialogue, listening, understanding, and relationship building also occur because they are more effective in resolving conflict than are one-way attempts at compliance gaining.

This is probably the most eloquent summation of two-way symmetrical communication to be found, and it leaves little to add.

Grunig *et al.* have further developed the excellence theory: 'As the underlying theory (my thinking) has developed ... I have begun to see the symmetrical model in broader terms. It has become a theory that goes beyond the description of one type of practice to a broader normative theory of how public relations should be practiced.' In the new **contingency model**, which takes in the two-way asymmetrical and symmetrical models, instead of asymmetry being, so to speak, at one end of the scale and symmetry at the other, *both* ends are occupied by asymmetric communication, and the symmetric appears *in the middle*. Each end is occupied by a 'player', the organization's senior management on the one hand and the organization's public on the other: each aims to dominate the other, taking an asymmetrical stance. The middle ground is the **win-win zone**, where *mixed motive symmetry* prevails, and as each party moves towards the middle, should it do so, it adopts increasingly symmetric communication with the other.

The organization sets out to manipulate or persuade the public to move towards *its* position, at the one end, while the public endeavours to draw the organization across towards *its* position, at the other end. The organization's communicators may try, however, to help the public with this ('the pure cooperation model'), but, since they are employed by the organization, presumably there has to be limits to this: it is improbable that the 'dominant coalition' which runs the organization is going to agree to taking a position that benefits the public at the organization's expense. The communicator's task as 'piggy in the middle' between their bosses and the public is to achieve a compromise somewhere in the win-win zone. 'Depending on the situation, asymmetrical tactics sometimes may be used to gain the best position for organizations within the win-win zone.'

Perhaps the most interesting aspect of this is that the senior management in the organization is treated as a *separate public*, which is to be influenced by communication. This implies a relatively impartial honest **broker role** for public relations, designed to serve the corporate greater good of establishing, fostering and maintaining quality relationships. Since the communicators are employees, or hired consultants, for this to happen much must depend upon the degree of respect in which they are held by the dominant coalition and its willingness to take part in, effectively, arbitration. Their role is based on corporate social responsibility and the need to secure mutually beneficial relationships in the win-win zone. The model is also a strategic tool, providing 'suggestions for strategies when [practitioners] find the relationship tipped toward one or the other end of the continuum.'

5.4 three levels and functions of public relations practice

Based on systems theory, summarized in Chapter 2 of this book, Ronneberger and Ruhl (1992), reported by Bentele (2004), developed an 'equivalence-functionalist' approach. This identifies *three levels of public relations practice*:

1 **The macrolevel**, the *function of public relations*: the relationship between public relations and society as a whole
2 **The mesolevel** of *public relations payments* '(and payments in exchange)': wherein occur the relationships between public relations and other functional systems, such as 'politics, economics, science, law, leisure, family, etc.'
3 **The microlevel** of *public relations tasks*: the relationships within and between organizations.

Public relations practice has the task of providing 'autonomously developed decision-making standards for the establishment and supply of effective topics or issues'. Much must surely turn here on the use of the word 'effective'. Public relations also aims to 'strengthen public interests ... and social trust of the [general] public through follow-up communication and interaction – at the least to manage the drifting apart of particular interests and to avoid the emergence of distrust'. This responsibility for being the glue that holds society together elevates public relations practice well beyond the degrees of importance hitherto commonly associated with it.

'The question of what impact or which function all organisational activities of all public relations departments of all organisations and all public relations firms in a society have on society seems to be a typical European question rather than an American one.' In an attempt to possibly answer his question whether this is a sociological or a communications 'challenge', Bentele (2004) reported that in 1998 he had developed a functional model *comprising three parts*:

1 The *individual* function
2 The *organizational* function, which is further divided into *primary* and *secondary* functions
3 The *societal* function, which is similarly sub-divided:
   a **Primary** functions are: monitoring (observation), information, communication and persuasion
   a **Secondary** functions are: 'the building of awareness, building of (public) trust, harmonisation, adaptation, integration, early warning (system), image functions, economic functions and the co-building of the public sphere.'

The *secondary* functions notably include socially orientated concepts that may strike a greater resonance among practitioners in some cultures rather than others, and with scholars who perceive public relations as being more about sociology than communication science.

5.5 conflict resolution

Whenever two people start communicating with one another there is *scope for disagreement* leading to conflict. So many relationships are played out within a predictable life cycle framework that begins with accord and ends in acrimony. The incidence of conflict appears to be growing, not only in international affairs but also domestically and regionally. Because public relations is concerned to **develop and nurture enduring harmonious interdependent relationships**, it has to take account of the *causes* of disharmony and the *degenerative processes* that follow. Grunig and Grunig (1992) cite Keltner (1987) as identifying six stages in the long slide downhill:

> *mild difference, disagreement, dispute, campaign, litigation, fighting and warfare.*

There may be some more in between, such as independent self-regulatory arbitration of the kind provided by trade and professional bodies.

In the first three of Keltner's stages communication comprises discussion, moving on to negotiation, then arguing and bargaining. Once the campaigning begins, it is the turn of persuasion and pressure. When litigation occurs, it becomes advocacy and debate. After that communication loses out to violence, all words having failed. There is a role for public relations *at each of these stages*, particularly *in the early ones*, but Grunig and Grunig complain that organizations that use the asymmetrical approach **usually wait until the campaigning phase has been reached** before they start to practise public relations. This assertion is *supported by widespread readily observable evidence*. So often the question is later asked 'Why didn't we do something about this earlier, instead of waiting until it became serious?'.

In the case of cause and issue-related pressure groups, however, the *opening* phase may be campaigning, the earlier stages having been missed. Out of the blue an organization may find itself under campaigning attack, but L. Grunig found that many such groups, after initially campaigning or seeking litigation or regulation, moved to negotiation as soon as their targets indicated a willingness to talk. The concept of win-win, developed in the 1980s, is about bargaining not from positions held by each side but on *interests*, each party trying to see ways of helping the other to achieve a satisfactory outcome; that is to say, an outcome that is perceived by that other to be satisfactory to it. This is widely recognized among managers to be a sensible way to approach these confrontational situations with external organized groups; pressing on to an outcome where one side wins and the other loses seldom provides enduring resolution, while 'win-win' negotiation may well provide the basis for a constructive future relationship.

The role of public relations in managing conflict, and thereby avoiding power struggles that intensify into moral crusades by each side, is probably underestimated and underused. It offers **a dimension of excellence** in practice that warrants greater recognition, for excellent public relations includes, as we have just seen, a two-way symmetrical collaborative process.

5.6 consensus

One means to managing conflict that is within the experience of most people is to try avoiding it in the first place. Hence the public relations interest in seeking to establish, ahead of any 'trouble', **mutual understanding**, which implies at least a *degree* of tolerance, if not acceptance, sufficient at least to permit the development of some modus vivendi, a *workable* relationship that reduces tension and allows both sides to 'move on'. This relative state of grace is usually dependent upon the abandonment by both sides of persuasive tactics, for they are likely to exacerbate tension and the adoption of inimical positioning stances that hinder progress or settlement.

Mutual understanding doubtless sounds like commonsense, but in practice it requires careful nurturing. Communication does not occur in a vacuum; the receiver evaluates a message *within the context* known to him or her at that moment in time. Furthermore, understanding and agreement, or at least tolerance, are *conditioned* by what is generally considered by the receiver to be both **current reality** and **socially acceptable**. So there may be plenty of scope for pre-receipt thinking and assumptions that need to be taken into account by the sender, particularly in what are *known* by him or her to be **controversial or contested situations** where disagreement is *more* rather than less likely to arise.

In the **theory of communicative action** (Habermas, 1981, summarized by Burkart, 2004), communication is always 'a multi-dimensional process' that depends on both sender and receiver fulfilling certain basic performance criteria: they have to make themselves intelligible to the other side; deal in the truth as both parties perceive it; act honestly and not misleadingly; and observe mutually accepted values and norms. *If only*, we might respond to this ideal: in the real world much communication may not really match this. 'Basic rules of communication are often violated and therefore there is a certain "repair mechanism" – the discourse. "Discourse" means that all persons involved must have the opportunity to doubt the truth of assertions, the trustworthiness of expressions and the legitimacy of interests. Only when plausible answers are given, the flow of communication will continue.'

Habermas identified **three types of discourse**, each identified by reference to the types of questions that the receiver asks. These relate to:

- **Intelligibility** (*explicative* discourse) – working out what the message *really* means and deciding how to interpret it
- **Truth** (*theoretical* discourse) – checking the *veracity* of the message, resulting in assertions and explanations

- **Legitimacy** (*practical* discourse) – asking 'why?' and looking for justifications.

He also identified the 'Trust me' type of statement, but this fell outside the range of discourse because truthfulness could only be proved by subsequent actions; in other words, 'actions speak louder than words', a common response given the rise in claims to trustworthiness of recent years, some people suspect in almost direct proportion to what they perceive to be a concurrent lessening of trustworthiness.

'Discourses must be free of external and internal constraints. However, this is what Habermas calls "contrafactual" because the "ideal speech situation" that would be required for this does not exist in reality. We only act as if it would be real in order to be able to communicate'. And understanding 'is not an end in itself. Normally we pursue the intention of putting our interests into reality'. It is a means to achieving coordination and synchronization 'on the basis of common definitions of a situation' (Burkart, 2004).

5.7 the public sphere

The historic German term *Offentlichkeitsarbeit*, meaning public sphere work, is interchangeable with 'public relations' but is usually used in the context of dissemination of information (Raupp, 2004). The word 'public', as in public relations, implies universal accessibility and has a state or government owned or managed connotation. The 'public sphere', though, 'denotes a domain appropriated by citizens and thus one which is not state-run or state-owned'. It is 'a space for communication, which in principle is available to all'.

This is where citizens can debate options and choices (Hutton, 2007):

> This public sphere is a whole network of 'soft' independent processes of scrutiny, justification, transparency and accountability that range from a free media to independent justice. Representative government in which the people regularly vote for their governors is but the coping stone of this structure. And the processes of scrutiny and deliberation do not stop just with the state – the same processes are extended to capitalism and the market economy, and through having to justify themselves, makes them more honest and better performing.

Habermas (1984) has been the most influential recent philosopher on the conditions for ethical dialogue (Day *et al.*, 2001). Burleson and Kline (1979) summarized Habermas as requiring the following:

1 Participants must have an equal chance to initiate and maintain discourse.
2 Participants must have an equal chance to make challenges, explanations, or interpretations.
3 Interaction among participants must be free of manipulations, domination, or control.
4 Participants must be equal with respect to power.

Habermas developed in 1990 a **public sphere theory** 'based on an ideal concept of the public sphere' (Raupp, 2004) that *took account of public relations*. How this space for rational discourse operates is influenced by the laws relating to freedom of speech and so on, what is needed to attract and retain the attention of others, how many people may be involved and the choice of subject matter.

It comprises **three 'arenas' or levels** (Gerhards and Neidhardt, 1991, reported by Raupp; there are alternative versions of this):

- The smallest comprises encounters between individuals in public;
- The next embraces public meetings and speeches;
- The largest is held by the mass media.

Each arena is distinguishable by:

- The degree to which it offers *scope for immediate response and feedback*,
- The extent to which it *conditions and constrains* how communication is undertaken, and
- The level of *organizational interest and involvement*.

In the first, there is scope for the fullest participation by each person; in the second, the receiver's range of responses is limited and the sender has to carefully craft content and delivery to suit specific audience requirements and circumstances; in the third, opportunities for direct feedback are limited, the communication processes are more complex, messages are standardized and the receiver is, usually, only required to pay attention.

This latter point clearly requires some qualification now, with the dramatic recent growth in the popularity of interactive media.

There is an *interdependence*, argues Raupp, between the concept of the public sphere and that of publics, each representing a dimension of communication, the one structural, the other 'pertaining to the theory of action'. Both are linked through 'the issues of public communication'. Public relations practice, in 'providing issues for public communication', is 'a societal function... related to the public sphere', while the 'organization-related function of public relations' addresses publics that are grouped around those issues.

Taylor (2001) points to the prominent role played by Habermas: 'Nessmann (1995)... identified the underlying assumptions of European public relations theorists and practitioners in the German-speaking countries. Nessmann found that many of the European assumptions about public relations are based on philosophers such as Sigmund Freud and Jurgen Habermas.' She rightly asserts that 'examining the assumptions behind theory serves to enrich our knowledge of the underlying communicative and human relationships in public relations at home and abroad'. It certainly does, and this applies universally.

5.8 the reflective paradigm

Given that 'differing and changing perceptions of legitimacy... are seen as the basic object of public relations practice' (Holmstrom, 2004), the **reflective paradigm** 'is based on an analysis of the diffusion of *reflection* as a specific social capability... to transform destructive conflicts into productive dynamics. We can define reflection as the core demand on organisational legitimacy today, and public relations as a specific reflective structure.'

Reflection in this context describes the more broadly considerate and thoughtful corporate assessment of the world about it. 'Reflection means a reference to the idea of a larger context.' A journey is being embarked upon, in which the organization progresses from a relatively narrow worldview, a 'mono-contextual perspective' hampered by established prejudices, and, we might add, conditioned thinking, to a 'poly-contextual perspective', in which 'the organisation inquires about the worldview of opponents' in order to better understand their reasoning. This long march takes the organization from a posture that can actually *induce* problems, giving rise to conflict, hostility and 'counter-action', to one in which 'sensitivity and respect for the socio-diversity' creates 'self-understanding in relation to the environment', without, nevertheless, changing the organization's fundamental worldview.

Progress is not without risk and expense, nor is it 'a natural social ability of organisations'. It involves questions relating to environmental and social impacts on profitability, 'as illustrated in the concept of *the triple bottom line*, [People, Planet, Profit] originally formulated by Sustainability, UK in 1994, and later adopted by, for instance, Shell (2000)'. The model embraces a 'tripartite synthesis' between:

> **Sense**: The sensor function; to increase reflection;
> **Integrate**: The leadership function; to integrate reflection;
> **Communicate**: The communicative function; to communicate reflection.

It calls for 'insight into the social and societal conditions, structures and processes in which organisations are embedded'.

In this poly-contextual perspective, two-way symmetrical communication and dialogue is intended to replace asymmetric communication; the environment is to be respected, rather than managed; relationships are fostered and maintained, rather than managed; and the talk is of shared responsibilities, partnerships and negotiation instead of persuasion. The organization *knows* itself, its 'own identity, role and function in society'; by implication, it is more aware and understanding of itself and its part in the bigger picture. Communication of this identity is central to this: 'Poly-contextual legitimisation is anchored not only in legality and functional sustainability, but also in complex and dynamic patterns of expectation involving a long and growing series of stakeholders. The perception of corporate legitimacy is the precondition of their trust in an organisation.'

This paradigm, it is argued, represents *enlightened self-interest*. It is not about harmony and consensus but 'mutual considerations' that take full account of differing ways of looking at the world and respect for the differences. It is about co-operation arising from mutual recognition of *interdependence* between independent, autonomous interests.

5.9 diffusion and effects

Of great interest to public relations practitioners are the *processes* that people go through when they are digesting news and information and trying to decide what to make of it. **Diffusion theory** suggests that there are five stages:

> *awareness, interest, evaluation, trial* (trying out the idea on others) and *adoption.*

This interest is keenest in the context of marketing: how do people move from first finding out about something to ending up purchasing it, or another product or service, and to resultant satisfaction? As Kotler (1991) remarked, 'The marketing communicator needs to know how to move the target audience to higher states of readiness to buy'.

There are several **response hierarchy** models, all comprising three stages:

» *Cognitive*, when the message content impacts on the receiver, what Kotler calls putting something into the consumer's mind
» *Affective*, attempting to affect or change the receiver's attitude
» *Behavioural*, prompting the receiver into acting in response.

Probably the best known of these is AIDA: *attention, interest, desire* and *action*. There are several developments of this, including the **hierarchy of effects**, in which the stages are: *awareness, knowledge, liking, preference, conviction* and *purchase*.

Kotler describes this as a '***learn, feel, do***' process that obtains:

» When the receiver, or buyer, has **high** involvement with a product category that is perceived to offer **high** differentiation between products.
» However, when there is **high** involvement but **little** perceived difference between products, an alternative '***do, feel, learn***' sequence occurs,
» and when there is **low** involvement and **little** perceived differentiation there is another, '***learn, do, feel***', sequence.

These cognitive, affective and behavioural stages may be related to *all* branches of public relations communication, not only MPR, and *all apply where specific behaviours are sought.*

5.10 two-step communication

A common feature of public relations practice is **two-step communication**, by which a message is sent not directly to the intended receiver but to a third party, such as an opinion former, 'reference group' or person who provides a 'role model' to the intended receiver. This third party in turn uses *interpersonal communication*, which can be more persuasive, in order to 'bounce' the message on to its intended recipient. In consequence the message is *likely to reach a wider audience* than might otherwise be the case, and it is *reinforced* in the process.

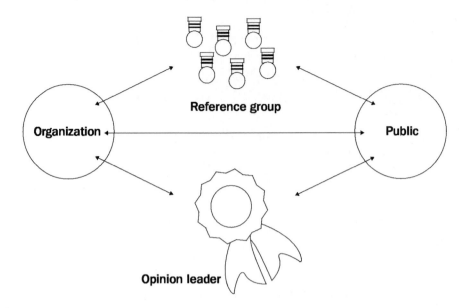

Reference group

Organization

Public

Opinion leader

figure **5.2** **one-step and two-step communication**

Fishbein's **reasoned action** model is relevant to this. It is based on the belief that the best way to predict a person's action or behaviour is his or her *intention to act*, and that *this* is conditioned by thoughts of what others, such as colleagues, families, partners and friends, *might think*. Would they approve or disapprove? In other words, intentions are determined by what **people who matter**, to the person concerned, *might* **think**, as well as his or her attitudes towards what is intended.

CHECKLIST

- The communication loop seeks to answer (1) who (2) says what (3) in what channel (4) to whom (5) with what effect?
- The key components of the model are: (1) sender, (2) message, (3) encoding, (4) channel, (5) decoding, (6) receiver, (7) distractions ('noise') and (8) feedback.
- Encoding and decoding of messages is influenced by distortion, owing to any of various factors, and selective attention, selective distortion or selective recall.
- Four types of practice have been generally recognized: publicity (or 'press agentry'); public information; two-way asymmetric; two-way symmetric.
- Excellent practice is said to comprise the two-way symmetrical model plus asymmetrical components when allowance is made for 'mixed motives' such as persuasion and 'managerial bias'.
- Three levels of practice have been identified: the macrolevel (with society as a whole), the mesolevel (with other 'functional systems' within society) and the microlevel (within the organization and with other organizations).

- Three functions of practice have been identified: individual, organizational and societal. Both organizational and societal functions are divisible into primary functions – monitoring, information, communication and persuasion – and secondary functions, relating to awareness, trust, harmony, adaptation, integration, image, economics, providing 'early warning' and 'co-building of the public sphere'.

- An important dimension of practice is the management and resolution of conflict when it arises, based upon an understanding of the causes of disharmony and the degenerative processes that follow in relationships.

- The achievement of consensus is intended to minimize the risk of conflict. To this end, communicative action theory states that both sender and receiver should meet certain basic performance criteria: intelligibility, truthfulness, honesty and respect of accepted values and norms. When these are not followed three types of discourse may be used: explicative (intelligibility), theoretical (truth) and practical (legitimacy). 'Trust me' statements are outside discourse; later actions establish veracity.

- The public sphere is a place of rational discourse open to all, without governmental involvement. It functions by reference to relevant laws and attention-gaining methods and to the number of participants and their choice of topic. There are three arenas, occupied by: individuals; public meetings and speeches; and the mass media. Each arena differs as to the scope for immediate response and feedback, the extent of constraints and conditions and the level of organizational involvement.

- There is an interdependence between the public sphere and publics. Practice has a societal dimension, in which it supplies issues for discussion to the public sphere, and an organization-related function, which addresses publics that have interests in those subjects.

- Reflective organizations seek to understand the worldviews of opponents in order to better understand them. They demonstrate particular interest in the environmental and social impact of their activities, develop heightened sensitivity and awareness, foster reflective cultures and prefer the two-way symmetric type of practice.

- The cognitive (information-processing), affective (emotions) and conative (will and intention to act, style of behaviour) stages of diffusion theory, which describes the processes of receiving, absorbing and deciding what to do about information, are relevant to all public relations communication.

- In two-step communication a message goes first to an influential intermediary, for that person in turn to use his or her interpersonal communication skills in redirecting the message to its intended final recipient. By this means the message is likely to reach a wider audience and be reinforced in the process.

- Future behaviour depends upon the intention to act, which is conditioned by expectations of what other people whose opinions matter (to that person) might think in consequence, as well as by attitudes towards what is intended.

CASE STUDY

THE DRIVE FOR EXCELLENCE

In civil administration the principal type of public relations followed is public information, telling citizens resident within the authority's area, where it supplies public services, what they need to know and are entitled to know, regardless of any political or other interpretation or construction. It is largely about communicating hard facts and figures on what is happening, where and why, so that the citizen may access services and make informed choices.

At Dorset County Council in southern England the new chief executive decided in 1999 to make effective communication a priority issue and a three-year strategy was prepared with the promise 'We will communicate clearly, openly and regularly with the public, with our professional partners, and with each other, in order to promote a high level of mutual understanding, and facilitate a better service to the people of Dorset' (some 700,000 residents). This was later amended to read 'with our citizens' rather than 'with the public'.

The strategy identified six functions that would be used to maintain the key principles and achieve key aims. These functions were simply stated: public relations – the core function; internal communication – the key that unlocks the door; consultation – the mandate for our actions; media relations – an essential channel; corporate identity – the framework that gives the message strength; and e-communication – the way forward.

Key principles described the quality of communication that was sought and key aims identified the five publics and groups of publics with whom clear and regular channels of communication would be developed. These comprised: external publics; internal publics; elected political representatives, known as members; other relevant branches of UK government, both national, regional and local; and publics comprising partners, suppliers and stakeholders.

In 2002 there followed a second three-year strategy. Benefiting from experience, the revised key principles contained some significant additions to: create meaningful dialogue with residents; consult well and act on the results; and concentrate on outcomes, not outputs. The strategy was written within a framework provided by the Improvement and Development Agency, a body advising the Local Government Association, to which UK local authorities, including Dorset, belong.

This framework for communication improvement by local civil administrators contained three tiers. The lowest requirement was to meet the legal duties for dissemination of information. Level two aimed at 'ensuring the [general] public is better informed' and enabled to obtain 'an understanding of the council's policies and priorities.' At the third stage, the highest level, communication had become a 'strategic issue'. It was 'two-way, enabling the authority to listen and learn'.

The Council considered that it had fulfilled the basic level one stage and was 'approaching level two'. The new strategy aimed to take its communication per-formance to the level three strategic grade within its three-year duration. To this end a substantial and growing department had been assembled, which was implementing an ambitious programme.

The second strategy sought to make a substantial adjustment to the balance between the public information model and the two-way asymmetrical model, by seeking to create meaningful dialogue and measuring performance by effects rather than process. Embarking on this journey towards excellent public relations practice coincided with the official recognition of Dorset as an 'excellent authority' by the Audit Commission, a government body that scrutinizes the performance of the constituent elements of the UK public sector. The citation was for 'a well-managed council and provider of good quality and cost-effective services'.

QUESTIONS

1 Why might some messages suffer more from noise than others?
2 Why might the two-way symmetrical type of public relations be seldom practised?
3 How might protagonists view the role of public relations in conflict resolution?
4 Why might the reflective paradigm's time have arrived?
5 When might the theory of communicative action truly apply, and why?

research, planning and evaluation

Research and evaluation – effectiveness – strategy and planning – situational theory – segmentation – consensus-orientation – cost–benefit analysis

6.1 research and evaluation

Most occupational groups have their traditions, and public relations people are not without one or two of their own, prominent among which is *equivocation about research and evaluation.* Theaker (2001b), writing about the British experience, traced the first interest of practitioners in research and evaluation way back to the early 1990s, when, coincidentally, public relations was emerging as an academic subject in the UK. 'As recession began to bite and budgets were slashed, public relations practitioners began to talk about whether or not PR could be measured, and so prove its worth. Up to that point, no one had really been concerned about measurement of results.'

For public relations practitioners with memories that stretched back a little longer than the early 1990s this was demonstrable nonsense. From the formative years of public relations practice in the UK, during the 1950s and 1960s, there had been repeated use made of research and evaluation. True, much research was secondary, that is to say, using published sources, but that was as much a function of limited budgets and ready access to marketing research already done than to any particular reluctance to undertake research.

Nor were early UK writers in any doubt. 'The first thing to put in hand is research... No good Public Relations can be done without sound research' (Lloyd, 1963). 'It is important that the public relations man should know the value, potential, and limitations of research ... Research can be an invaluable extra shot in the public relations man's locker' (Bowman and Ellis, 1977).

Probably *evaluation* received more attention than research, for, from the outset, the public relations practitioner was expected to identify and discuss **the value of outcomes**. Much has been written, as well as said, over the years about the difficulty of evaluating public relations owing to its supposed ephemeral qualities. Typical observations included: 'Much of the doubt about the value of public relations arises from the difficulties in assessing the results of public relations activities and the absence of suitable yardsticks by which these results can be measured accurately' (Black, 1989). And, describing 'self-evident results': 'These are results where nothing has to be spent on a marketing research survey to check, i.e. they are to be seen or experienced... sometimes the facts can be so plain that, given clear objectives, PR cannot be intangible and unaccountable. Results can literally stare you in the face' (Jefkins and Yadin, 1998).

The claimed absence of suitable yardsticks is unsustainable; there are more than enough evaluation methods available. So it cannot explain why '"Gut feeling" was felt to be an acceptable gauge of whether a PR campaign had succeeded' (Theaker, 2001b). Could the explanation for this combination of supposed inability to measure and apparent lack of concern have less to do with not wanting to bother about evaluation and more about *reliance on accumulated knowledge and experience*, on confidence born of practice, as in other occupations; the kind of assurance that comes from familiarity with 'self-evident results'?

Public relations practice is concerned with attitudes and perceptions, based on images and reputations. These may be researched, traced and measured for the purposes of public relations, given an adequate budget. But there is the rub. Could the supposed reluctance among some public relations practitioners to commission or undertake primary research for the purpose of evaluation be explained by insufficient funds allocated for the purpose? If so, why should this be? Could *competitiveness* be a root cause, resulting in a reluctance to make an adequate allocation within a competitive consultancy fee quote and to specify research when selling on knowledge and expertise already acquired at the expense of other clients or previous employers?

Whatever these uncertainties, a few observations may be offered with some confidence:

- Public relations without research is *pure adventure*, and practitioners know it
- *All* public relations outcomes are measurable, by one means or another
- Practitioners most certainly *do* undertake research and measurement, consistent with what they assess to be the requirements of the specific circumstances
- Selling on 'You know when it works' cannot explain the *dramatic growth* of public relations, whatever the pressures of rising pluralism
- In the face of *incontrovertible* evidence to the contrary, persistent generalized allegations of immeasurability have to be treated with caution.

Not only outcomes, but also all the variable factors that influence those results need to be carefully scrutinized.

EXAMPLES

Public sector media campaign relating to road safety: well, *was* there a reduction in death and injuries caused by dangerous, reckless or just plain stupid driving over the relevant period? If so, to what extent? And what about the weather conditions during that period, the amounts of daylight, holiday and work patterns, and so on?

Private sector exhibition and demonstration programme at selected public events: *was* there an increase in enquiries, invitations to tender, new business opportunities, orders placed or some other yardstick? By how much? And how might those results have been influenced by the choice of venues, seasonal commercial factors, competitor activity and so on?

Voluntary sector lobbying campaign to raise awareness of local homelessness: *was* there an increase in expressions of official interest, invitations to meet with local bureaucrats, offers of help from property landlords, media enquiries or funding donations? What did it all really come down to? And did the lobbying capitalize on government promises, increased social unrest, bad weather, prior media interest, city centre redevelopment plans and so on?

6.2 effectiveness

Public relations activity contributes to the effectiveness of the organization, but *effectiveness is susceptible to multiple interpretations* and therefore **difficult to define and manage**. Grunig *et al.* (1992) considered effectiveness in terms of four perspectives: systems, competing values, strategic constituencies and goal-attainment, or rational systems.

It has been widely asserted, and is readily observable, that the structure and environment of the organization *determines the flow of information* both within it and between it and its external publics. So when an organization seeks to maximize its effectiveness by matching its structure and functions to its external environment its public relations *should* gain in effectiveness. However, this *systems* approach appeared to remain more an ideal than a reality, for otherwise 'the role of public relations practitioners as boundary spanners, mediators, and participants in managerial decision making would be more highly valued'.

The *strategic constituencies* approach also had particular relevance for public relations. It also focuses on interdependencies, but specifically on the most *threatening* elements in the external environment and how well the organization handles them. That in turn depends upon the *detection* of those strategic publics. Successfully responding to them could help reduce uncertainty and conflict by creating stable relationships upon which the organization depends.

Their conclusion was that **public relations could increase the effectiveness of an organization** by two means:

- To 'enact an environment that includes the stakeholders most likely to constrain or enhance the ability of the organization to carry out its mission – to meet its goals'
- By developing communication that built enduring quality relationships with strategic publics.

'These relationships help the organization manage interdependencies, simultaneously limiting and enhancing the autonomy of the organization. The better the organization manages its interdependencies, the more likely it is to succeed in meeting its goals – although factors other than public relations contribute to that success as well.' Note that here the terms 'public' and 'stakeholder' are used interchangeably and that goals may be interpreted as (general) aims and (specific measurable) objectives.

This evaluation of effectiveness in the public relations context is an admirable attempt to lasso a jelly. Most discussion about effectiveness dwells on the minutiae of practice, is generalized and contains little specific explanation much beyond 'it worked'. 'Effective communication' is widely interpreted as asymmetrical persuasion, with or without the dialogue, redolent of quick fixes, but to the experienced practitioner that reveals a fundamental misunderstanding, for public relations is correctly about finding *enduring solutions* through communication.

More specifically, Moloney (2000) complained that 'Modern PR lends itself to manipulative communications' and identified common features that by implication are thought necessary in order to achieve effectiveness. Messages:

- Frequently fail to declare sources, to 'appear to be free-floating from any originating interest'
- Often assert data, rather than reference or argue it
- Often use negative emotions, to achieve persuasive effect and downplay reason.

'The removal of these manipulative flaws in the internal construction of PR communications constitutes the case for reform through education and regulation.'

Here 'effectiveness' acquires an entirely different dimension, for it is allegedly sought through non-disclosure of interests, exploitation of data and arousal of emotions to impair reasoning. However, the failure to reveal sources *contradicts the primary aim* of most practioners to *identify the interests* they serve. For the rest, the objection appears to be against rhetoric and advocacy per se.

6.3 strategy and planning

Another subject of, at times remarkably deep, equivocation among public relations people is **strategy**. There is *frequent confusion between strategy and tactics*. Repeatedly, tactics are dignified by being described as strategic when in truth they do not satisfy any readily recognized definition of strategy, and frequently 'strategy' is slipped into proposal documents, reports and speech as if its *mere presence* will enhance the sagacity and credibility of whatever it is attached to. Perhaps the problem lies in making the link between corporate and public relations strategy. The latter serves the former, but what exactly *is* strategy? Oliver (2001) ventured 'the means or process by which an organization aims to fulfil its mission', but this is necessarily general and therefore susceptible to wide interpretation.

Fifield (1992), in addressing marketing rather than public relations strategy, found that 'every author seems to start from his or her own premise and lays down a new set of parameters and definitions ... The one thing that many definitions do is to confuse'. He concluded that marketing strategy 'will mean different things to different organizations. It will fulfil different needs both within the organization and in the marketplace'. Although it might be objected that Fifield's observations are about marketing, they have a ring of familiarity about them for public relations practitioners. And marketing is itself *probably the major source of confusion*, because MPR serves the *marketing* strategy; however, customers, albeit critically important, are but *one of many* publics that concern public relations.

This heavy involvement with marketing – to the extent that many practitioners specialize solely in MPR – can throw the PR strategic planner off the scent. In reality the public relations and marketing strategies *each* respond *directly* to the corporate strategy, as do all other function strategies: hence the strong interest of public relations in the organizational vision and mission, because *they* provide the starting point for developing the public relations strategy.

strategy development

Not that deciding the strategy is necessarily left to the experts. Most times the **dominant coalition decides what type of public relations it wants**, and if the public relations function is *not* represented at that exalted level it *may not be heard* and almost certainly will have to *forego any final decision making* about such fundamentals. This harsh reality could be interpreted favourably, as indicating that PR is considered so important that senior managers dare not let anyone else decide, or, unfavourably, that PR is seen as purely a technical service that is not competent to handle strategic decisions. Public relations people aspire for membership of the dominant coalition not without good cause.

Larissa Grunig (1992) developed a **power-control model of public relations** to depict the factors that *influence which type of public relations is adopted*. She makes several key observations about the power play within the organization:

- *The dominant coalition adopts a worldview, or mind-set, about PR*, which is based upon a broader set of suppositions, the corporate culture and the potential of the public relations department itself. This worldview about PR therefore determines the *scope* of the function to show what it can do.
- *The dominant coalition also adopts a view of the organizational environment*, to the extent that 'the environment is in part at least the subjective perception' of this group of senior managers. They decide what bits are, in their minds, crucial and then 'choose strategic publics for public relations programs from that perceived environment'.
- Other managers, including those in public relations, gain power 'in part because they have knowledge and skills relevant to a crucial problem in the organization's environment'. In other words, *what they have to tell impresses the dominant coalition*.

- 'If organizations choose the most appropriate public relations strategy for communication with strategic publics, then that strategy will help the organization to manage critical environmental interdependencies and make the organization more effective.' In other words, **there is a critical link between strategic management of public relations and organizational effectiveness.**
- **The dominant coalition, particularly the founder, creates the corporate culture,** which is also conditioned by social culture and by the environment. Managers do not gain power if their values and ideology *differ substantially* from that of the organization.

The parameters within which the public relations strategy is developed are, therefore, subject to a variety of internal influences. And 'if a culture is essentially hierarchical, authoritarian and reactive, the dominant coalition will generally choose an asymmetrical model of public relations. Furthermore, it will choose not to be counselled by the public relations expert who traditionally is not seen as having enough strategic awareness and is therefore of limited value' (Oliver, 2001). This depressing picture is well within the experience of many talented public relations people, but by no means all.

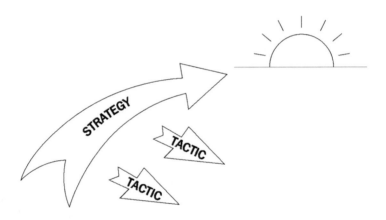

figure **6.1   strategy and tactic timescales**

A very practical means by which strategy and tactic may be differentiated is that the former deals with the 'bigger picture' and the *longer-term,* whereas the latter is more concerned with obtaining short-term effects.

The dominance of consultants numerically over in-house people in some countries may be yet another factor, because invariably consultants are tasked to provide short-term solutions, often through one-off limited period instructions, responding to detailed briefs that fit the strategy, and are not invited or encouraged to offer a longer-term view by commissioning in-house practitioners.

Strategy development, in contrast to implementation, is a demanding process that is subject to many forces and pressures, not only from within but also without the organization. Grunig and Repper (1992) cited a model developed by Pearce and Robinson, in which they identified the steps that a strategist takes. These provide a useful structure and may be briefly summarized as:

1 *Corporate mission* development
2 *Corporate profile* development, to reflect 'internal condition and capability'
3 *External environment* assessment
4 *Interactive opportunity* analysis, to identify options
5 *Desired options* identification, compatible with the mission
6 *Long-term objectives* and *grand strategies* decided, to meet the options
7 *Annual objectives* and *short-term strategies* decided, compatible with the previous objectives and strategies
8 *Implementation*
9 *Review* and *evaluation.*

The model does not mention vision, so presumably for mission read also vision. The mission is very much linked with the environment, and public relations has a key connecting role here. 'Short-term strategy' may appear to be contradictory, but there is no prescriptive period for a strategy. They are often set long-term, typically for three years, although duration of one year is common.

6.4 situational theory and segmentation

Weighing up the situation before plunging-in sounds sensible enough. 'The kingpin of the exercise is understanding the situation, i.e. asking: Where are we now? What are their misunderstandings?' asked Jefkins (Jefkins and Yadin, 1998), who clearly anticipated trouble ahead. To address the 'classic PR situation [which] confronts most PR practitioners' he developed his **PR transfer process**, which describes the conversion of four negative attitudes into four positive ones: hostility to sympathy; prejudice to acceptance; apathy to interest; and ignorance to knowledge. 'Ultimately, knowledge creates understanding: the principal PR objective is *understanding*. Sometimes this may be even of things people dislike or with which they disagree.'

This is familiar indeed to most practitioners and many who undertake public relations on a voluntary basis. Understanding does often allay anxieties, fears, even hostility, but in this increasingly fractious world situations can be, and often are, more complex than might be inferred from this relatively simple exposition. Grunig's **situational theory of publics** (Grunig and Hunt, 1984) sought to reflect the complexity. 'Publics come and go' and, what is more, organizations *create* them, when what they do have *consequences* for others. Publics form when there is a *shared perceived problem*, but if this is not recognized the public is latent: 'a potential public relations problem waiting to happen... Active publics are the only ones that generate consequences for organizations' (Grunig and Repper, 1992).

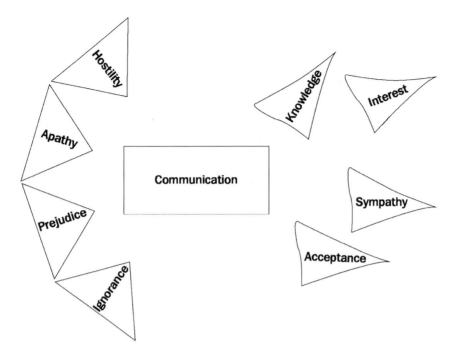

figure **6.2** **converting negative attitudes into positive, after Jefkins**

'The theory states that the communication behaviours of publics can be best understood by measuring how members of publics perceive situations in which they are affected by such organizational consequences as pollution, quality of products, hiring practices, or plant closings.' Three major independent variables distinguish people who are:

» Members of publics from those who are not in any publics
» Prepared to speak up from those who remain quiet about an issue.

These three variables are:
(1) *Problem recognition*: this relates to the degree of realization that something's wrong and needs dealing with; then people communicate most because they seek information to help solve their problem. From the initial detection there follow successive phases: construct, define, select and confirm. This process is divisible into two dependent variables:

» *Information seeking*, or 'active communication behavior', when information is sought and effort is then made to understand it and use it for planning ahead – because there's a job to be done; and
» *Information processing*, or 'passive communication behavior', when there is no search as such for information, but that which is available may be processed effortlessly – in other words, it comes in handy.

'The members of a public exert less effort to understand information they process than information they seek. Thus, processed information has fewer communication effects than information that is sought.'

(2) *Constraint recognition*, when people weigh up the apparent obstacles to their potential actions. The worse this looks to them the less they bother about seeking and processing information.

This second independent variable

> represents the extent to which people perceive that there are constraints – or obstacles – in a situation that limit their freedom to plan their own behaviour. If people realize that they have little choice of behaviour... [this] lessens the likelihood that [they] will *seek information* about an organizational consequence or that they will pay attention to and *process information* about the consequence that comes to them randomly.

(3) *Level of involvement*, which is about determining whether 'the person's communication behavior will be active or passive'. It is about involvement, being bothered enough.

'A member of a public who perceives a strong involvement in an issue generally also has high problem recognition and low constraint recognition for that issue.' This can result in more rather than less activity, often in the form of organized response with others who share the same concerns. Awareness, and activity, can arise, however, without *any* involvement, because we randomly process information about issues that are of *no* direct affect or consequence to us.

On the basis that a public is a group of people who share a similar problem, recognize that it exists and organize to do something about it (though not all three elements may be present), Grunig identified three types of public:

- A *latent* public, where only element one is present;
- An *aware* public, where elements one and two are present – members have 'cottoned on'; and
- An *active* public, where all three elements are present.

Grunig also identified *nonpublics*, where the organization has *no consequences* for members of the group, *and vice versa*, the other way around.

In 1992 Grunig and Repper described **four kinds of publics**, which may be summarized as:

- *All-issue* – active on all fronts
- *Apathetic* – not interested in any of the issues
- *Single-issue* – active on one issue, or small subset of issues, of minority interest
- *Hot-issue* – active on one issue of widespread concern and big media interest.

In 2001 Hallahan, reported by Raupp (2004), added to Grunig's original theory a further classification of publics, with the addition of 'informedness', meaning, *by just how much* a group is informed, a subtle and valuable dimension, for partial information might well impair or distort the development of a public and its consequent response.

There are many **segmentation theories**, but most others are used in marketing. 'As a result, techniques of *market* segmentation are used more widely in public relations than are techniques to segment *publics*' (Grunig and Repper, 1992). Which is very true. This is although 'most of [the segmentation] theories are poorly developed' and the situational theory of publics being 'the only segmentation theory that has been researched extensively'.

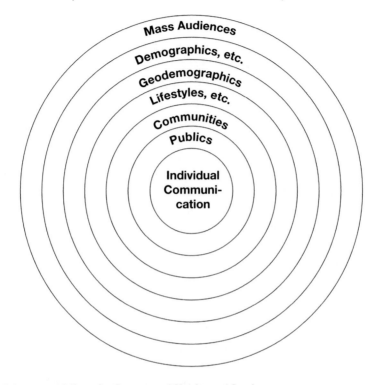

figure **6.3** **segmentation, after Bonoma and Shapiro, and Grunig**

A most important rider to this is that organizations choose their markets, 'but publics arise on their own and choose the organization for attention'. They 'organize around issues and seek out organizations that create those issues – to gain information, seek redress of grievances, pressure the organizations, or ask governments to regulate them. As publics move from being latent to active, organizations have little choice other than to communicate with them; whereas ... organizations can choose to ignore markets if they wish'. This may appear overstated, but the point is well-made. It is a fundamental difference between public relations and marketing. Some publics do not spring upon the organization, rather as depicted here, but *many do*, and **in turbulent environments the incidence of publics forming and reforming around issues is ever present**.

Adapting Bonoma and Shapiro's nested model for analysing industrial markets, Grunig has produced his own version to suit the needs of public relations. In this there are **nests**, arranged similarly to Russian dolls, in which the innermost contains **the variables of *individual communication behaviour*** *and effects* **that are the more effective in communication planning**. 'Decision makers should begin with the inner nest and work outward only when resources are not available for the research and time needed to work with the inner nests.'

Starting from the centre, the outer nests contain (1) publics; (2) communities; (3) psychographics, lifestyles, cultures and social relationships; (4) geodemographics; (5) demographics and social categories; and (6) mass audiences. 'The best segmentation concepts lie in the second nest, that of publics, but ... the behavior of publics can be understood only by understanding the individual behaviors in the innermost nest.'

6.5 consensus-orientated public relations (COPR)

This model is a planning and evaluation tool (Burkart, 2004) based on Habermas's 1981 theory of communicative action. It 'relies on two prerequisites and their consequences for PR': rising popular demand for organizations to earn their 'public legitimacy', similarly to the 'licence to operate' concept mentioned in Chapter 4, and the recognition that human communication generally is 'a process of mutual understanding', which public relations practitioners should heed 'if they take their jobs seriously'. In the model, which was developed in the context of a public dispute about a proposed landfill waste disposal site, the public relations senders offer information on *what, who* and *why*. The receivers of this information doubt it: they question the *truth* of *what*, the *trustworthiness* of *who* and the *legitimacy* of *why*.

Four **planning steps** are identified, each adaptable to individual circumstances. These may also be used for **evaluation** by the practitioner, both during and at the end of the period of communication (formative and summative assessment). The *what, who* and *why* categories are considered under *information, discussion, discourse* and *definition of the situation*. In the first three steps, there are both planning and evaluation questions to be addressed; in the fourth, there is in each case a 'to what extent has consent been achieved?' question. This is asked in relation to facts and fact-based judgements (*what*), the trustworthiness of the communication/company (*who*), project goals and value-based judgements (*why*). The final question, across all three, is: 'Has the result been communicated adequately?'

Following the landfill dispute, using COPR, a survey established a firm correlation between understanding and acceptance. This is unlikely to come as any surprise to the seasoned practitioner, although it would be unsound to assume that acceptance is an assured consequence of understanding, which might lead the relationship in quite another direction. The model's questions may appear to be 'commonsense' through their familiarity in practice, so its particular value is more likely to be measured by its very sound theoretical as well as practical basis. Under the heading 'Dimensions of understanding', it provides a clear and disciplined structure that captures key elements to be considered.

The *social* benefits of public relations practice are well rehearsed and often repeated in the context of corporate social responsibility and community relations, but they should not distract from consideration of the *economic* benefits, particularly now that there is growing pressure upon practitioners to demonstrate a satisfactory 'return-on-investment' (ROI) for their activities. Public relations budgets have grown significantly during the past decade. In the UK it is not uncommon to encounter internal departments comprising 35–40 and more people and some consultancies claim annual revenues in the order of £35–40 million. This underlying growth trend is also observable across Europe and in many other parts of the globe.

The historic tendency has been to view the cost of public relations as a necessary burden to be bravely borne, an administrative overhead in running the organization, and to waive questions about specific financial returns. Scrutiny of the economic benefits was discouraged by assurances, as we have seen, that PR outcomes were not in any event accurately measurable.

But although public relations may have thereby *evaded more rigorous evaluation* this **did it no service in the longer run**, for it had the effect of *relegating PR*, in the perception of other functions, to *the status of a technical support service* for the primary powers in the corporate hierarchy, such as finance, HRM and marketing. And invariably *they* set PR's agenda accordingly.

This was made most apparent in the marketing context, where public relations was subsumed into a simplistic publicity role, from which it is having great difficulty in extracting itself. So much so that many marketers still consider PR to be no more than a small part of marketing, less expensive, often by far, than the other marketing communications – direct sales, advertising, direct marketing and sales promotion – and something to resort to mainly when budgets are limited.

At such times the popular euphemism used to placate the PR people is 'tight', a word designed to foster their sympathy for the travails of a supposedly underfunded, struggling marketer. Marketers also see some other benefits to them of public relations, for instance, in helping to bolster or 'save' indifferent (and usually far more expensive) advertising, but whatever its immediate purpose, MPR is *primarily* about helping to achieve sales; not surprisingly, therefore, it is often mistaken for sales promotion.

Another well-entrenched perception of public relations also discourages any meaningful analysis of outcomes. It is the preoccupation with 'doing PR' as *both a means and an end in itself*, as though the activity had some therapeutic or similar quality that bears no further inspection. This view is shared by many, including more than a few practitioners who should, and almost certainly do, know better.

It results in many managers approaching their first use of public relations much as they might decide to start going to regular religious worship or taking routine exercise. 'Doing a bit of PR' becomes its own reward, needing no evaluation. While this can serve to postpone discussion of public relations and how it is done, as Ehling (1992) points out, 'it cannot eliminate the question of what should one seek to attain by means of communication.'

Before any **cost–benefit analysis** may be undertaken it is first necessary to dispense with such inhibitions to evaluation and to focus instead on the *core purposes* of public relations, devoid of any substitutions or additions sourced by other functions. Ehling reminds us that in their sixth edition Cutlip and Center (Cutlip *et al.*, 1985) sharpened up their definition of public relations, which we encountered in Chapter 1, away from 'a planned effort to influence opinion' to being about *mutually beneficial relationships* with publics on which *the success or failure* of the organization depends. *That* was the *primary* purpose of public relations.

compensating variation

Although some outcomes nevertheless may appear to defy rigorous economic analysis, Mishan's concept of **compensating variation** 'theoretically provides an optimal solution to placing dollar value on communication program effects'. **Break-even** is reached where the *cost of communication* designed to maintain a harmonious relationship and avoid conflict *equals the subjective benefits* gained from harmony and co-operation.

At this point there is indifference about continuing with the expenditure and effort. If communication costs rise, disharmony and conflict may seem less costly than the programme designed to reduce them. Should the relationship deteriorate, the compensating variation then required is the amount of cost to be incurred in order to regain the same subjective break-even point, when there is renewed indifference about continuing or ceasing the communication effort.

In using this approach there are two obvious difficulties:

▸ A monetary value has to be assigned to non-monetary effects, and
▸ Everyone affected by the programme has to be treated fairly or compensated.

Nevertheless, compensating variation probably offers the most satisfactory method, because it is based on how much gainers would pay for their benefits or would be needed to compensate losers. Alternative attempts to assign monetary values to non-traded goods (outcomes) by reference to traded products and services are based on flawed assumptions about their values being equal to those prices.

Taking positive compensating variations as benefits and negatives ones as costs, it is possible to arrive at the **net benefit** (benefit less cost) and at the **benefit–cost ratio** (benefit divided by cost). Ehling is not prescriptive about their use in deciding upon expenditures; sometimes one or the other is useful, sometimes neither. He recommends benefit–cost ratios, however, for choosing between competing mutually exclusive alternatives, selecting first that with the highest ratio.

He also touches upon **opportunity costs,** where the benefits of *alternatively spending elsewhere* arise. In practice this can occur remarkably often and present difficulties, for the concept is based on *missed* opportunities to obtain better return elsewhere, which in public relations practice may prove particularly demanding to calculate.

CHECKLIST

- All public relations outcomes are measurable, by one means or another, and persistent generalizations of immeasurability have to be treated with caution.
- The effectiveness of an organization is increased by the enduring quality relationships nurtured with strategic publics, which assist in the management of interdependencies, by which PR contributes to organizational success.
- Public relations practice is concerned to achieve enduring solutions through communication, not short-term fixes.
- Factors that influence the overall direction and purpose of the public relations function may depend upon where control of power lies within the organization.
- The dominant coalition of senior managers who run the organization most often decides what type of PR it wants, whether or not PR is represented or consulted.
- The coalition relies on suppositions, corporate culture and the function's perceived potential, in its worldview of PR that then determines the PR scope.
- The coalition also adopts a view of the organizational environment, which parts are crucial and what it considers to be the strategic publics for PR attention.
- Public relations strategy development is also subject to external as well as internal forces.
- The situational theory of publics measures communication behaviours by reference to problem recognition (information seeking and processing), constraint recognition (perceived obstacles) and level of involvement (degree of identification with the problem). From these variables publics may be identified, ranging from apathetic through latent to aware and active.
- Publics may be segmented into: all-issue (active generally); apathetic (inactive); single-issue (active on one issue, or a small subset, that is of limited concern) and hot-issue (active on one 'major' concern attracting wide interest).
- Whereas companies choose or ignore markets, in many cases publics choose companies, and other organizations, and so cannot be chosen or ignored by them.
- The innermost nest of the nested model for analysing publics contains the variables of individual communication behaviour and effects that are the more effective in communication planning.
- In the consensus-orientated public relations model, the practice output is grouped under three headings, what, who and why, to which receivers respond by questioning the truth of what, the trustworthiness of who and the legitimacy of why. Four adaptable steps are identified, information, discussion, discourse and definition of the situation, on which questions for planning and evaluation purposes are based.
- Research and analysis advances progressively from the centre, nest-by-nest, concentrating on the inner nests. The successive nests contain, in turn, (1) publics; (2) communities; (3) psychographics, lifestyles, cultures and social relationships; (4) geodemographics; (5) demographics and social categories; and (6) mass audiences.

□ Cost–benefit analysis may be applied using compensating variation, when the cost of communication designed to maintain a harmonious relationship is compared with the subjective benefits gained from harmony and co-operation.

FIGHTING FIRES

When in the autumn of 2002 the UK full-time firefighters' labour union, the Fire Brigades Union, announced publicly its demand for an across-the-board 30 per cent wage increase, it had a carefully laid public relations strategy and plan for what it anticipated, correctly, would be a major battle ahead for public opinion.

Firefighters are employed by local government authorities, which, in turn, rely on national government for funding. So the union was technically in dispute with a mixed bunch of political representatives scattered around the country, most of whom individually belonged to one or other of three major and two minor political parties. They formed a disparate, large negotiating team in which priorities were mixed, and historically the firemen had experienced little difficulty in obtaining what they wanted from this somewhat ineffectual body, the government meeting the cost of the resultant settlements.

But 30 per cent was bound to take some swallowing, with official economic inflation running at around 2.5 per cent and the government determined to limit public sector pay increases to little more than that. The union employed as its head of policy the domestic partner of a former government public relations 'spin doctor' who had felt obliged to resign as adviser to the Chancellor of the Exchequer, or finance minister, when he found that he 'became the story', rather than remaining out of sight, 'behind the story', where PR people much prefer to be. He denied that he was advising the union, although its leader was a long-standing friend.

The PR strategy called for a rapid insurgence into the national media and public consciousness, with a depiction of the union on terms calculated to best attract public sympathy and support for the pay increase and thereby advance the negotiations to a successful early victory. A 'formidable public relations machine' was assembled and the plan of action was woven around a series of strikes and whistle-stop morale-boosting tours by the leader, using pseudo-events, mainly of men burning wood fires in braziers on the forecourts of fire stations.

'By first threatening to strike and then undertaking a relatively modest two-day walkout, the firefighters have focused attention on their cause and mobilized some sympathy from those who feel that they perform a valuable service for what sounds likely relatively modest money.' On 15 November, in answer to the survey question 'Has the strike this week made you more or less sympathetic to the firefighters, or has it made no difference?' 39 per cent said that it had made them more sympathetic, compared with 23 per cent, who thought it had made them less sympathetic (*The Times*, 16 November 2002).

'The employers', as they were repeatedly described, spent a whole night in negotiation, resulting in acceptance of the full increase. But the government had insisted that it was involved, since it had to pay, and when a senior minister was awakened to hear the news he refused to accept it, instead commissioning an enquiry that would take weeks to report. Worse, for the union, it would be looking at the total picture, terms and conditions as well, with a view to identifying some tradeoffs for any increase. The government had bought time, designed to slow the pace of events.

It worked: the vital momentum had been stalled, and the union struggled for weeks thereafter, with lessening success, to maintain a grip on the 'news agenda', what interests the mass media day-by-day. Worse, facts began to emerge that damaged its cause. It appeared that, owing to the nature of the occupation, much if not most time spent on duty did not comprise work but mere attendance, waiting for a fire to happen. It was suggested that firefighting accounted for only five per cent of the time.

This in turn left the firefighters with plenty of spare energy, and most of them had second jobs, which was made possible by work timetables negotiated by their leaders. So the seemingly modest wages told only part of the story, and the media soon located men working at their second jobs who were willing to talk about it. This also gave credence to the employers' claim that on average 48 people applied for every vacancy in the service. Nor was the cause assisted by the details that emerged about the rulebook, the various working arrangements and agreements, which, it was argued, collectively increased costs unnecessarily and necessitated a hunt by the employers for economies.

The union's public relations campaign had well fulfilled its purpose, to create an environment that provided the optimum conditions for the negotiators, but it had failed to adequately anticipate and prepare for the government's response. The media began to discover the part-time firefighters, people who provide a service to smaller communities, whose union contested imputations that their members were amateurs and deflected public sympathy away from the full-timers. And attention also turned to the army, tasked to operate 50-year-old 'mothballed' well out-of-date firefighting machines manned by young, hastily trained soldiers, who were denied use of modern publicly purchased equipment by the strikers.

There was an offer of around 15 per cent 'on the table', much as there had been during the previous summer, but now it came attached to various conditions, so instead of 'quitting while ahead' the union leaders campaigned on, with successive strikes further eroding public sympathy. The media largely lost interest, as negotiations continued. A year after they rejected an unconditional deal at around 16 per cent, the leaders recommended to their members acceptance of much the same with strings attached.

QUESTIONS

1 What would prompt expenditure on primary research and why?
2 Why could strategy mean different things to different organizations?

3 How might public relations influence power within the organization?
4 When might publics 'come and go', when might they stay, and why?
5 What might be gained by evading evaluation of public relations effects?

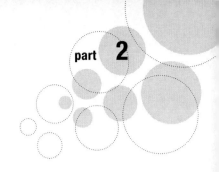

part **2**

the customers

Relationship objectives – dialogue with privacy – loyalty – lifetime customer value – consumers' decision-making process – the decision-making unit – relationship care

7.1 relationship objectives

Relationships can develop from the least likely beginnings and some of the most fulfilling may be the least well planned or sought after. People, though, usually allow relationships to develop because they *want something out of them*, and the relationships that organizations cultivate with their customers, and they in turn consider that they enjoy with those organizations, are no exception. There is *calculation* afoot, often rather deep calculation, and it is *mutual*.

Customers, it has often been remarked, come in all sizes and shapes. The principal division is between those that *consume* the products and services, who account for the vast majority of sales by volume, and those that use them to *in turn add value* in some way that they then offer on to others. This, however, is a fine distinction.

Firstly, the **consumers** are generally thought to be those who *finally* consume, or use, the product or service, but consumers may also buy for others, and quite a lot of people consume but do not purchase, although they had a hand in deciding what they consume. Secondly, other **customers**, those aiming to add value by processing, also have much in mind the *consumer* interest. Every product or service must find its ultimate user, so everything done to bring it to this happy outcome is geared to that harsh reality. Such customers may be referred to as **corporate, trade** or **industrial purchasers**, although many are organizations that are neither businesses nor engaged in industrial processes: they include institutional and government buyers, for instance, as well as manufacturers. The term **business-to-business (B2B)** is widely used to describe these markets.

'The central ideas of marketing are universal and it makes no difference whether we are marketing furnaces, insurance policies or margarine'

(McDonald, 1989). What unites all types of customer is that they have **needs and wants which must be satisfied**:

▸ The consumer is increasingly driven by *personal wants* as well as needs, owing to increasingly sophisticated marketing directed at creating and stimulating consumption, and hopes to be totally *delighted*

▸ The B2B customer is focused on *specificity* to meet often complex requirements, and expects to be *fully enabled.*

Public relations practice reflects this division, through **consumer relations** and **B2B public relations**. The first is thought by practitioners to be the glamorous, even exciting, 'action', and it accounts for far the greater proportion of expenditure devoted to customers, while the second is usually seen as the opposite, although in reality B2B is often more complex, demanding and professionally fulfilling.

There is a further category of customer: the 'internal customer', as marketing prefers, what public relations people regard as the *internal publics*. The link between employees and sales, however, might be considered tenuous or inappropriate, since it implies that employees are captive targets for being sold at, when in reality they are there to do their jobs. Public relations adopts a rather different perspective on this, not regarding employees as being also customers.

CERP has no doubt about the importance of **consumer relations**: 'People, generally speaking, more and more frequently consider corporate behaviour as a key element to identify and qualify the enterprise, but corporate behaviour itself is first and foremost expressed by the quality of the consumer relations' (CERP website, 5 November 2002).

Usefully, given this emphasis, it offers four definitions, starting with:
'Consumer relations is corporate or business activity aiming at:

▸ Matching the corporate and product image as close as possible with that expected by the consumer targets

▸ Ensuring the best quality of products and services, to achieve consumer satisfaction.'

In other words, consumer relations may take the form of *organizational* communication, ongoing interaction between the organization and one of its key publics, or *marketing* communication, part of product or service promotion.

This combination is reflected in CERP's three further definitions, which describe consumer relations as being:

> planned programmes designed to establish, handle and develop appropriate two-way communication channels with consumers of products and services, with Consumer Groups and Associations and with public Authorities and Bodies whose responsibilities involve consumer protection and information rights.

> a significant asset to a Company or business which recognizes consumer protection and information rights as a fundamental principle to be respected and developed in the Company or business managerial practice.

planned and permanent pro-active and post-active action addressed to consumers as individuals or groups, aiming at improving consumer confidence in the quality of products or services.

Here the emphasis is on addressing **consumerism**, developing and maintaining reputation for fair dealing, responsible behaviour, reliable performance, all to create the climate of confidence in both the source and its offerings that provides the optimum environment for marketing of those products and services. It is about '**building brands**' by adding those extra qualities, in the perception of consumers, that give the supplier competitive advantage.

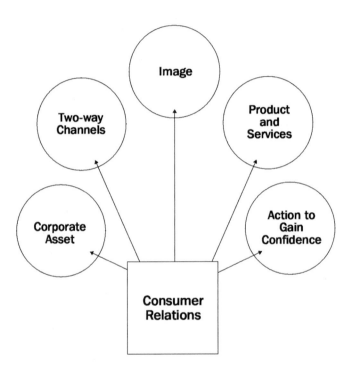

figure **7.1   consumer relations**

And CERP is uncompromising in its strictures about this; for instance, clause 15 of its Code of Conduct, 'Specific Responsibility to Consumers', states: 'Any attempt to deceive consumer opinion or its representatives is forbidden'.

Public relations in connection with non-consumer customers is similarly centred on relationship building. Accordingly, it takes account of the *detailed circumstances of each customer* to a degree that is very unlikely to be matched, or necessary, with a consumer. This gives rise to the development of **specialist knowledge about specific sectors**, to the extent that many public relations practitioners are recognized experts in the fields within which their customers operate.

Their skill sets also tend to differ, to the extent that they are likely to be talking with *very informed and knowledgeable* customers, usually have to *understand technical detail* and frequently need to communicate *complex information and arguments* that are variously encoded to be understood by a variety of receivers.

Customers tend to be **individually more significant** owing to their *purchasing power* and *scale of influence.* There are multiple *business practices* and various *regulatory codes* that apply specifically to different sectors, all of which have to be well understood and observed. Communication is more likely to be *two-way* **through opinion formers** and to include **presentations to key decision-makers**.

7.2 dialogue with privacy

If customers are to consider that they have a worthwhile relationship with the organization, whether as consumers or organizational purchasers, they must be able to recognize those qualities that they would expect to find in a *valued interpersonal* relationship.

EXAMPLE

If an airline passenger wants to e-mail his or her preferred airline, the one always chosen to fly with, to offer a brilliant tip about passenger comfort, *first* there has to be a feeling that the airline is **really just like a friend** who *deserves* this tip. In other words, that making this generous gesture is going to be *appreciated.* In fact, airlines receive many such communications, perhaps because their passengers are so grateful to be safely carried, and they are skilled at knowing how to respond, sounding really appreciative.

And the same applies, but *more so*, with other customers, where very often there is a formal ongoing relationship, probably based on after-sales service, phased delivery or some form of partnership agreement. Routine and regular contact tends to encourage relationship bonding, bringing forth *expectations about interpersonal shared values,* much as occurs between work colleagues. If the customer contact person wants to offer a comment or tip, and many do, he or she needs to be *sure* first that **the relationship is *right***, so that its delicate mechanism may not be put at risk. This is potentially very sensitive, because any disturbance to perceived ability to relate successfully one with another in these situations can result in significant consequences.

There is therefore a *quality dimension* to *successful* consumer and customer communication that can be characterized as **dialogue with privacy**. This is about having the confidence to converse one-to-one with each other *as if old friends*, knowing that each will respect the position of the other and bring to the exchange that level of commitment. Where it occurs, it begins to satisfy the requirements of the *two-way* symmetrical approach to communication; that state of grace described as **excellent** public relations.

7.3 loyalty and lifetime customer value

The proliferation of **loyalty** schemes is evidence enough of the importance attached to not only attracting consumers but also *keeping* them. And there are also many similar schemes for other types of customer. As marketers never tire of pointing out, it is generally estimated to *cost around five times as much to find a replacement customer as to keep an existing one.* So in customer relations, *loyalty is a core purpose* of communication.

Modern loyalty schemes, however, are about more than mere loyalty. Direct marketers seek **one-to-one relationships for commercial gain**, so loyalty programmes are devised that facilitate this through *segmentation* of customers, to the extent that *each is profiled* and thereby 'known' to the organization. McCorkell (1997) identified seven key ingredients for 'the truly successful scheme', of which two are of particular relevance to public relations:

> 4) *Recognize individuality of customer.* Include rewards, benefits and courtesies that recognize the customer as a person.

> 7) *Use data collected for intelligent marketing.* Schemes can be used to provide data that drive communications recognizing customer shopping patterns, preferences, breaks in continuity and so on. They can also provide useful area data to retailers, improving catchment area definition and permitting accurate targeting of competitive customers.

The direct marketer's database is therefore a potential cornucopia of valuable information about customers. Although it is preoccupied with sales, and so full of useful nuggets about, for instance, shopping preferences, it should greatly assist the public relations practitioner by providing the quality of information required to assist in initiating relevant and meaningful customer relations programmes.

In most businesses the bulk of profit comes from transactions with *established* customers, which leads to the conclusion that over time specific **values can be assigned** to each one. Some customers say as much themselves, usually when they are dissatisfied, with comments such as 'To think how much I've spent with you'. The concept of **lifetime customer value** (LCV) aims to optimize the *total net revenue that may be obtained from each customer*.

In determining LCV, the ***anticipated future worth of each customer*** is calculated by forecasting:

- The period over which the customer will remain loyal and
- The customer's *spend within that period*, usually calculated in present-day prices.

'Very often this spend will increase for a while, then reduce before the customer severs the relationship.'

This concept has direct relevance also to the conduct of customer relations programmes, *particularly those with consumers*, many of which include enhancements such as complementary deals, exclusive invitations, memberships, customized magazines, educational leaflets and information access.

7.4 consumers' decision-making process

To marketers, consumer behaviour is of eternal fascination. The term is used to describe how people act not only when they are searching for and buying products and services but also *how* they use, evaluate and dispose of products, services and ideas that they expect will satisfy their needs. Three major *comprehensive* models of consumer decision-making help explain what happens. These describe the stages people go through, from:

▸ The source of the message and the consumer's attitude: (1) the attributes of the *company* that is the message sender, and (2) the attributes of the *consumer* that affect her or his perception of the message, especially predispositions such as personality, motives, experience, and thus knowledge and beliefs (the **Nicosia** model).
▸ The consumer's existing level of knowledge and whether he or she has already a strong preference or brand loyalty, or fairly well-defined criteria for making a choice, or either no preferences and/or perceived high risk of making a mistaken purchase (the **Howard-Sheth** model).
▸ The initial search for information in differing degrees of complexity, relying on relevant variables such as memory (the **Engel-Kollat-Minniard** model).

For public relations practitioners engaged on customer relations programmes, these provide a particularly useful *broad frame of reference*. Like all models, they provide *simplified* representations of reality and they may indicate gaps in knowledge and understanding that might need filling. Sheth also produced a model that describes **how families make decisions**. It lists seven factors that influence whether a decision to purchase will be shared or taken independently of others. These factors are: social class; lifestyle; role orientation; family life cycle; perceived risk; product or service importance; and time pressure.

A 'family' may comprise **two adults** living together:

▸ Who have **no children**, either because they have not produced any or the children have grown up and left home
▸ With **one or more children**, all living together ('the nuclear family')
▸ With **one or more children** and **one or more other relatives**, such as grandparents ('the extended family').

The family can be viewed as a

▸ *Social unit,*
▸ *Network of relationships*, or
▸ *Reference group.*

The latter exerts critical influences during the *formative years* of life in relation to, for instance, social standards and behaviours, self-awareness and perceptions and interpretation of environment.

Within the family, *various roles are adopted* in relation to decisions about purchases:

▸ *Influencer* – introduces information, starts up the interest

- *Gatekeeper* – controls the flow of information in the following search
- *Decider* – has the power, 'final say', on what is to be purchased
- *Buyer* – executes purchase decisions
- *Preparer* – converts the purchase for family use, for example, 'flat pack' assembly
- *User* – consumes or uses the product or service purchased
- *Maintainer* – keeps the product fit for purpose
- *Disposer* – prompts and implements disposal of the product or termination of the service.

These roles, and the number and type of persons who adopt them, vary according to circumstances, such as the *type of family structure* and *how roles are assigned by reference to gender*. Often one person fulfils several roles; sometimes the decider and the buyer are two different people. Often users are neither deciders nor buyers; children are said to exert great 'pester power' as influencers and potential users.

The *family life cycle* (FLC) reflects the evolution of families over successive generations. There are common stages of development, which are reflected in changing economic circumstances. This has been variously described, including this commonly used seven stage version:

- *Young*
- *Young single* without children
- *Young couple*, whose youngest child is *under age six*
- *Young couple*, whose youngest child is *aged six or older*
- *Older couple*, whose children are *aged 18+* and still living at home
- *Older couple*, whose children have all *left home*
- *Older single*, living alone.

While all this is of abiding concern to the searcher after consumption variables, it also has great relevance to customer relations programmes.

figure **7.2** **the family decision-making team**

7.5 the decision-making unit

The **decision-making unit** within any organization comprises 'all those individuals and groups who participate in the purchasing decision-making process, who share some common goals and the risks arising from those decisions', according to Webster and Wind, cited by Kotler (1991). Accordingly it can be *much larger than* that of a family, and the processes may be *very much longer, more detailed and complex,* with **greater risk attached to outcomes.**

However, the roles are similar:

> *Influencer* – often contributes to the preparation of the specification, as well as providing information; typically a technical expert

> *Gatekeeper* – frequently interprets the role as being to keep out sales, other contacts and information, possibly to doubtful advantage

> *Decider* – sometimes well removed from 'the action' and not readily identifiable from the outside

> *Buyer* – selects the supplier and negotiates the deal, may also contribute to preparation of the specification

figure **7.3   the organizational decision making Unit**

> *Approver* – authorizes the proposed actions of deciders and buyers

> *User* – often initiates the process by identifying a need and contributes to the preparation of the specification.

'When a buying center includes many participants, the seller will not have the time or resources to reach them all. Smaller sellers concentrate on reaching the *key buying influences.* Large sellers go for *multilevel in-depth selling* to reach as many buying participants as possible. Their salespeople virtually "live" with their high-volume customers.'

For many public relations people, this tends to translate into generating communication with *specifiers*, who may appear in various guises and at one or more remove from where the products or services are required. Architects provide an obvious example. They seldom finance or construct anything, but they design, and to do *that* they have to specify. There are numerous similar examples.

7.6 relationship care

In World War II the UK government advised its citizens to restrict their conversation in public places, for fear that enemy agents overheard something to the country's potential disadvantage; its famous slogan was 'Loose talk costs lives'. Judging by the lengths to which some people go to obtain valuable marketing intelligence, loose talk still has its dangers, a fact that many public relations people recognize very well. The consequences for lapses can be serious, particularly if the words come from the lips of senior managers, whether of their own devising or placed there for them to utter. In fostering and maintaining customer relationships, the practitioner is *acutely aware* of the importance that must be attached to *all interactions* with customers, whether through customer magazines, chief executive comments or any other communication.

The organizations that really do *not* appear to care much about this, those who seem to fly in the face of the conventional wisdom about corporate reputation, seldom mince their words. But surprisingly often those that clearly *do* care nevertheless manage to commit some startlingly clumsy gaffs. And claiming afterwards that words and comments have been taken 'out of context' is of little avail, because the damage is done, and in any event both sender and receiver can variously interpret 'context'. The *reality* is that communication with customers, whether direct or mediated, *has* to be Handled With Care, increasingly so given deteriorating perceptions of poor 'customer care' and the reputational damage that it is doing undeservedly to many organizations. The customer relations programme has a heavy responsibility to bear.

CHECKLIST

- Customers may be consumers or business-to-business (or industrial) purchasers with needs and wants which must be satisfied. The first hope to be totally delighted, the second to be fully enabled.
- There are substantial and significant differences between the two types of customer. Consumer relations accounts for far the greater PR spend on customers; B2B public relations is often more complex, demanding and professionally fulfilling.
- All customer communication benefits from achievement of a quality 'dialogue with privacy' similar to that attainable within a valued interpersonal relationship.
- Gaining customer loyalty is a core purpose of communication and is sought by reference to customer lifetime value (LCV), the forecast future worth of the customer based on duration of loyalty and estimated spend during that period.
- The interactive Nicosia model of consumer decision-making depicts a communication cycle comprising four fields: (1) consumer attitude towards the product; (2) pre-action search and evaluation, leading to motivation; (3) the act of purchase; and (4) feedback, indicating predisposition towards further messages.
- The Howard-Sheth model distinguishes between extensive problem-solving, limited problem-solving and routine responses. The basic version includes inputs, intervening variables and outputs.
- This model identifies many of the variables that influence consumers but is suited to choosing within a specific product or service category, not between two or more related alternatives.
- The Engel-Kollat-Minniard model has four basic stages: (1) search for information, (2) evaluation of alternatives, (3) choice and (4) outcomes. It describes what occurs in varying degrees of complexity.
- Sheth listed seven factors that influence family purchase decision-making: social class, lifestyle, role orientation, family life cycle (FLC), perceived risk, product or service importance and time pressure.
- Eight purchasing roles are adopted within the family: influencer, gatekeeper, decider, buyer, preparer, user, maintainer and disposer. Often one person fulfils several roles, which vary according to circumstances.

- The family life cycle (FLC) describes the evolution of families over successive generations. A commonly used seven-stage version includes: young, young single, young couple with young children, young couple with older children, older couple with adult children, older couple and older single.
- Six purchasing roles, comprising the Decision-Making Unit, are adopted within the organization: influencer, gatekeeper, decider, buyer, approver and user. One person may fulfil more than one role.
- PR communication is often with specifiers, who may appear in various guises and at one or more remove from where the products or services are required.
- In fostering and maintaining customer relationships, it is necessary to be acutely aware of the importance of all interactions with customers, without exception.

CASE STUDY

PRINCE CHARLES'S CHRISTMAS PUDDINGS

When the delightfully named Puddings & Pies, a privately owned 'Country Fresh Food Company', embarked upon a PR-led brand awareness programme it little supposed that one outcome would be to become a supplier of Christmas puddings to His Royal Highness Prince Charles, The Prince of Wales, the next British monarch.

Puddings & Pies, located at Sherborne in the English rural southwest, produces a wide range of high-quality foods, which are sold mainly into the catering trade and to food retailers, including delicatessen shops, traditional English teashops and farm shops, within approximately 50 miles' radius of its kitchens. Everything is made to order by hand.

The company's policy statement states simply: 'We only use free range eggs, local farmhouse cheese, butter, milk and cream. All our flour is traditionally ground at a local watermill or a family miller's in the Cotswolds. All our meat is supplied by local farms. We do not use any flavourings, any additives, any colourings, any genetically modified products.'

The company uses a friendly Grandma symbol, to imply that all the food is prepared 'just like granny does'. With only a very limited budget, Puddings & Pies embarked on an intensive round of exhibiting at agricultural and other country shows and at UK catering trade exhibitions. This led to invitations to participate in local farmers' markets and, at its peak, the programme included an average of 10 shows each month, which represented a major commitment for this microsized business.

Apart from selling retail every product it displayed at these events, confirming that it had accurately identified an attractive niche market for 'proper food that looks home made', the principal objective was to attract trade enquiries. These came in abundance, from a wide variety of sources, some 'out of area', searching for premium-priced quality.

This was achieved for a fraction of the cost of advertising and has contributed substantially to a trebling of annual turnover and more than trebling of profit. That in turn has led to investment in additional plant and premises designed to maintain handmade production while expanding capacity. The exhibition programme has been adapted over time and is now complemented by marketing activities that include point-of-purchase displays, very successful retail product sampling and some advertising.

The Christmas puddings tasted so good at Prince Charles's country estate that, from being a private customer, he became also a trade customer, through his quality foods company, Duchy Originals, for which Puddings & Pies is developing an exclusive range of products, for sale under the Duchy Originals brand. This 'royal endorsement' is also leading Puddings & Pies into invitations to supply direct some of the leading London food halls. The Puddings & Pies experience demonstrates the remarkable brand awareness impact that can be achieved by diligent use of low-cost PR techniques with very limited financial and labour resources.

QUESTIONS

1 When might dialogue with privacy be more attainable, and why?
2 How might LCV influence the design of a customer relations programme?
3 How might intervening external variables in decision-making determine the choice of communication channels in customer relations?
4 How relevant is the FLC likely to be in framing customer relations communication?
5 What measures might the PR person take to avoid quotation 'out of context'?

chapter **8**

within marketing

The promotional mix – marketing public relations – areas of support – brands – integrated marketing communication – Cause Related Marketing – the relationship between public relations and marketing

8.1 the promotional mix

To briefly recap: much public relations activity is directed at supporting marketing, where it is assigned to that part of the 'marketing mix' called *promotion*. There it works alongside other forms of marketing communication, which is one of the three categories of corporate communication, the others being management and organization communication. Public relations in this guise, together with all other marketing communication, contributes to the creation of shareholder value, which is about building sustainable competitive advantage.

The '**marketing mix**' is also known as the **seven Ps**. These comprise:

- *Product*
- *Price*
- *Place* (distribution) and
- *Promotion*

all of which relate directly to the offering, plus

- *People* (because everyone who has a customer interface influences purchase decision-making)
- *Process* (reflecting the involvement of the customer in the production processes) and
- *Physical evidence* (since less tangible services often need to be made more apparent). So *promotion* is but *one of seven* components of the marketing mix.

The various forms of marketing communication in turn comprise the '**promotion mix**'. This comprises:

- *Direct sales* or personal selling
- *Advertising*
- *Sales promotion*
- *Direct marketing*
- *Public relations* and
- *The Internet*.

Of these marketing communications, in the UK direct sales account for the greatest expenditure: many companies have substantial sales forces. In 2000 estimated total UK expenditure was: sales £20 billion, sales promotion £14 billion, advertising £13 billion, direct marketing £5 billion and public relations £2 billion (Doyle, 2000). This puts the PR contribution to marketing *by expenditure* well into perspective, although the relative differences indicated reflect UK conditions and cannot be readily assumed elsewhere. For instance, sales promotion in the UK is heavily used, yet in Germany use of sales promotion is very limited indeed.

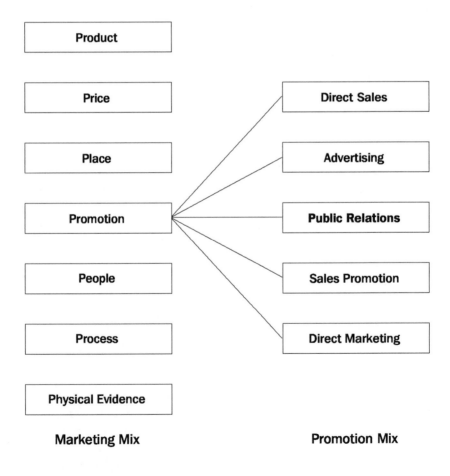

figure **8.1 the marketing and promotional mix**

Moloney (2000) points to a growing use of public relations by marketers (which is observable in many countries) and suggests that this is 'because they believe that advertising alone is not persuasive enough, when the consumer is better educated, is seen as "active" and "ethical", and is considered to be "compassionate". Certainly all the indications are that the *hunt for more persuasiveness* lies at the heart of marketing's growing interest in public relations, but there are several other, more mundane, factors that, where they apply, also explain the take-up. These include:

- The availability of appropriate advertising media,
- Rising costs of advertising production,
- Inapplicability of sales promotion,
- Sales force reductions, and
- Smaller audiences to reach.

Compared to other marketing communications, however, this 'tool', as marketers call it, is judged primarily on 'physical economics': put bluntly, both research and practice confirm that for most marketers using public relations is a cheap alternative to what they generally prefer. 'Quite literally, marketers are being forced to consider PR's applicability to marketing products, brands and services' (Kitchen, 1997b).

But there is another factor at work as well: *the rise in importance of corporate reputation*. How customers think *about the organization itself* is having a big impact on how they decide to view its products and services. *That* makes public relations seem rather more interesting from a marketing standpoint.

8.2 marketing public relations

Time was when public relations in support of marketing used to be known simply as publicity and its purpose was to support sales through media coverage. The term stuck until the 1980s, when it was superseded by the conflation of marketing and public relations to produce MPR.

But what *is* MPR? Kotler (1991) defines this 'tool' as

- 'A variety of programs designed to improve, maintain, or protect a company or product image.'

This represents a substantial advance, adding *images*, including their *protection*, both those that apply to organizations *and* to what they have to offer.

This important point is now widely accepted and understood: MPR adds up to more than its predecessor. Hart, for one, took it further:

> Overall, one may say that public relations is concerned with creating a favourable image, or, to use a less emotive word, a favourable reputation ... The emergence of reputation as a factor in the marketing mix leads onto the extension of the classical 4 Ps into Five. The fourth P of promotion (which more properly anyway should be 'perception') now has to be considered as those activities which are involved with the product (brand image) and those concerned with the company (corporate image). It can be

said that whether or not a product is purchased is dependent on five factors – the product, its price, its availability, the brand image and the corporate image... Insofar as PR is the function which builds reputation or corporate image it can be seen then to have a direct correlation to sales and hence to profit. (Hart, 1995)

This represents a quantum leap in the argument for deploying public relation skills in the service of marketing. MPR is not only about adding to the battery of techniques and tactics, it is gaining in *marketing consequence*. To reinforce his point, Hart quotes Levitt's identification of 'sixteen areas in which a good reputation can be shown to have a positive benefit' in B2B markets. In practice reputation factors have always greatly influenced commercial and institutional purchasers, but the point is well made, and such factors are also of growing interest and concern to consumers.

Various definitions of MPR abound, and a prosaic summary such as '**the marketing component of public relations**' is probably entirely adequate for all practical purposes. *However*, among marketers it is still often seen as 'free advertising', an impression that not a few public relations practitioners encourage by seeking to 'value' the published editorial coverage that they have secured by reference to the alternative cost of advertising in the same space or time. The problem with this is that

▸ The space or time may not be buyable,
▸ Receivers attach markedly more credibility to editorial than to advertising, and in any event
▸ Public relations is not without its own costs. So whatever else MPR is, clearly it is *not* free advertising.

8.3 areas of support

From a marketing perspective, public relations is part of the marketing communications mix, but if that is so, what *exactly* is it doing there? Marketers talk about **exchange theory**, as well as communication theory, so whatever public relations practitioners contribute is likely to be judged within that *commercial* framework. Kotler (1991) argues that MPR can contribute to four marketing objectives:

▸ Awareness,
▸ Credibility,
▸ Stimulation of the sales force and dealers, and
▸ Holding down promotion costs.

'The smaller the company's promotion budget, the stronger the case for using PR to gain share of mind.'

That memorable last phrase, 'share of mind', may be compared with the commonplace and less subtle 'share of shout' allusion to noise. MPR, then, has a *cerebral* contribution to make to marketing, and is not entirely, or necessarily, about publicity. But nevertheless that sits alongside its *cheapness* as one of

MPR's contributions. It appears that no matter how subtle MPR may become at influencing customers to purchase, if it is not downright inexpensive, relatively, most marketers are not *that much* interested.

How, then, may this low-cost marketing communication tool contribute in practice to the marketing tasks? Kotler offers six suggestions 'beyond simple publicity':

▸ Assist in the launch of new products
▸ Assist in repositioning a mature product
▸ Build up interest in a product category
▸ Influence specific target groups
▸ Defend products that have encountered public problems
▸ Build the corporate image in a way that projects favourably on its products.

Here too the corporate image obtains a mention, as being part of MPR's workload, as also is *defence* as well as promotion. Nevertheless, most marketers prefer a simpler view of MPR as being *the delivery of successive good news*, faithfully reproduced by the mass media with extra credibility attached. And *that* creates a problem for them in valuing MPR, a problem that is neatly summed up by Doyle (2000), for whom MPR's main features are:

▸ *Credibility*, because 'news stories and features are more credible sources of information to buyers than ads and promotions that are obviously biased and paid for'
▸ *Imprecise*, being more difficult to control the message and target it accurately than with 'conventional commercial communications'
▸ *Low cost*, owing to 'free media exposure'
▸ *Difficult*, because 'it depends upon the perceived importance and interest of the message'.

In other words, in his view, on the one hand MPR is cheap and effective, but on the other it is less controllable and certain, because its very strength, the 'free' mass media 'exposure', is *also* its very weakness: mediated communication has to be *subjected to the filtering process* of the mediators, usually journalists. Marketers recognize practitioners' media relations skills – for instance, Kotler observed that 'PR practitioners are able to find or create stories on behalf of even mundane products', and indeed they do – but worry that messages have to satisfy media criteria first. They assume that all messages have to jump this hurdle, although in practice MPR very often communicates *direct* to customers and consumers, for instance, through exhibitions, literature and events. This, therefore, is a *defective element in marketers' perceptions of public relations*, one that is now being reinforced by the introduction of instruction in the art and mystery of writing press releases as part of marketing training.

Public relations practitioners are in no doubt about this media challenge. They spend very many hours trying, sometimes with growing desperation, to dredge interest for the reader, viewer or listener out of information and other material that holds fascination for only a limited circle of people within the organization. Then often only to find that the message source insists on *filleting the facts* that create the media interest, out of anxiety about control, sometimes extending to rampant 'control freakery'.

Public relations contributes **topicality, credibility** and **involvement** through *interactive opportunities,* the aim being to achieve topicality, some link with current news, but many non-PR managers find this difficult to understand, much less accept. As Oliver (2001) remarked, 'Public relations can only be effective if it has a credible story to tell'. And *some* managers find that to be too great a challenge for them, typically concluding that it is better to 'keep it simple some other way'. Furthermore, for them talk of 'the broader and more strategic function of public relations [that] is concerned with corporate image' (Hart, 1995) usually falls on deaf ears.

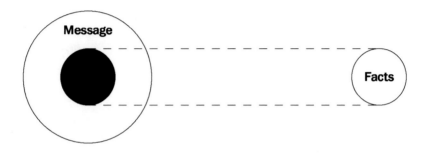

figure **8.2** **extracting, or 'filleting', the facts from the message to leave a hole**

EXAMPLE

To launch the new version of the Range Rover motorcar, what the British motor industry calls a 'four-by-four' that is designed to travel across difficult terrain as well as roads, the MPR effort entailed persuading motoring writers from a variety of media to travel to Scotland in mid-winter in order to 'test run' the new product. A 'plane was chartered and repainted, part of a military airfield was rented, as was a country estate in the Highlands, an expensive castle-turned-hotel was fully booked, a special 'off-road' course was built, a famous explorer was hired to give an 'adventurous' after-dinner speech and several senior managers were assigned to act as hosts.

Some five hundred journalists were flown to the venue over a period of five weeks, where one hundred attendant staff engaged in 'being nice, cleaning cars and repairing the inevitable prangs'. So reported one of the journalists, who remarked that in three years as a professional road tester it was the most sumptuous launch he had experienced. 'Almost every car maker will mount a similar PR offensive to mark the arrival of a new model. Exotic locations, excellent food and Grand Luxe hotels. The free bars never shut, the room service is paid for, and there's almost always a gift ... to help you remember it all.'

'My best estimate of £2 million for the extravaganza works out at a cool £4000 per journalist. Still, compared to the Range Rover's £1.5 billion engineering costs, it's a drop in the ocean. ... So does this multi-million-pound niceness campaign work? ... With my hand on my heart, resting over a Land Rover fleece, Skoda wallet and Mercedes watch I can tell you that it has absolutely no effect on my impartiality whatsoever.'

(Financial Times, 5 February 2002)

8.4 brands

Now that **corporate** brands are being brought to the attention of consumers alongside **product** brands, those broader public relations responsibilities are adding to MPR's potential contribution, for 'corporate and brand images inter-act to enhance overall ambience and [PR in respect of both types] influence the bottom line [profitability]' (Kitchen, 1997b). Accordingly corporate brands are being brought to the consumer's notice, even where the product or service has sold very well for many years without it.

The term 'brand' is so generously used, but what *exactly* is a brand? At its most prosaic, a brand is simply a name and all the qualities that are perceived to attach to it. But that needs qualifying. According to Doyle (2000), brands:

> reduce perceived risk, simplify the choice process and save time. This relationship [of trust] is based on the image customers have of the brand. A *brand image* is a set of beliefs about a brand's attributes and associations. A customer's image of a brand is built up from four types of sources: experience ... personal [endorsements and tips] ... public [mass media coverage and consumer report analysis and] ... commercial [marketing and sales].

Doyle goes on to place brands and brand images into three categories:

- An *attribute* brand – the image generates confidence through beliefs about functional attributes
- An *aspirational* brand – the image indicates who buys the brand and their enviable lifestyles
- An *experience* brand – the image shares emotions and associations with the consumer.

In B2B markets the emphasis is on *attributes*, more down-to-earth about function and performance, whereas consumers are more interested in *lifestyle* and *experience*. 'Experience brands have a number of advantages over attribute and aspirational brands. ... Consumers are becoming more individualistic ... Experience brands are more robust because they do not depend on a product or a "look". ... The archetype of an experience brand is Richard Branson's Virgin brand, which stands for an unstuffy, irreverent, us-against-them attitude.'

The role of MPR in enhancing brands was addressed by Houtman (Harris, 1998, cited by DeSanto and Petherbridge, 2002). Houtman, whose title at Chrysler was Manager of Corporate Image and Brand, identified five rules for building brands through public relations:

1 Know what the product, and the campaign that surrounds it, stands for.
2 Target those buyers who have a passion for your product.
3 Understand how the industry to which your product belongs has evolved.

4 Integrate the timeless qualities that have helped make the brand successful.

5 Reduce cross-considerations by targeting an exclusive market and audience.

Viewed this way, where there is already a successful brand with 'timeless qualities', MPR is primarily about **filling any gaps of uncertainty about purchase** that are resulting in hesitation and hovering over the **corporate elements** of the **product surround**. But the brand does not have to be long established for MPR to bring these 'extra' dimensions to the marketing effort. Just as public relations is the eyes and ears of the organization (and its voice, too), so also it can bring the bigger picture to bear on brand promotion and defence, trying to *make sure that marketing is wholly consistent with all other messages.*

8.5 integrated marketing communication

This matter of *integration* is critical, on which PR practitioners place great emphasis; they know how destructive can be inconsistencies, in generating *perceptions* of confusion, incompetence, even deceit. There is need of 'a consistent corporate message and tone that appropriately reflects the organization in the way that the organization wishes it to be reflected' (Oliver, 2001). This public relations priority is shared with marketing. 'At its most basic level, integrated marketing communications [IMC] means integrating all the promotional tools so that they work together in harmony... Their sum is greater than their parts – providing they speak consistently with one voice all the time, every time.' In addition to 'the basic communications tools', integration may be horizontal, vertical, internal, external and in relation to data (Smith, 1999).

These may be summarized as:

- *Horizontal*, across the marketing mix and subsystems, so that different functions send out consistent messages through their various decisions and actions
- *Vertical*, so that both marketing and communication objectives are consistent with the corporate mission and objectives
- *Internal*, keeping everyone relevantly informed and motivated
- *External*, providing a single, cohesive message through the close collaboration of external partners such as advertising and public relations agencies
- *Data*, to ensure a marketing information system which collects and shares relevant data across subsystems.

Much importance is attached by marketers to this simple precept. Smith asserts that 'it can create competitive advantage and boost sales and profits, while saving money, time and stress'. That is certainly borne out by experience, as is the prospect of the alternative: 'disjointed messages which dilute the impact of the message [and may] confuse, frustrate and arouse anxiety in customers'. The most relevant benefit of IMC from the public relations standpoint is its *effectiveness*. 'At its most basic level, a unified message has more impact than a disjointed myriad of messages [and] a better chance of cutting through the "noise" of over 500 commercial messages that bombard customers each and every day.'

Kitchen (1997b) asked seven marketing and seven public relations executives, drawn from seven companies on average each employing 17,000 people, what IMC meant to them. The conclusion was that IMC 'extends beyond marketing to corporate activities too. For many FMCG [fast-moving consumer goods] firms, there is a significant need to *market the corporate brand*. Thus while PR can be utilized by marketing, marketing can also be utilized by PR.'

8.6 Cause Related Marketing

The BITC's annual Awards for Excellence scheme includes an award for 'Marketplace Impact' called the **Cause Related Marketing** Award, 'for using the power of the brands in partnership with charities or causes to address key social issues'. Moloney (2000) quotes BITC's definition of CRM as being 'a "commercial activity" to "market an image, product or service for mutual benefit. It is an additional tool for addressing social issues of the day." It emphasizes goals such as "enhanced reputation", "awareness, improved loyalty".'.

He cites by way of example the supply of 29,000 computers to UK schools by multinational grocery retailer Tesco. In fact the scheme is said to have supplied £77 million-worth of computers, yet it still has its detractors. A consumer organization calculated that it took 21,990 vouchers, acquired by buying groceries, to provide a single computer worth £1000. A similar scheme introduced vending machines containing packets of Walkers potato crisps, or chips, into school hallways by offering free books in exchange. This was met with substantial dietary criticism; it also resulted in 93 per cent of 15 and 16 year olds ranking the brand as their highest 'top of mind' food snack (*The Guardian*, 30 April 2003).

Donations, in cash or in kind, are tied to purchases, which, it is intended, will be stimulated by the seller's association with a 'good cause'. But the causes have to be 'right' and the linkages have to be 'real'. For example, the UK National Lottery is promoted heavily by reference to the many good causes it 'supports' (the government requires that a proportion of proceeds is given to a wide variety of social purposes) but repeatedly research has demonstrated that only a small minority of the customers, or gambling 'punters', take any account of this; *the vast majority simply want to win*.

CRM should not be confused with **social marketing**, which describes what charities and other not-for-profit organizations – many of which are beneficiaries of CRM – undertake for themselves. Social marketing describes communication with members, donors and other *non-consumer* publics with a view to developing and maintaining beneficial relationships. It is, in effect, an alternative term for public relations in the voluntary sector.

8.7 the relationship between public relations and marketing

The relationship between public relations and marketing can be sensitive territory. Many writers on marketing over the years have asserted the dominance of marketing, interpreting MPR as simply part of 'promotion management', a minor role within a much more significant and senior function; only lately has there been much of a let up, owing to the rise of pluralism and resultant knock-on effects for marketing. Those effects (Seitel, cited by Kitchen and Papasolomou, 1997) include:

▸ Consumer protests about value and safety
▸ Government scrutiny of marketing claims
▸ Product recalls, giving rise to media coverage
▸ Food ingredient scares
▸ Advertising claims being questioned, in social and civil dimensions
▸ Rumours about companies
▸ Media criticism of companies and 'business'.

Practitioners of MPR undoubtedly can bring considerable added depth to marketing campaigns, and some perceive MPR as having a *corrective job* to do, protecting marketing from *the consequences of its actions* where these appear to contradict overall corporate well being. They often mention by way of illustration controversies relating to **environmental issues**, where marketing has brought embarrassment or worse upon the organization.

In the final analysis, how do marketing and public relations relate one with the other? The dispassionate empirical view is likely to be that both are *equally important and separate*, similarly to all other functions, such as finance, law, human resources, production and so on. The fact that the public relations function spends more of its time, in aggregate, with marketing than with any of the others does not, of itself, make the case for subsuming it into the marketing function, which in any event, should that occur, would eliminate much of the *value and purpose* of public relations.

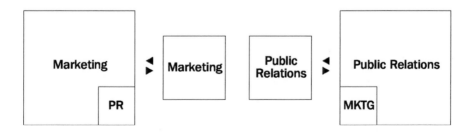

figure **8.3   the relationship between public relations and marketing**

This is an argument borne of rivalry that doubtless will persist interminably. In the meantime, assuredly, marketing will continue to concentrate on attending to customer needs and wants of its products and services by way of exchanges, while MPR will persist in its focus on generating and enhancing relationships through meeting customers' expectations and fostering awareness, understanding and goodwill towards the company and its offerings.

CHECKLIST

- ▢ MPR is part of the 'marketing mix' called promotion, one of several tools of marketing communication, in turn a category of corporate communication.
- ▢ Wherever it is formally located internally, the PR function spans boundaries, both within the organization and between it and the external environment.
- ▢ For Kotler MPR is about: publicity, new products, product repositioning and defence, product category awareness, publics and corporate image.
- ▢ For Doyle MPR's main features are: added credibility, weaker delivery control ('imprecision'), lower cost and news/topicality imperative.
- ▢ In its essence MPR is primarily about filling any gaps of uncertainty about purchase that are resulting in hesitation and hovering over the corporate elements of the product surround, all the many additional factors perceived by the buyer.
- ▢ Integrated Marketing Communication (IMC) describes, at its simplest, the integration of all promotional tools to optimize harmony and therefore impact.
- ▢ In many markets there is a significant need to promote the corporate brand as well as product brands; the IMC concept may be extended therefore to include corporate activities, for marketing purposes.
- ▢ From an overall PR perspective, all messages must be wholly consistent one with another; this applies universally to all corporate communication, including marketing, and extends also to tone and style of delivery.
- ▢ Cause Related Marketing (CRM) is designed to address and remedy social issues and ills while generating product sales through achieving enhanced reputation, awareness and customer loyalty.
- ▢ Social Marketing is communication by third sector organizations with their members, donors and various non-consumer publics.
- ▢ Marketing concentrates on customer needs and wants by way of exchanges; MPR on meeting customers' total corporate, product and service expectations.

CASE STUDY

AEROSYSTEMS COMMUNICATES ITS OWN MESSAGE

For 15 years Aerosystems International, which manufactures computer software-intensive systems for a variety of military and civilian transport, was to all intents and purposes an invisible company. Then in 2000 it decided to change all that. At the time it had but four customers, and all of them built aircraft. The time had come to find more customers and to enter new markets; first it had to generate awareness.

The company had been formed in 1985 by IT company Cap Scientific and the long-established Westland Helicopters at Yeovil in the English southwest. The company was established to provide real-time-embedded command and control solutions, primarily for Westland, and its identity therefore was unclear to the market, its products being largely credited to the parent companies. Three ownership changes resulted in BAE Systems becoming both a new parent company, alongside GKN Aerospace Services, and a new customer. This in turn led to work for Boeing and Lockheed Martin, resulting in there being four OEM, or mainframe, manufacturing customers.

In 2000 the first move was to create a public relations function; the second to instigate a thorough review of the corporate identity, starting with that most fundamental detail, its name. Most people in the defence community perceived Aerosystems as being 'part of the OEMs' and when they did recognize any difference they called the company Ael for short. The review resulted in a decision to keep both the 'proper' name and the logo design too.

Then attention turned to making sure that all ID applications were mutually consistent, itself a major advance, since until then the logo and typography had been interpreted very loosely by each department and unit, scattered across five separate locations, with no overall policing to enforce consistency. The task of establishing a uniform, satisfactory corporate identity extended to a newly built office building, opened in 2001 to house all company personnel, apart from one outstation located some 80 miles away.

The accompanying brand awareness campaign focused on three publics: ground maintenance staff, pilots and specifiers within the decision-making units.

Two primary communication channels were identified: technical journalists writing for a host of, often, arcane publications, primarily serving the defence industries; and exhibitions such as public flying demonstrations by the Royal Air Force and the Fleet Air Arm of the Royal Navy, which, apart from attracting large general public audiences, are attended by key military and civilian personnel who exercise purchasing influence.

Owing to the nature of its business, Aerosystems has been able to mount highly engaging interactive exhibitions, both on-site for visiting journalists and at shows, which are seen not as sales platforms but valuable networking opportunities. Two PR-specific results have been identified: quality relationships with key journalists, resulting in substantial press coverage of the company and its developments; and greatly increased awareness and favourable recognition of the company in its key markets.

These PR outcomes have served the corporate strategy well. The company has entered new markets, in army, naval, rail and automotive applications, and achieved sales in the USA and several European countries, while strengthening its position with its four core customers. PR has also materially assisted internally. Employee loyalty is high, with an annual 'attrition', or loss, rate of 10 per cent, a particularly significant factor in a knowledge-based company where recruitment and retention are key factors. Some 70 per cent of staff members are graduates and one-third hold doctorates.

The PR effort has been widened to embrace CSR and corporate community involvement, or CCI. This is focused on three further publics: civic opinion formers, local schools and environmentalists. A variety of educational projects designed to assist recruitment include work experience placements, funding and instruction in website construction and graphic design. The company has gained civic recognition as a major local employer. And it is committed to tree planting schemes following the 'Year of Promise' in 2000, when the company undertook to plant sufficient trees to offset its annual paper consumption.

It could be fairly argued that, since previously Aerosystems had not undertaken any promotion, the results were bound to be substantial. Equally, given the circumstances, it seems reasonable to suppose that even modest budgets would provide the means to generate significant results. However, the company's grasp of the scale of the challenge and what was needed, working on a relative 'shoestring', might well have been rejected as impractical by another organization that was more accustomed to working with substantial marketing budgets and advertising expenditure.

At Aerosystems it is argued that every £6000 that could be spent on a whole page corporate advertisement is better spent where it can complement the company's existing resources. So it is, for example, that aircraft maintenance personnel and pilots are invited to experience hands-on simulated use of the company's products at show stands, senior military personnel are encouraged to ask searching questions about practical applications and journalists are welcome to spend a day at the company's premises, checking up on what's new at first hand. This skilful MPR is closely interlinked with corporate PR, starting with identity awareness and extending to CSR and community relations.

QUESTIONS

1 Why should interest in corporate reputation make MPR more valuable to marketers?
2 How might MPR protect a product's image and why?
3 Why might MPR 'never sell a bad product'?
4 When could marketing be utilized by public relations, and why?
5 What could make PR and marketing look one and the same?

public affairs

'In the public interest' – government public relations – propaganda – lobbying – issues management

9.1 'in the public interest'

'Let's start with image. In politics it is everything. And if you want to get on you need a good head of hair. And the simple fact is that baldness is a political loser. Since the early days of television the only bald [UK] prime minister ... was 40 years ago and he wasn't even elected. He inherited his job.' Thus explained Kelvin MacKenzie, a former national newspaper editor, describing the leader of the largest opposition party as 'the loser in waiting' owing to his premature and pronounced baldness (*Kelvin saves the Tories*, Channel Four, 7 June 2003).

It is nearly half a century since President John Kennedy reputedly won power in the USA by a narrow margin after he had appeared live on television, sporting a suntan, to point-score against an opponent, the (later) President Richard Nixon, who looked as if he needed a shave. The *radio* audience thought that Nixon won the argument, but the majority of *viewers* opted for the better-looking Kennedy; appearances counted more than mere words.

This degeneration of political debate to mere *spectator entertainment* appears far removed from the earnest arguments in the assembly rooms and coffee houses of 18th-century London, where, it is said, first the 'public sphere' took root. There, and increasingly elsewhere, 'men of affairs' gathered to discuss the issues, gossip and rumour of the day, encouraged by the appearance of the early newspapers and magazines. They formed opinions, began to organize around issues of concern to them, sought to influence the government, established the early commercial and intellectual societies and generally began the slow process that led to universal suffrage, the vote for all adults, which continues to this day around the world.

The public places where this occurred were in aggregate small, not many people participated at first, and those that did were rich and privileged, or, at the very least, earnestly intent on becoming so. But they laid the foundations to modern interpretations of democratic free speech and representative government that were to spread rapidly and for which both men and women have laid down their lives. In 1929 every UK adult finally won the right to vote, so what has gone wrong? Why *do* so great a proportion of UK voters now consider that their only means of influence is to *abstain from voting*, to throw away that long-fought-for right? In the last UK general election, for example, less than 62 per cent of voters bothered, and how many of *them* were deciding on looks, not content? In the previous election turnout was less than 60 per cent. And is this mass disaffection spreading to other democratic countries and cultures?

It is the agreement of the vast majority of people to exercise their right to vote that gives legitimacy to the political class. Without *that*, public affairs are reduced to illegitimate assertion of authority by a tiny minority, as in many non-democratic countries. The mass involvement necessary for democracy evaporates, and politics becomes a spectacle, the source of prime-time satire and gossip, in which promises are greeted with ridicule, announcements are generally mistrusted and motives are deeply distrusted. In short, democracy becomes for the vast majority of people, those who are not paid-up members of one or other faction, a hoax, a sham designed to give a few people a very good living indeed and also, in the UK and some other countries, self-awarded honours and titles in abundance.

This degeneration has its origins long before the advent of widespread television. In *The Century of the Self* (RDF Television/BBC, 2002) Ewen observed

> [Edward] Bernays's and [Walter] Lippmann's concept of managing the masses takes the idea of democracy and it turns it into a palliative. It turns it into giving people some feel good medication that will respond to an immediate pain or an immediate yearning but will not alter the objective circumstances one iota. I mean ... the idea of democracy at its heart was about changing the relations of power that had governed the world for so long and Bernays's concept of democracy was one of maintaining the relations of power, even if it meant that one needed to sort of stimulate the psychological lives of the public, and in fact in his mind that was what was necessary. But if you can keep stimulating the irrational self then leadership can basically go on doing what it wants to do.

Later in the four-part documentary series Ewen observed that Bernays has thought 'the man in the street' was 'driven by the spinal cords'. Lippmann, who had declared 'Democracy has to be changed', had fascinated him.

Habermas described the public sphere in simple terms as being where private people gather as a public. Raupp (2004) is clear that this space is not 'state-run or state-owned', but that differs from blatant appropriation, or misappropriation, by political parties, led by the one in power. This transformation from a venue for rational debate between concerned and interested citizens to the current circus was, thought Habermas, the consequence of the burgeoning mass media and public relations. Somewhere along the line, certainly, politicians changed from being sober men and women, earnestly debating the issues of the day, often at such length as to challenge all but the most ardent and committed to stay listening, into *performers* obsessing on appearances, who attach more importance to being on television than to speaking in Parliament, assiduously courting the glitterati of cafe society and industriously copying the lifestyles of the celebrities their electors adore. They have become a specialized branch of show business, with whose members they enthusiastically mix.

McNair (1996) identified the first political public relations consultancy as having been established in Los Angeles in 1933, 'since which time the industry has expanded throughout America and the rest of the democratic capitalist world. Now ... it is axiomatic that no serious contender for public office can afford to do without the services of his or her "spin doctor" or media adviser. Once the politician is in government, the role of the political public relations specialist becomes even more important.'

According to Moloney (2000), in 1999, as the UK prime minister was about to reshuffle his government, 'one minister's promotion prospects were reported to be diminished because his team of press officers was not as good as others'. Indeed, the British press frequently discusses the relative merits of this or that government department's public relations performance, as if tipping runners and riders in horse races.

While public relations clearly has become a, possibly *the*, most important component of modern politics, attention to any passing political utterances quickly indicates that the probable causes for this degradation lie in **consumerism**. Why otherwise should baldness be a bar to office, or 'five o'clock shadow' or any other alleged or implied presentational failing? Why otherwise are policies advocated primarily or wholly on the basis that they serve the results of opinion research? And if consumerism *is* the source, should it be allowed free rein in a 'market' where, ostensibly, nothing is bought or sold, in that votes are cast as of right and not for, at least direct, payment? Is the contemporary 'telling people what they want to hear', which is serving the current generation of politicians so well, a new version of buying votes, a practice that in the UK supposedly ended in 1832?

9.2 government public relations

This modern condition of public discourse is not confined to the UK. There is, however, probably a greater *intensity* of political PR activity in the UK than in most other countries. The advent of 24-hour news has been accompanied by the emergence of *round-the-clock government news output*, seeking to continually 'set the news agenda'. Seldom does a day go by without politicians trying to occupy the thoughts of those they rule over or hope to govern in the future. Pretence of dialogue is frequently used as part of this relentless intervention, with repeated use of catch phrases such as 'national debate'. Claims to be engaging in dialogic activities are used in order to enhance reputation and justify the abuse of public patience; in practice, much of the time dialogue occurs, contradictorily, only within party political circles and not between politicians and individual citizens or subjects.

In the UK as in many other countries there has been a **government information service** provided by civil servants for many decades. 'Public relations in a government department has two main tasks: to give regular information on policy, plans and achievements of the department; and to inform and educate the public on legislation, regulations and all matters that affect the daily life of citizens. It must also advise Ministers and senior officials of reaction and potential reaction to current and proposed policies' (Black, 1989). It is essentially non-political, a position that, as expected of civil servants, is jealously guarded. Or at least it *should* be, for in the past decade or so there has been significant change.

Job rotating civil servants 'did a turn' at public relations as part of their careers, working in about 30 government departments. The type of public relations they were engaged in was of the informational type, so they were, in effect, journalists-in-residence, for the moment, before passing on to what were considered to be more senior tasks. As public relations practice gathered greater status, this approach has evolved into a much expanded, dedicated public relations **information management** operation. This has been accompanied by a quantum leap in resourcing, resulting in some 1,200 press officers and an estimated £200 million aggregate annual budget, according to Budge *et al.* (1998), quoted by Somerville (2001). There is every likelihood that the increase in expenditure has continued. All this to run the delivery of what the UK government and its agencies wish the public at large to know about, and, by the same token, to withhold what is *not* intended 'for public consumption'.

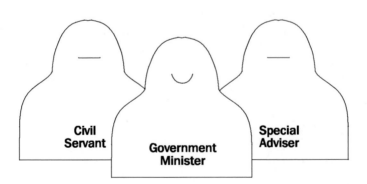

figure **9.1** the role of special advisers

Greater interest, however, has been focused by the media on the 'special advisers', most of whom have at least a partial public relations role. We are told that they are relatively few, less than one hundred, although their number has trebled under the present government, and most if not all of them are *former employees of the governing party.* Their activities are the source of much controversy, since they appear to be primarily employed to promote favourable images of government ministers and their wives, but are paid out of taxation, and to this end they are involved in media output. They are empowered to instruct civil servants but are not technically part of the civil service, although it is mooted that this power may be withdrawn sometime. A committee of members of Parliament has declared that they perform a valuable function but that 'the boundaries between their work and those of career civil servants do not appear to be well understood'. Their work can come to explicit public notice in unfortunate circumstances.

EXAMPLE

On 11 September 2001, an hour after the first terrorist-controlled civilian passenger airliner had been flown into the World Trade Center in New York, a special adviser, Jo Moore, e-mailed colleagues advising: 'Media handling. It's now a very good day to get out anything we want to bury. Councillors' expenses?' The reference to 'councillors' expenses' related to a minor 'U-turn' on pension rights for local government politicians.

A former governing party official, Moore kept her job, confessing an 'error of judgement' but, it was widely thought, showing little contrition. According to at least one national newspaper, her chief error had been in getting caught. Subsequently, however, she was again embarrassed and was dismissed. The civil servant head of the department's public relations function was 'resigned' and subsequently received very generous compensation. (*The Daily Telegraph*, 10 October 2001, and *The Times*, 8 May 2002)

The '**spin machine**', as the media describes it, has provoked many public rebukes, with headlines such as 'When the spinning had to stop' and 'Spinners are now out of control'. Wrote one prominent political editor: '"No spin is the new spin" has become this year's brittle joke. There is some truth in it, though it is hard to be a spokesman in such an adversarial climate. "You lot are much harder on the spokesmen than we are in Berlin," a German reporter told me the other day after attending a briefing' (*The Guardian*, 16 December 2002).

But government is not alone in its heavy use of public relations. *All* the **political parties** are very actively engaged, nationally, regionally and locally, in seeking to communicate with voters.

> The proactive public relations pursued by parties as they campaign for election (or re-election) represent the visible, truly *public* dimension of political communication. Much political public relations work remains hidden from public view, however. Aware that information, and access to it, is a power resource, parties in government have become enthusiastic custodians of a vast machinery for suppressing, censoring and at times falsifying information which, it might be thought, the citizenry of a democratic state has a right to receive in relatively unadulterated form (McNair, 1996).

Most governments demonstrate both reluctance to be entirely forthcoming and a taste for classifying information, at their sole discretion, as being officially secret, on grounds of 'national interest'. UK governments are reputedly among the most secretive in the world; they compare badly, for instance, with those of the USA, despite Ewen's (1996) 'revealing social history of the thinking of professional communicators' that 'American democracy could not function based on the rational thinking of the common man' (Day *et al.*, 2001). 'For American society, the area of greatest concern might well be the impact of public relations practice on the democratic process.'

Attempts in various countries to improve the quality of democracy through legislation that promises **unhindered access to non-classified government information** can meet with arbitrarily imposed obstacles, such as rationing to a very small number how many questions will be answered over a given period. UK Prime Minister Tony Blair 'complained this week: "What's important to realise is this [Freedom of Information Act] generates an awful lot of work for government." ... The act is beginning to work. Yet ministers plan to introduce regulations that will choke off the growing number of information requests. They claim that they take up too much time and cost a fortune' (*The Guardian*, 4 December 2006).

Official effort to staunch the flow of inconvenient information is not always successful, though.

> Over the next two years a ground-breaking decision by the council of ministers and the European Parliament will result in the biggest release of information held by governments to the public and the media since the creation of the European Union. All 27 EU countries will disclose data revealing details of some 100bn euros given in subsidies by the Eurotaxpayer every year to farmers, food companies, industrial regeneration schemes and the fishing industry, from the Black Sea resorts in Bulgaria and Romania to the Canary Islands and Madeira. The decision is the result of a rare example of journalists cooperating with each other across Europe to bring pressure ... using national freedom of information laws. (*The Guardian*, 22 January 2007)

Technology advances are central to this. Starck and Kruckeberg (2001) anticipate that 'despite cold war victories, democracy and democratic principles will be challenged as never before'. They foresee 'more nebulous, and potentially more insidious, technological and economic challenges' that 'will have a direct impact on the concept of democracy and on contemporary forms of government' and they quote Sclove (1995), who contended, 'If citizens ought to be empowered to participate in determining their society's basic structure, and technologies are an important species of social structure, it follows that technological design and practice should be democratised ... Procedurally, we require expanded opportunities for people from all walks of life to participate in shaping their technological order'.

Owing to local and personal knowledge and awareness, public relations in the service of government and its institutions is often most apparent *below* the national or state level, particularly in relation to manipulation of facts and figures, and the withholding of information. As is often the case elsewhere, in the UK **local government** is often the *largest local employer*, and certainly this is so in the outer regions, further removed from the seat of national power. In a small administrative area that is predominantly rural this is highly likely; in another such 'authority' with a larger population and broader mix of commercial activity, local government is typically one of the three largest employers. Stone (1995) asserted that the typical higher tier administrative body employed 35,000 people; there are also lower-tier authorities within the same geographical area.

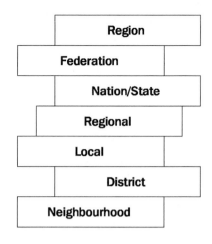

figure **9.2   multiple layers of government**

This civil administration is further increased by the presence of **regional government**, which, as in the UK, may constitute a further upper tier. Federalist states such as Germany are all too familiar with the costly burden of democracy when it spawns *multiple layers* of government. And in Europe there is the *additional layer* represented by the **European Union's institutions**. None of this, however, appears to do much to overcome *widespread public mistrust and resentment* of the political class, which is viewed as being wholly self-serving, as its members are seen to scramble for these multi-layered job opportunities. Nor does the laboured intrusion of government into daily life appear to most electors to result in any *commensurate* benefits for society.

This is of the greatest relevance to the future development of public relations practice in government, which is a burgeoning on-cost for every elector to help bear, for each bureaucracy seeks to promote itself and its activities and to protect its interests. The size and intensity of public relations activity at the *national* level should not obscure the very substantial activity that also occurs at *regional* and *local* levels, and at the *continental* level, as with the European Union.

9.3 propaganda

It has been argued that propaganda is not public relations, that is to say, it is not synonymous with practice. This is a position that is generally asserted by public relations practitioners, perhaps not so much from an ethical standpoint but more on practical grounds: propaganda can be very effective, but if it 'goes wrong' its consequences can be dire for the propagandist. For many of them it recalls the saying *those who live by the sword usually die by the sword*, the meaning of which may be also interpreted from an ethical standpoint.

Critics assert that propaganda is the dark secret in the public relations cupboard, the embarrassing Bernays inheritance PR people must always deny. That modern public relations practice is, technically, *not* propagandistic may be argued in the context of the various theories based on two-way communication. The importance of **dialogue** between the parties is pivotal. Where the two-way dialogue is missing, the possibility arises of propaganda being present, and Grunig and Hunt (1984) argue that this is the case with *publicity*, when the sender feels free to be 'economical with the truth' in the pursuit of desired outcomes. That may have a relatively benign intention.

In government, publicity is widely used, at all levels, and to that extent propaganda is present, but it is usually well intentioned and harmless. But publicity is not the only mode of communication used by practitioners; in public affairs all four types of public relations practice are deployed in the service of political rhetoric, which is heavily permeated with propaganda, well-intentioned or otherwise. The phrase 'economical with the truth', significantly, emanated during the 1980s from the highest level of the British civil service, during a trial relating to 'official secrets'.

EXAMPLE

The British public was overwhelmingly opposed to military invasion of Iraq in February 2003. Only 16 per cent supported the government, but 62 per cent said that it would come round *provided* there was first a UN Security Council resolution in favour. To combat this opposition the government published a supportive 'dodgy dossier' that included plagiarized sections of a doctoral thesis. 'The dodgy dossier was a public relations disaster for the Prime Minister,' claimed an opposition politician who was a former Defence Secretary. The chairman of the all-party parliamentary committee on public policy, a government supporter, said of the dossier: 'It breaks every rule of integrity in public life.'

And when the government found that it could not secure an affirmative vote in the UN Security Council, having previously advanced several differing arguments in favour, it reverted to claiming that Iraq not only had weapons of mass destruction but the *capacity and intention to use them at 45 minutes' notice on a British military base*. That *imminent threat* persuaded parliament in March to endorse the government's position, the widespread supposition being, among politicians and citizens, that the prime minister had secret intelligence to justify his claim.

Subsequently it became self-evident that this had not been so. The government sought to expunge the claim, but television footage provided the evidence. Under the military occupation of Iraq no such weapons could be found, much less any that could attack the British at 45 minutes' notice.

(Sources: UK national media, in particular *Channel 4 News*, 7 and 11 February 2003)

When are communicators in the 'public domain' public relations practitioners and when are they propagandists? The careful and prudent selection and use of facts, figures and arguments in order to inform or to achieve two-way dialogue is clearly distinguishable from plain assertion of political propaganda, which, by definition, relies on deceit and trickery in pursuit of gaining a following, and has little time for two-way anything, total acceptance and obedience being the priority. Since national governments never encounter domestic publics that they can recognize as being *relatively equal* to them, the degree of sought-for symmetry is likely to be fairly limited in any event. Why bother, when the power of the state lies behind the communication? Millions of people, for instance, marching in orderly, civilized, democratic protest against a political policy may not necessarily provoke a governmental desire for greater symmetry of communication with them about it, or indeed for any dialogue at all.

It may be argued that this is really a matter of *degree*; that propaganda is not so inimical, more a *natural development* of public relations, 'just' the greater use of hyperbole and better-calculated advocacy (many politicians are lawyers) in order to be more effective, that is, achieve greater beneficial outcomes for the message sender. But, quite apart from any ethical objections, in an increasingly pluralistic age such an amoral position is unlikely to be sustainable, as is observable in politics, where politicians and their supporters concentrate on the shortest of short-term outcomes and effects, giving the impression that they are engaged in some 'snatch and grab' operation and will not be around for long to deal with the consequences. They think within *timeframes dictated by political convenience*, such as the periods between one election and the next, yet they deal in matters that have *major long-term implications*, such as public health and education standards; and the economy.

The conceptual thinking about public relations in its formative early years kept reverting to its *applicability to democratic government*. If, as McNair (1996) asserted, 'the public relations function is a necessary dimension of the modern political process', the heavy *use of propaganda appears contradictory*. Given the 'enhanced tendency' of politicians 'to seek to "manufacture our consent"' within a 'media-assisted mass democratic participation', public relations people employed in the service of such masters might be expected to concentrate on trying to achieve two-way communication that effected mutually rewarding exchanges. And brought voters back to the polling booths. Or is all the talk by politicians about public debate and dialogue a reflection of the degree of their aversion to any such 'infringements' of their 'licence to operate'?

9.4 lobbying

Anyone can **lobby**, according to the politicians. By 'lobby' they mean make representations, aimed at *influencing decisions of government* about laws and regulations, but most lobbying is *not* undertaken by concerned individuals, usually constituents of the person being lobbied, but, particularly in the UK and USA, by organizations or their paid representatives, an activity called **public affairs**, which is that part of public relations which embraces **relations with government** at all levels. The terms 'lobbying' and 'public affairs' are often used interchangeably.

CERP says public affairs are 'the planned and formalized efforts of a company to exercise its rights and duties as a corporate citizen in the community, the nation and the society and to encourage employees to discharge their rights and duties as individual citizens' (CERP website, 5 November 2002). This definition involves the employees as well as the organization they work for; although in practice lobbying is *primarily an organizational activity*, as CERP acknowledges in one of its three further definitions. This spells out more precisely the purpose of public affairs as 'a corporate activity designed towards

‣ Improving the business climate surrounding corporate operations to the extent by which that climate may be influenced by government, thought leaders, and the general public, and
‣ Minimizing the adverse effect of government's involvement in matters of economic and social concern to the corporation in question.'

Lobbying is also, according to CERP, about **greater social cohesion**. It is concerned with:

‣ matters of 'significant and substantial concern' to 'individuals, business, labour, foundations, private institutions and government'

and also:

‣ 'relations between an organization and government, parliament, civil servants and special interests and pressure groups at both national and trans-European levels.'

So, one way or another, lobbying seems to involve all manner of organized interests, whether governmental, bureaucratic, corporate, institutional or representational of causes that arise outside those structures.

Lobbying has been developed over many decades (since the 1870s in Austria) primarily as a means, according to Moloney (2000), to enable '"insider" groups to maintain public policy in their favour'. It is widespread throughout the world and recognized as a legitimate part of democracy, although the legitimacy of such claims depends upon the *level of accessibility* available to the less advantaged, poorer funded interests. One way around this is through *association*; typically companies rely upon trade bodies representing their industries to lobby on their collective behalf, much as labour union members employ their officials to represent their aggregate interests.

This mechanism 'to rebalance the contest between interests of different power and influence' has been credited by lobbyists with some highly principled social contributions. Certainly, in so far as it *unsettles the political class* to the extent that it **exposes its policies to external scrutiny and adjustment**, such supposedly altruistic mediation is entirely consistent with excellence in communication. The reality, though, is rather less about altruistic lubrication to improve the operation of democratic machinery and much more about self-interested pouring of cans of oil into well-targeted engine parts, otherwise known as 'pressure points', for purpose of competitive advantage.

The concentration of lobbying effort might be expected to be found at the federal or national government level, on the assumption that what happens there exceeds in importance any policies or activities at any other levels of government. However, *proximity* appears to play its part, for the further away lies the seat of power the greater the likely need to exert effort in finding out what is going on there and the possibility that something may happen that has far-reaching consequences little envisaged or noticed nearer home. This certainly applies within the EU: in the UK, for instance, it is estimated that half of all legislation is decided at EU level and that British civil servants' workload is substantially EU-orientated. Most significantly, EU law takes precedence over national legislation, and the European Commission in Brussels is ever proactive in bringing forward proposals. Significantly, although policy formation is relatively transparent, national civil servants 'behind closed doors' make nearly all EU decisions.

Lobbying is a lucrative expertise; hence the large number of public relations people who are specialist lobbyists, or public affairs advisers and consultants. And the demand for their services grows. It requires a thorough understanding of the relevant political system and the critical interrelationships between differing elements. Information flows, the sources of policy initiatives, the parts played by various officials and advisers, the differing decision-making structures and procedures: all the arcane detail of government is the stock-in-trade of the lobbyist.

↑ Lobby Entrance

figure **9.3   the lobbying maze**

Outsiders of 'the system', including many senior managers, often mistakenly assign *far too much importance to the politicians*, the 'front line-up', and fail to appreciate the importance of the 'back office personnel' who deal in the detail, where so often lie the nuances that can make all the difference. Similarly, they may *underestimate the need to prepare* the case as thoroughly as they would for litigation, and that includes taking into account how 'the other side' is likely to respond and why, given its circumstances and existing pressures.

So the skilled lobbyist, in seeking to make **private, one-to-one representations**, is more likely to tread the back corridors of the less obvious offices that lead to bureaucrats than the well-presented main 'corridors of power' frequented by politicians. But companies that employ lobbyists as consultants are more likely to seek their *advice* than to send them forth as *advocates*. That role is more usually performed by in-house people employed within specialist public affairs units, who are well versed in corporate culture and adept advocates of their causes. Personal influence is exercised through interpersonal forms of communication.

In researching standards of performance among public relations practitioners, Grunig (2001) found that the correlations of the original two-way asymmetric and symmetric communication models with the excellence factor were lowest for the governmental public. 'We think that this is because government relations, especially lobbying, tends to be managed by lawyers or the CEO directly and because lobbyists and other public affairs specialists typically rely more on their contacts in government than on their knowledge of communication principles. Thus, governmental relations programs may be relatively autonomous from the rest of the public relations function.'

Lobbyists have tended in the past to see themselves as a group apart from public relations practitioners, and some even deny that they have any connection with PR. There is a widely held assumption among them that what they do is innately superior to other branches of public relations practice, although, viewed from a distance, that might seem implausible, for to many people the lobbyist is simply a fixer who is paid to jostle for position. It is certainly the case that chairmen, corporate presidents and chief executives, particularly the latter, are all likely to become involved in lobbying at the most senior levels of contact, while specialists engage with civil servants and bureaucrats at lower hierarchical levels. And senior managers are not communication professionals, although most have a public relations dimension to their job specifications. Rather, they belong to the dominant coalitions that communicators may view as a discrete public.

This trend by public affairs advisers towards giving strategic advice rather than taking lobbying action reflects the growing *scale, complexity and fragmentation* of government. Lobbyists identify seats of power and encamp there, from which multiple vantage points they may provide perspectives denied to their corporate clients. This geographical spread also better equips them to become informed of grass-roots developments, particularly the emergence of locally based pressure groups.

A further trend is the *greater integration of public affairs with public relations consultancy*; this despite any lobbyist reservations. Public affairs advisers are seeking to **exert more pressure** on behalf of their clients **through media relations**, for they are finding that as governments become ever more driven by public relations considerations they are also becoming more **sensitive to media coverage and comment**, which can be as influential, or more so, than representations by lobbyists.

9.5 issues management

Lobbying is a prominent feature of **issues management**. This is 'the process of identifying issues, analyzing those issues, setting priorities, selecting pro-gramme strategy options, implementing a programme of action and evaluating effectiveness' (Cutlip *et al.*, 1985). In other words, it describes the attempt by organizations, but particularly companies, to try to **identify and anticipate issues and do something about them before they turn into crises**.

As Bland (1995) observed, *issues and crisis management are similar* in that they broadly involve the same considerations and techniques. 'The biggest differences are the time scale and the sense of panic.' Generally, issues develop over months, crises over minutes. Issues management ideally therefore prevents crises.

But identifying the issues requires practised skill and **much careful scanning of the** *environment*. It has been argued that issues only 'go live' in the public imagination when someone chooses to 'make an issue' out of a problem that they perceive. And opinions differ as to where issues are most likely to arise: **pressure and cause-related groups** are often cited, but so too are organizations themselves, who, so often portrayed as 'sitting ducks' just waiting for someone to shoot at them, are, on the contrary, thought by some to be the *major* source. And many people think *government* is the prime originator of issues.

Grunig and Repper (1992) cite Chase's three strategies:

▸ Reactive (oppose change),
▸ Adaptive (try to satisfy outside demands), and
▸ Dynamic.

This last is 'clearly asymmetrical: "This strategy anticipates and attempts to shape the direction of public policy decisions by determining the theater of war, the weapons to be used, and the timing of the battle itself"'. The military imagery accords with how issues management is often perceived: Chase was 'a veteran public relations practitioner' who coined the term issues management in 1977. However, avoiding war is less expensive, distracting and potentially ruinous to reputation. After all, issues are primarily disagreements that need to be resolved to the mutual satisfaction of all concerned.

'Issues management, in practice, essentially is another name for the external component of strategic management.' Chase later argued that issues management was the culmination of an historical process that began with press relations and led on to first public relations and then public affairs, but others contested this. Not surprisingly, since public relations people have been paying particular attention to these issues since the earliest days. The more pertinent point is: *what can they do about them?*

Issues come and go; their incubation periods vary and, rather like products, they can hang around a long time. If they are adequately anticipated and properly addressed, issues *can* be positively helpful. Whether they represent potential opportunities or threats, for sure just talking about them is not enough, and nor is neglect, however well intentioned.

CHECKLIST

- ☐ Habermas defined the 'public sphere' as where private people gather as a public.
- ☐ The degeneration of democratic politics into media entertainment has coincided with the rise in the use of mass psychology and in consumerism.
- ☐ Public relations has become a, or possibly the, most important component of modern politics, at all levels (supranational, regional, federal, state, regional, local and district).
- ☐ Impartial government information sources have become politically partisan.
- ☐ In the UK the use of propaganda as a communication component is concentrated in government public relations.
- ☐ Public affairs describes PR-driven communication with government at all levels.
- ☐ Lobbying is making one-to-one representations to politicians, civil servants, bureaucrats and other public policy planners by concerned individuals, organizations or their paid representatives, who are lobbying experts, mostly public relations consultants described as public affairs advisers.
- ☐ The term 'lobbying' is often used to describe all public affairs activities, although these may include other public relations activities, notably media relations.
- ☐ Issues management is the monitoring of the operating environment in order to identify and anticipate relevant issues in order for the organization to address them in a timely and effective manner. It is 'another name for the external component of strategic management'.
- ☐ Crisis management is planning in anticipation of foreseeable crises, the implementation of those plans in the event of crises and the evaluation and addressing of resulting consequences.
- ☐ Issues and crisis management are complementary and share some similar characteristics; the former should reduce risk of crises but does not obviate the need for planning in anticipation of various crises scenarios.

CASE STUDY

COMMUNICATING IN A CRISIS

In 2001 Foot-and-Mouth Disease (FMD) swept through British livestock. It was probably the most serious animal disease epidemic in the UK in modern times; the virus is likely to have been imported in a contaminated food product. The impact of FMD was particularly pronounced in some regions, being all pervasive, catastrophically destructive and traumatic for those concerned.

It occurred at a low point for livestock farmers, who were recovering from the economic consequences of the recent BSE disaster, which had set in train a reduction in UK consumer demand and the loss of European markets. For some farmers, the arrival of FMD indicated that it was time to quit the industry. Their representative body, the National Farmers' Union (NFU), said it was difficult to overstate the overriding profound sense of loss and waste, emotional as well as financial, and that many farmers were also angry.

Across the world's media the story was graphically depicted, as piles of cattle were burnt in order to eliminate the disease, not without criticism from some farmers in other countries. The carnage continued for many weeks, during which time farmers and their families were confined to their homes, large parts of the countryside were shut off to visitors and the UK's tourism trade collapsed. Who would want to visit a countryside enveloped in foul black smoke and stench, even if they could be allowed in?

In its evidence to the subsequent government enquiry the NFU included communications among the matters it addressed. It complained of inadequate liaison and co-ordination of activity between the veterinary experts and the administrators in the agricultural government ministry and between government departments and agencies. This had led to inadequate management and resource response, some misapplication of resources and 'in some regions no effective involvement of stakeholders'. Only over time had matters improved, with the involvement of the army 'after a serious delay of nearly a month', the appointment of two regional operations directors and the establishment of the Cabinet Office Briefing Room (COBR) to co-ordinate activities among government ministers. A Joint Co-ordination Committee (JCC) had as its mission 'to create and maintain an accurate ground picture, to create an all-informed network and to facilitate passage of information flows, information management and dissemination of instructions.'

Communication had been patchy and inconsistent and 'delays in tackling problems and obstacles were rooted in failures in communications. ... With a wide number and variety of actors involved in a complex and evolving disease outbreak and control programme, it was inevitable that there would be gaps and lapses in communication from time to time. Much was very successfully implemented and achieved. But, in our view, there were still too many failures of communication.' Examples of failures cited included:

- Considerable confusion in the (general) public's mind about the animal health and welfare consequences of FMD. 'This lack of understanding in turn led many people to question the need to slaughter infected animals since "they will recover". This belief distorted their view of [the government department] and of farmers.'
- Confusing and apparently conflicting statements issued at various times, giving rise to rumour and speculation, for instance as to future slaughter plans.
- Poor maintenance of the ministry's information website.
- Guidance to cattle valuers, contractors and government field staff inconsistently distributed, interpreted and applied.

- Reliance on trade associations to communicate guidance and other messages, but 'some operators were not always members of these trade associations'.
- Telephone help lines frequently jammed and inaccessible. 'In some instances, the advice given was frequently incomplete or inaccurate.'
- A video film explaining biosecurity (provision of washing and disinfection points) distributed to farmers as the general ban on public access to the countryside was lifted, which had 'to some extent undermined the message' on the need for farmers to observe appropriate care.

The lessons to be learned were:

1 In civil emergencies, government information websites should be constantly updated
2 Easily accessible and authoritative help lines should be established at an early stage
3 Clear, consistent guidance to government field staff, farmers and other operators on operational and environmental procedures should be widely disseminated.

The NFU's evidence to the enquiry concluded that 'the overriding message is that government communications with farmers was very patchy at best and poor and unreliable most of the time.' It quoted the comments of a farmer in Cumbria, where the outbreak was severe. These included: 'From my work I know how bad communications were at the start of the outbreak, how families were left on their farms without help or information, often surrounded by carcases. This should never have happened and it must never be allowed to happen again.'

QUESTIONS

1 Is the conduct of 'public life' attributable to public relations, and if so why?
2 Should government 'invest less in public relations and more in public services'?
3 How appropriate is the use of public relations in delivering local public services?
4 How may lobbying rebalance the contest between interests of differing power and influence?
5 Is 'making an issue' the cause or consequence of pluralism?

community relations

Corporate community involvement – objectives – the environment – community action – valuing donations – the voluntary sector

10.1 corporate community involvement

When talk of **corporate social responsibility** (CSR) turns to specifics, a number of differing areas of activity are mentioned. For its Corporate Responsibility Index, for instance, Business in the Community (BITC) identifies:

▸ The physical environment,
▸ The workplace,
▸ The marketplace,
▸ The community, and
▸ Human rights.

Beyond that there is also widespread and frequent reference made by companies, respondents to surveys and others to matters such as:

▸ Charity donations,
▸ Ethical practices among suppliers,
▸ Workforce diversity, and
▸ Corporate risk control.

So CSR has multiple dimensions, and each organization places the emphasis where most appropriate for its purposes.

The **community** is high on most CSR priority lists, because it is largely about the practicalities of corporate life; it can seem an obvious choice, particularly to the organization that operates among many neighbours in a highly populous, not to say overcrowded, city or region, a circumstance familiar enough in many parts of Europe and Asia. What used to be known as *community relations*, about corporate getting-on-with-the-locals, has acquired greater importance since the 1970s, not least owing to some very well reported disasters that might have been avoided. And it has acquired a new name to match: **corporate community involvement** (CCI).

The term 'community' is widely used, but to what *exactly* does it refer, and where does communication fit in? Heath (2001b) cites an explanation offered by Kruckeberg and Starck (1988): 'A community is achieved when people are aware of and interested in common ends and regulate their activity in view of those ends. Communication plays a vital role as people try to regulate their own activities and to participate in efforts to reach common ends.' The aim of communication in this context is to foster 'social involvement and participation.'

Use of the term 'corporate community involvement' implies, therefore, an organizational proactive interest in identifying and sharing with others a *communal* interest and in taking measures together with them in furtherance of those interests. The shared interests may be identified by reference to geographical or other considerations; in other words, the community of interest need not be necessarily neighbourhood-specific. CCI is 'the face of corporate social responsibility in practice' (Theaker, 2001a), one that is plainly more visible than most other CSR activities. And CCI touches upon a number of *practical aspects of operations* that apply to *all types and size* of organization, including:

▸ Workforce recruitment and retention,
▸ Physical expansion,
▸ Operational parameters and
▸ Consultation on local issues.

To a local community, an organization's credentials and credibility for being a 'player' that shares and advances common interests with it is likely to depend upon how its members perceive the 'beast' in their midst. The organization might be seen, for instance, as:

▸ A large, friendly, somewhat benign herbivore, grazing gently and wishing only the best for everyone around, always approachable provided not too much effort is called for.
▸ Or it might be a lean, hungry-looking hunter, always on the lookout for the next opportunity to leap in and take an initiative, in the hope of recognition and reward.
▸ Again, it *might* be a very large, avuncular creature, very much a local fixture on the skyline, with a substantial track record for defending smaller fry and worrying about the whole neighbouring herd.

In other words, **companies set their own *scale* of agenda** to reflect their circumstances, as they perceive them.

Once the dominant coalition within the organization has decided to treat CCI seriously, its options can seem almost limitless, particularly when its interest becomes known. Typical activities that may be volunteered by the organization or suggested to it include:

▸ Funding landscaped local roundabouts
▸ Decorating old people's homes

- Reading aloud to young children
- Secondment of staff to work with local organizations
- Raising funds for local causes through sponsored activities
- Open days with hospitality and entertainment
- Sponsorship of local events
- Seed funding for local community activities
- Providing a venue for local organizations to meet regularly
- Contributing trees to local landscaping schemes
- Offering work experience to young people
- Creating bursaries and scholarships at schools and colleges.

figure **10.1** **varying perceptions of the organization as neighbour**

All these activities do not occur in a vacuum. They *speak volumes* about the organization, for better or for worse. Heath sees this community-orientated involvement and participation as rhetorical enactment.

> Rhetoric is the voice of the community. It is dialogue, statement and counterstatement. It is the self-correcting and self-maintaining process by which people in each community derive the expedient truth and policy that they need to achieve concurrence and to coordinate their activities. ... As rhetoric, public relations enables various entities to become meaningful to and influential for one another. That is the rationale for a socially responsible view of public relations.

10.2 objectives

Being known locally as an organization that is open to suggestions for its CCI programme can bring hazardous exposure to the vagaries of human nature and the enthusiasms of the few, if there is no forethought about objectives, just what they are and how they are to be measured. **Clear, concise objectives** make possible the identification of the *particular* potential CCI areas of activity that are **of interest** *to the organization* and to prioritize them accordingly. *Then* the approaches that are received may be assessed within a structured framework, much as a person may refuse one charity a donation because he or she has already selected and committed to another.

Community needs are, understandably, open to interpretation: that is to say, some are obviously more pressing, have wider applicability or will benefit greater numbers of people than others; some address long overdue improvements, while others are opportunistic and marginal; some are properly the responsibility of the civil authorities, others are rightly within the compass of community action. And 'evidently some things are beyond any company to provide. Business can only pay its local and national taxes and rely on government to supply such things as law and order; schools; healthcare and social services' (Newman, 1995).

CCI, it seems, is 'perhaps one of the "softest" and most intangible of CSR activities' but it 'can be used as a strategic business tool in managing a company's relationship with the community' (Portway, 1995). Her CCI objectives at the UK operation of IBM in central southern England were to:

1 Contribute towards a favourable social and economic environment for IBM's business,
2 Be recognized by selected target audiences as a leader in corporate community involvement, and
3 Promote the morale and motivation of employees.

These objectives were met through:

▸ Education and training in schools
▸ 'Voluntary sector empowerment' with training, consultancy projects and employee support in voluntary work
▸ Support for the disabled via 'The Computability Centre', established with two partners as a national UK charity in 1992 to give advice and information
▸ Support for good environmental practices, awareness and research.

Portway's 'manage and measure' approach, using objectives to report to relevant 'audiences' on progress, should ensure that CCI evades the risk of falling into a potential quagmire of tendentious pleading and sentimentality. To assist in this, Cutlip *et al.* (1985) advocated **segmentation**, both of the locals as a whole, according to their relative importance to the organization, and of the 'prime movers', the people that *really* matter.

The *first* such analysis should indicate **how, and perhaps *why*, power is distributed**. Predictably, the landowners and big business head the list, with SME managers following up in the rear. But in between these they suggest placing people like public relations executives and journalists, as well as local administrators and bureaucrats, that is to say, people who are supposedly in *positions of influence for a living*. But this has to be a generalization. There are plenty of people who exert influence that might not be *that* obvious, and local power structures can be remarkably deceptive, particularly in areas where traditional forms and values have been swept aside by modern changes in demography and culture.

The *second* analysis is probably closer to most CCI planning, for it identifies and confirms **the people that any programme *should* address**, starting with the employees, or members, and their families and friends. These people have always been at the centre of community relations priorities. Then there is, inevitably perhaps, the local media, and the various local cause-related and pressure groups and individuals who, for one reason or another, are the 'crusaders', a potentially unflattering term for a variety of local residents that ranges from the well-intentioned proactive citizen to the scurrilous rumour-monger.

The prime movers that interest many companies are the key politicians and local officials who run the most relevant parts of local government, such as urban and transport planning, and the various welfare and similarly unincorporated groups, typically connected to military, religious, cultural and social interests; the list can be long and varied. This intensity of interest is likely to be *reciprocated* by local government, and government departments locally, for any company with a substantial presence is a source of wealth generation: it pays local taxes, provides local employment and indirectly stimulates the whole economy. In consequence it is welcome to participate through memberships of various advisory and other bodies. 'It has become common practice for senior members of the firm to take an interest in local politics, and it is good policy to make it equally possible for workers to serve on local councils or boards' (Black, 1989).

This involvement with local people is depicted by Stone (1995) as a 'three-cornered tug-of-war ... between self-esteem, altruism and commercial advantage. Get any one of these wrong and you are in trouble. It is only when *feeling good, doing good* and *doing well* are in balance ... that community relations can be truly effective'.

10.3 the environment

A substantial amount of CCI time and effort is accounted for by concerns relating to the **physical environment**, and with good reason. Environmentalism, that is to say, interest in the world ecosystems and mankind's treatment of the planet, came of age with the landmark United Nations conference on environment and development held in Rio de Janeiro in 1992, the 'Earth Summit' that was attended by politicians and civil servants from 178 nations, very nearly *every* nation at that time. More significantly, no fewer than 118 heads of state attended.

The ensuing UN conferences and EU 'green directives' have generated much talk and some do at the 'supersonic' level of human affairs, but probably the greater impact has been more *localized*, not only in the worried advanced countries but also in other states, where there may be some scope for learning from the mistakes of others in matters of industrialization, infrastructure, food production and so on. There is ample evidence of **widespread public awareness, interest and concern about environmental issues** around the world:

'On the whole, the environmental issues are seen as real "values", identified and accepted by the public opinion all over Europe, even though to a different extent and with a different impact, because they represent the search of quality to every society in all European countries' (CERP website, 5 November 2002). 'Today, all enterprises must consider the environmental issues in their communication processes owing to the impact that these issues have in each community, involving public opinion, prompting judgements and views.' Worries about the physical environment are widespread and growing. And in consequence corporate positive action to meet such concerns can **benefit brands**; it all depends upon the detailed circumstances.

EXAMPLE

When the Australian wine producer BRL Hardy purchased 1,700 hectares (4,250 acres) in South Australia's Riverland it became involved in wetland conservation with Australian Wetland Care, a conservation organization already on site, which includes over 12 kilometres of mainly wetland river frontage. This link largely shaped the Banrock Station brand when it was launched in 1995. The environmental theme was carried through to cardboard tags impregnated with the seeds of a local flowering shrub, attached to the bottles, and part of the sales revenue donated to Landcare Australia and Wetland Care Australia. In the UK this wetlands association has led BRL Hardy to support the UK's Wildfowl and Wetlands Trust, to mutual benefit: the charity has secured substantial extra funds and Banrock Station has become the UK's fifth largest wine brand and sixth fastest-growing grocery brand. (BITC/FT guide, 2002)

10.4 community action

As part of its Better Britain Campaign, Shell UK sought to assess the '**community sector**', prompted by the World Summit on Sustainable Development in Johannesburg in 2002. The company calculated that in the ten years since the initial conference at Rio de Janeiro there had been a two- to three-fold increase in activity in the UK (alone), although the absence of baseline data defied certainty. Shell's own scheme, however, had grown from some 10,000 projects in 1992 to 26,000 in 2002.

Its report 'describes a strong and growing movement, locally based and focused but working in a global context. Thousands of organizations and hundreds of thousands of people who are stepping forward and doing what they can for their neighbourhood, for their friends and neighbours and, ultimately, for all of us across the planet... The next step must be to consider how the sector can be supported and developed' (*The Quiet Revolution*, 2002).

Schemes described in the report include:

▸ *A car sharing scheme*, whose 50 members aim to reduce traffic by sharing journeys by road. 'The group hope to have the same success that Europe has had with similar schemes – that five car club members reduce the need for one privately owned car, bringing less reliance on private cars, fewer parking problems, an increased incentive to walk and cycle and a better quality of life all round!'

- *A furniture recycling scheme,* one of some 300 supported by Shell. Household items and electrical appliances are collected, restored or renovated and 'recycled' to young, disadvantaged people aged 16–25 years. There are also training schemes associated with the work and its administration.
- *A bicycle recycling scheme,* that rescues discarded bikes from public refuse tips and elsewhere, then cleans, repairs and resells them. The scheme also runs a bicycle taxi service.
- *An environmental improvement scheme,* run by Bangladeshi women, who have created an organic vegetable garden in part of a public park. The scheme also has a social dimension linked to environmental issues and horticulture.

Shell supports a variety of schemes elsewhere around the world.

EXAMPLE

One such Shell scheme is The Flower Valley Conservation Trust in the Cape Floral Kingdom, South Africa. This is said to be one of the world's richest but most threatened botanical regions, containing some 7000 species, of which 70 per cent are not found anywhere else. Only four per cent of the area is formally protected.

The Trust has acquired 550 hectares, with help from Shell and a UK conservation body, Fauna and Flora International. The management project includes conservation of endangered flora, known as 'fynbos', in ways that benefit the local Cape community, where there is 50 per cent unemployment. This is done through harvesting flowers and wood for papermaking and other related microenterprises. (Shell, 2002)

10.5 valuing donations

In 1998 BITC initiated the **PerCent Club**, whose initial 38 UK member companies pledged to *donate at least one per cent of their annual pre-tax profits to the community*. In 2002 148 organizations indicated their intent to fulfil this commitment, either to good causes or **some form of community involvement**. Giving at least one per cent is *not mandatory* for members but those that do so are entitled to display a specially designed logo to proclaim their benevolence. A substantial proportion of them are in the [London] *Financial Times/*Stock Exchange list of 'Top 100' companies.

At the beginning of the 1990s 'leading [UK] companies were contributing 0.42 per cent of their pre-tax profits to the community, much of it in cash,' reported *The Guardian* on 25 November 2002. 'These were the days before business gave a monetary value to gifts in kind and staff time. [Owing to more accurate measurement] you would expect contributions to be considerably higher. While this is true in money terms, the £499 millions contributed in 2000–01 is exactly the same percentage of pre-tax profits as the £225 millions contributed in 1990–91.'

Four years on: 'The total expenditure on corporate responsibility from all the

FTSE 100 companies is £985.76m, up 3.9% on last year and showing a huge rise in money terms since 2002 of 59%. However, these companies 'earmarked 0.79% of pre-tax profits for financing their social and environmental responsibilities, down almost a full point from last year's 0.87%... This year's figure is the lowest since *The Guardian* began monitoring in 2002, when it recorded 0.95%. Pre-tax profits have doubled in money terms since then' (*The Guardian*, 6 November 2006).

Whether like is being compared exactly with like here is in doubt, since 'community' has become 'social and environmental'. No doubt about the reasons for this expenditure, however: 'The growth in interest in corporate responsibility has come from consumer pressure and campaigns, coupled with a push from institutional investors such as pension funds, concerned about the ethics – and therefore the reputations – of companies in which they hold shares'.

10.6 the voluntary sector

The **voluntary sector** in the UK employed 563,000 people, or two per cent of the workforce, in 2001, when it accounted for £5.4 billion of the country's gross domestic product, or economic output. Total income was £15.6 billion, of which 4.9 per cent was received from business, *less in real terms than ten years earlier*. 'Research by the National Council for Voluntary Organisations (NCVO) shows that support from companies is in fact the only source of charitable income that has declined in real terms in the past decade' [up until then]. The British people, by contrast, had donated £5.41 billion (34.7 per cent) and the UK government another £4.52 billion (29 per cent). The charities managed to raise £3.53 billion (22.6 per cent) by their own efforts and received another £1.37 billion (8.8 per cent) from charitable trusts.

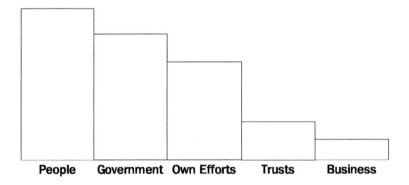

figure **10.2   the voluntary sector's sources of income**

NCVO wanted the government to force companies to give more, but there was evidence from another body, the Charities Aid Foundation, that the value of *gifts in kind* nevertheless rose by 25.4 per cent between 1999 and 2000. This raises the question of whether it is worthier for companies to hand over the money and have done with it or use their other assets to help. The latter route may be more economical and controllable to the donor, but that does not mean it is any the less, or more, beneficial to the recipient. Furthermore, it may be a means to being able to do more in real terms.

During 2002, its 20th year, BITC consulted with over 500 businesses in an attempt to review its role and responsibilities and to see where it might enhance its effectiveness. This exercise occurred in the wake of the September 2001 terrorist attacks in the USA, a period in which 'an increasingly disappointing performance in all the major economies of the world started to push the argument [for CSR] in the opposite direction' (Lambert, 2002). 'With profits and budgets under pressure just about everywhere, the question was how far companies would be able to sustain, let alone increase, efforts to support their different communities.'

The dialogues that BITC had with these companies' senior managers, who included over 300 chief executive officers, indicated that there was plenty of scope for improvement in the relationships between the voluntary and private sectors.

> People from the private sector complained about the complex political relationships within the voluntary sector; there were too many agencies doing roughly the same thing, and there was a need for consolidation and takeovers. Their counterparts in the voluntary sector tended to regard business people as innocents abroad, who spent their time trying to reinvent the wheel. To this observer, at least, it seemed that both sides were missing a number of opportunities by going down their separate tracks.

This conclusion entirely coincides with the commonplace experience of most managers in both sectors, in their dealings with the other over the past two decades and more:

▸ Company managers can find the complex, often Byzantine, decision-making structures frustrating and daunting and the duplications of effort frankly tedious. When they also encounter the amateurish vagaries and occasional outbreaks of internecine warfare that characterize not a few charitable bodies the temptation is for them to run.
▸ Voluntary sector managers for their part can become thoroughly rattled by the apparent ignorance of their daily realities, particularly where managers from a large corporate culture fail to understand, much less appreciate, that results have to be achieved by different means when most of the time everything is done on a shoestring budget and/or with dependence upon volunteers, who may, or may not, quite feel like it on the day.

The one side thinks 'What's *wrong* with these people?' while the other asks itself 'How do these people *ever* manage to tie their shoelaces?' It is a chasm to cross.

- ☐ Corporate community involvement (CCI) is CSR in relation to local communities, a development of community relations 'good neighbourliness'.
- ☐ Companies set their own scale of agenda to reflect their perceived circumstances.
- ☐ Community needs are open to wide and self-interested interpretation and some are properly the responsibility of civil institutions, not companies.
- ☐ Corporate CCI objectives provide the framework for using CCI as a strategic business tool, with proactive, not reactive, programmes to match.
- ☐ Effective CCI is said to result from achieving a balance between managerial self-esteem, corporate altruism and commercial advantage.
- ☐ Local communities are segmented to identify (1) the distribution of power and influence and (2) the publics, starting with employees, their families and friends.
- ☐ Issues relating to the physical environment account for much CCI activity, which is then called environmental relations. Positive action can substantially enhance corporate brand recognition, image and reputation.
- ☐ The BITC's PerCent Club corporate members donate at least one per cent of their annual pre-tax profits to the community.
- ☐ The differing cultures of the private and voluntary sectors give rise to differences in perceptions of each other that may result in lost opportunities to collaborate.

CASE STUDY

MAKING UP FOR LOST GROUND

The Prince's Trust was founded by HRH The Prince of Wales in 1976 and is the leading UK youth charity, offering 14–30 year olds opportunities to develop confidence, learn new skills, obtain employment and start businesses. The Trust targets people who are unemployed or facing barriers in life, and over 450,000 have participated in its programmes.

In 2002 the communication team developed a strategy to position the Trust more clearly as a leader and solutions provider on the key issues that affect socially excluded young people, the client group that the charity aims to help. One of the Prince's Trust's key target groups is young people with no or few qualifications, so educational under achievement was identified as a priority topic for a communication campaign.

Every year over 30,000 young people in England leave school without any qualifications at all. They are at increased risk of unemployment, homelessness and crime, unless they are able to get their lives back on track with support. The team's aim was to bring the facts to public attention, highlighting the social and economic impact and the potential solutions that the Trust and its partners could offer young people in these circumstances.

It was decided to capitalize on the existing 'news agenda' by mounting an awareness campaign that coincided with the next annual August announcement by the government of the results of the main secondary education public examinations (GCSE). The focus of the campaign would be to counter the traditional media treatment of these results, which concentrated on over achievers. This campaign would offer a message of hope for the 30,000 without any examination passes, reassuring them that they could still succeed in life, and explaining the Trust's volunteers' programme.

The programme provides a 12-week training course for 16–25 year olds, most of whom are unemployed, which is designed to develop their confidence, motivation and skills through teamwork in the community. The various activities include a community project, a fund-raising activity and a residential outward-bound week (rugged outdoor adventure). Further elements include work placement experience and support with employment interviews and writing personal profiles for job applications.

The Trust compiled a media briefing paper on educational underachievers, drawing on its existing research and external data relating to underachievement, truancy and exclusion. The paper considered the impact of a lack of qualifications on life chances and the potential social and economic costs. It summarized the Trust's £5 millions three-year programme and what various government agencies were also doing about the problem; these included the Connexions Service, the Learning and Skills Council and the Basic Skills Agency. The briefing paper and an accompanying press statement was forwarded to journalists specializing on education and social affairs ahead of the announcement of the examination results.

Next the Trust's team drew on its resource of 'celebrity ambassadors' to help promote the campaign to young people. The boxer Prince Naseem participated in a radio feature, produced for national distribution to radio stations, which included a case study of a young person who had failed all his examinations the previous year and then undertaken the Trust's course and commentary by a Trust representative. The footballer Rio Ferdinand, then currently high profile in the media owing to his recent transfer to play for Manchester United, gave an exclusive interview to BBC Radio One, a mainly pop music national station for young people.

The Trust's website was amended to include a pop-up page signposting the Trust and other support for anyone who had failed the examinations. And the Trust's local offices were briefed on how to respond to a potential influx of telephone calls.

The overall campaign reached over 12.5 million people. Coverage included news on both BBC terrestrial television channels, live and taped interviews on not only Radio One but also 52 regional radio stations, features in two national newspapers and reports in 25 regional newspapers, over 41,000 website visits during August (up 350 per cent on the same month of the previous year) and a high volume of direct enquiries into both free phone services and local offices. Two months later the BBC sourced from the Trust case studies on truancy and both the Trust's policy and fundraising departments received approaches from several potential partners, keen to collaborate. The campaign had increased recognition of the Trust as a specialist on educational underachievement and had been deemed an all-round success.

1 What might be common sources of friction in CCI?
2 Why might CCI be one of the softest and most intangible CSR activities?
3 To what extent might segmentation of the local community assist CCI, and why?
4 How might 'environmental relations' impact on employee relations?
5 Should companies have to give a higher percentage of their pre-tax profits?

the media

Serious media and entertainment media – media values – mediated communication – online media – the relationship between public relations and the media

11.1 serious media and entertainment media

> [He] switched on the television news. An important decision by the government was to be reached in twenty-four hours, but until this time – nothing. So nearly all the news was about this nothing. Special planes had been chartered so that reporters could land in distant places and talk about this nothing. Men spoke about it from Paris and Washington. There were expensive and complicated nothing interviews. Never had more been done for nothing. 'You don't want this nonsense, do you?' he asked Hazel. 'Of course not. I'll turn it off.'

Seldom has the banality and contrivance of television news been so well captured as in this depiction, by J. B. Priestley in *The Image Men*, of what has become an all-too-familiar wearying routine for viewers the world over. This is **'news' as entertainment**, thinly disguised as being serious. *Strangely unnecessary at weekends*, when it might interfere with the observance of rest and play, yet *in abundance on weekdays*, morning, noon and night, round the clock: all the news fit to print, shout, look deeply significant about, illustrate with computerized graphics; in short, attach to reality like some life-enhancing ritual observance.

Mass communication is probably nowhere more prevalent than in the UK, where until recently people read more newspapers per head of population than any other nation on earth and:

- Two out of three people are said to have a mobile, or cell, telephone
- 99 per cent of all households have a colour television
- 50 per cent of homes have at least one computer
- Mobile text messaging is thought to be more prevalent than anywhere else
- There is certainly no lack of interest in radio, particularly popular music interrupted on the hour, every hour, by news

- Television news output on the five main channels has increased by 80 per cent in less than a decade.

Not to mention the satellite television stations, the cable television stations, the thousands of magazines and umpteen radio stations. The British, it seems, have plenty of mass communication, all carefully contrived, packaged and presented for their edification, but *why?* Nor is the UK alone in this; around the world there is an 'explosion' of media. This is a boon to the public relations practitioners, but, as in any market, there can come a time when supply exceeds demand.

The modern media have five characteristics (McQuail, cited by Oliver, 2001) that offer some perspective on this. They may be summarized as:

- The media are, collectively, *the main source of information*. In consequence they exert **power**, for 'knowledge is power'.
- The media provide the venues of the modern **public sphere**, where the issues of the day are presented and debated, argued and explained, in studio discussion, documentaries, political advertising and speeches.
- The media *'tell it how it is'* about contemporary mores, changing values and cultural influences, so what they have to say about this or that **social reality** provides the framework within which people think about people, places, organizations, issues.
- The media are the major delivery systems for **projecting images** that entertain and inform, giving rise to *fame and subsequent fortune*.
- The media **represent 'normality'**, which is of particular consequence in matters touching upon morals and ethics. People *use as points-of-reference* for determining their own attitudes and beliefs what the media represent to them as being currently socially acceptable.

It is in the depiction of news that these characteristics are most clearly discerned. For instance, the main nightly radio and television news bulletins are relied upon by countless millions of people as their main source of information from beyond their immediate life experience. And the 'normality' represented there can determine how *whole nations* of people *think about this or that*, from the great issues of the day to minor trivialities.

Television news is supposedly impartial, unbiased and therefore trustworthy, differentiating it from newspapers, but 'impartiality helps to explain why TV news is so predictable and unadventurous and, more importantly, why TV news is growing less and less attractive to large cross-sections of the viewing audience', according to a senior UK television executive (Shaw, 2002). 'Television news should be accurate, fair, honest and respectful of privacy but that should not stop it from campaigning or pushing a particular agenda that concerns its audience. ... Why shouldn't there be a news programme slanted to one or other particular point of view?' This is known in the USA as **advocacy journalism**, 'in effect, taking sides or a particular point of view, and it is proving popular, if controversial'.

This is nothing novel in print journalism, where particular, often self-serving, interpretations of social reality and normality are energetically advanced, with commercial benefits. Although newspaper (not magazine) readership is said to be in overall, steady, year-on-year decline in a number of countries, there is copious research evidence of readers buying newspapers that carefully pander to their worldviews; these include, to judge by the public print, generous quantities of bias and bigotry. Such editorial policy places a strong filter over all content, resulting in distortions, hyperbole and omissions, and it sells newspapers and news magazines.

This carefully calculated 'talking back' to readers uses several stylistic devices, perhaps the most obvious being the 'Daily Wind-up', in which social and political 'outrages' are identified or contrived, then heavily exaggerated. This may account in good measure for the **'grumble culture'** that, in the UK at least, particularly afflicts people aged 35–54: the deepening dissatisfactions and discontents that relentless 'bad news' can foster in even the most resilient and purposeful readers. The 'grumpy generation' cites 'the sterility of popular culture' as one of three main causes of their dissatisfaction (*The Daily Telegraph*, 26 August 2002). Opinion surveys indicate people consider the world to be far better in the context of their own lives, based on personal experience, than it is generally, as derived from what the media tell them.

The media have **three basic 'duties', to inform, educate and entertain**, so when they are not being serious they are trying to be entertaining, even frivolous. This particularly exercises public relations people. They contribute both *serious* material, about, for instance, matters relating to the environment, company results, politics, redundancies and so on, *and* they are the source of much *lighter* content, relating to, say, show business, celebrities, readers' competitions and pseudo-events. They *also* provide plenty of the **information that fills the middle ground**, usually about products and services, such as travel features, fashion stories, lifestyle depictions, explanations of how things work, guides on where to go for what and interesting facts and figures on all manner of subjects. In short, **content and its sourcing is multidimensional and reflects the culture it serves.**

11.2 media values

Is the quality of television content deteriorating? The majority of people in the UK certainly think so, and they consider four or five terrestial channels quite enough; they have no need of any more, terrestrial or satellite. If this applied solely to news and current affairs, the cynical and shallow collaboration between politicians and broadcasters to fabricate news to their mutual satisfaction would provide explanation enough, but the criticism extends across *all television* broadcasting.

A recent Director General of the state-owned BBC has argued against reliance on 'the economic marketplace' or allowing advertisers 'to make the total running'. In March 2003 he criticized 'tame, flag-waving coverage of the Iraq War on American television and radio'. This had happened 'because the US became obsessed with regulating the economics rather than the content of broadcasting; it is not meant to be the British way of doing things. "If you allow economic factors to weigh heavily you would never have had the British television system anyway. ... We spend more money per head in this country on original television production than any other country in the world, even America'" (*The Guardian*, 11 June 2003). Given this overall level of expenditure, could the *content* and *production standards* be the source of so much dissatisfaction?

EXAMPLE

The BBC is also not without criticism of its handling of the military invasion of Iraq, despite its very extensive reporting of it in the UK and in the Middle East. In a confidential internal memorandum dated 6 February 2003, its senior management had cautioned relevant staff 'to "be careful" about broadcasting dissent', wrote a media researcher (*The Guardian*, 22 April 2003). 'A study of coverage in five countries for the *Frankfurter Allgemeine Zeitung* shows that the BBC featured the lowest level of dissent of all. Its two per cent total was even lower than the seven per cent found on the US channel ABC... As Baghdad fell on April 9, BBC reporters could hardly contain themselves in their haste to endorse the victors... Here the BBC enunciated a version of events very similar to that of the [UK] government.'

All such matters so central to popular culture arouse much debate in every country, but they are of *particular interest* to public relations practitioners. If, as some critics assert, PR provides an 'information subsidy' (Gandy, cited by Moloney, 2000), it is **empowered to exert some influence**, for better or for worse, and, like advertisers, it has a need to be *associated with successful output*, that is to say, broadcasting of a standard that appeals to the audiences it seeks. Mass disaffection is emphatically not in the interests of public relations, which, *given its involvement*, must accept some *responsibility* for media values, including ethics.

EXAMPLE

'The latest news on propaganda: The US is being bombarded by video news releases – fake TV packages that are actually stealth marketing', runs the headline to the article, which begins '"Hurricane seasons for the next 20 years could be severe, but don't blame global warming," intoned the news anchor for WTOK-11, a rural ABC affiliate in Meridan, Mississippi, on May 31. The clip aired nine months after Hurricane Katrina devastated the region, knocking WTOK off the air. The anchor was reading an introduction to a report, Global Warming: Hot Air?, which was narrated by Kate Brookes. "There's a lot of debate as to what's been causing all these hurricanes," she says. "Some scientists say it's a naturally occurring cycle, while others have made the claim global warming is to blame."' There followed an interview with a hurricane expert, who 'firmly rejects the latter possibility. He blames the "cycle of nature itself", and insists satellite data shows "no significant change" in the frequency or intensity of hurricanes worldwide during the past 20 years.' Narrator Brookes completed the item with: '"This year the probability of a major hurricane is about 81%. And while this number is a prediction, it's based on science and research, so it never hurts to be prepared. I'm Kate Brookes."

'No word on [the interviewee's] detractors, who cite compelling evidence that global warming has spawned ferocious hurricanes. And while Brookes never identifies herself as "Kate Brookes for WTOK-II News," or "Kate Brookes for ABC News," she has quite a reputation. Not as a reporter, but as a flack for PR company Medialink Worldwide Inc, the world's largest creator of Video News Releases, or VNRs, corporate propaganda designed to look like legitimate news. ... Her prints are all over fake news stories, aired on affiliates for ABC, CBS and Fox, as she "reports" on medical devices and ethanol plants from electronics giant Siemens AG. The WTOK clip was one of 54 VNRs identified by a Centre for Media and Democracy (CMD) report called Still Not the News: Stations Overwhelmingly Fail to Disclose VNRs, which was released on November 14. In April, CMD's report Fake TV News identified 36 VNRs.' The US government uses VNRs, revealed the *New York Times* in 2005, and CMD estimates that some 5,000 corporate VNRs 'were offered to TV stations between April and October 2006'.

(*The Guardian*, 4 December 2006)

The *visual imperative* of television has long been a significant factor, giving rise over the years to ever-greater compression of messages, through devices such as the 'nine second sound bite', flashing imagery and sound and monosyllabic two sentence drama scenes. This has laid fresh demands upon the skills of the public relations practitioner as well as the screenwriter and script editor.

And this use of vision to contrive urgency and pace has extended to radio, using sound instead, and to the printed media, where photography has become cinematic in its proportions and treatment. Overall design and layout of the printed page is undergoing a transformation as well, to present the content in compellingly attractive formats that find favour with advertisers as well as readers.

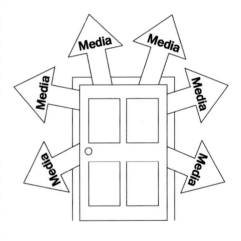

figure **11.1**   **the all-pervasive media**

Media values are highly pervasive. Newspapers and magazines have to decide what is *ethically* **appropriate for them**, which is translated into *editorial policy*. The quality of *self-regulation* by the newspaper industry varies from country to country, culture to culture.

EXAMPLE

An American war photographer in Iraq promptly, and very publicly, lost his job when he 'used his computer to combine elements of two photographs, taken

moments apart, in order to improve the composition', against his newspaper's editorial policy, which forbade the alteration of news photographs.
(*Los Angeles Times*, 2 April 2003)

Yet writers may expect to *keep* their jobs if they **refuse to disclose their sources**, for this is widely considered to be a fundamental principle of journalism that may only be breached in extreme circumstances; these are often created by government hostility in reaction to damaging public disclosures. This principle appears to extend well beyond protecting sources of 'leaks' and other valuable information. Nor do most journalists reveal the entertainment and gifts that they receive, the 'freebie' travel and holidays, the unreturned motorcars and other products lent for purposes of review. Occasionally one is dismissed, when it becomes 'too embarrassing' for the employer.

EXAMPLE

'A very big corruption in all British journalism is the network of friendship and obligation between people who write and the people about whom they write. We have no codes and we make no declaration and we leave our readers in the dark,' admitted a prominent *Times* feature writer and former member of parliament.
(*Writers' News*, February 2003)

Ethical questions also arise over such devices as the **infomercial**, television advertisements that are presented in a programme format, usually comprising two presenters introducing and talking about products in a studio setting. Does their pretence to be just like other programmes represent a true deception upon the viewing audience or merely a congenial device for distraction? Are infomercials an incursion into 'editorial' airtime that could be filled with a 'real' programme, and, if so, what of their production quality?

Product placement also raises questions about what is appropriate. And questions arise also concerning **advertising features**, editorial that promotes products and services, and **advertorials**, paid-for advertising in editorial format, often in the form of a flattering report, offer of free samples or reader competition. All three are routinely used by public relations in support of marketing. Any deception about their purposes is likely to be relatively innocuous, and readers' competitions are very popular. But to the extent that they risk *corrosion of editorial values* they are questionable practices of which both the media and public relations should be wary.

11.3 mediated communication

These practicalities are but the small detail of daily **media relations** when compared with the 'spin policy' of each media player, those agendas that they pursue, often with a political intent and always with an eye to a market for their product. How the media interpret events, any events, can be most instructive for discerning how they are likely to perform their role in **two-step communication** between the organization and its publics.

The **two-step flow** concept of communication has been modified to depict what happens when the third party is *a journalist or similar 'gatekeeper'*, the person who is to pass on the message to its intended recipients. This person also has access to information from other sources, which he or she may care to exercise, and in practice often does, in search of an '**angle**', that is to say, an interpretation that will be **distinctive to him or her** when compared with that of rivals elsewhere in the media who are in possession of the same original information. The journalist may also have *contact with the receivers*, and *they directly with the original public relations source*, so in effect the gatekeeper may not be the *sole* means by which the message may reach its destination, and nor may the gatekeeper *solely rely* on the originating public relations source.

Once the media become involved in the communication process, there is ample scope for *variation* to the original message. That is why public relations people endeavour to supply messages that are so well conceived and timed for the purposes of the media involved that they *will be passed on with minimal alteration*, by which means a **greater degree of control** is retained by the sender but with the *added-value endorsement* of the media attached. The *greater the confidence* that journalists repose in their sources, the less likely their probable inclination to alter the 'copy' before 'filing' it for use.

How receivers approach receipt of mass media messages may be at variance with what the media intend. Thus:

▸ News that is intended to be serious may be considered risible
▸ Intended humour may be thought distinctly unfunny
▸ Educational facts and figures may be met with grave suspicion.

Although the very source imparts status to the message, as it is seen, heard or read, that does not mean that it is *necessarily that well* received or accepted. Letters to the Editor provide ample evidence of that.

People condition how they receive media messages by how they *use* the media. They select from the vast choice before them by reference to what they want out of it. The **uses and gratifications theory** identifies five use classifications (Baskin *et al.*, cited by Harrison, 2000). In summary, the media may be:

▸ A source of entertainment
▸ The place to find items that are of particular personal interest
▸ A diversion
▸ A substitute for social relationships
▸ A check on personal identity and values.

If the 'telly' or radio is only on for *background companionship*, for example, there is **little prospect of much attention being given to content**, and there is heavy use made of these media for this purpose. Similarly, skimming for specifics or types of content serves to filter out much else, as where, for instance a newspaper is 'read' but not a single advertisement is seen. The public relations practitioner is, therefore, always at pains to assess the likely *effectiveness* of his or her output, and to use this in considering beforehand the likely value of intended effort. A common temptation is to mistake the placing of a message with the media as an end in itself, when it is *how* the end-receiver will receive that message and its *effect* that is the primary consideration.

This, together with agenda setting, whereby the media seek to identify the current topics and tastes that drive contemporary discussion and interaction, are key elements of mass communication. In other words, the media are very active in **constructing how receivers see the world**, and therefore they can not only filter but also *distort* messages in the process of communication, and this may be intentional as well as accidental. Public relations seeks to counter this through **repetition of key words and phrases, images, sounds and symbols**, offering **rewards** for the receivers' **attention** and providing *credible representatives* on behalf of the organization to present the message.

McQuail (cited by Oliver, 2001) developed a framework for taking into account two independent dimensions that determine differing views of both the media and society:

figure **11.2** **repetition of key words and phrases, images, sounds and symbols**

▶ The first separated the media that seek to be significant players in *achieving social change* from those that tend to be more *reflective of the contemporary* economic, political and social *conditions*
▶ The second distinguished between *culture and ideas* on the one hand and *material forces and factors* on the other.

This assists the media relations planner to **plot a position for a strategy that best fits the media**; whether:

▶ More campaigning and focused, or reserved and wider in its perspective
▶ More orientated toward *societal influences* on the content and effect of communication or on the *technological advances* in the means of communication.

The original **process of communication**, discussed in Chapter 5, conceived of a simple exchange between two people, but when the media become involved *in reality* much more is going on: the mass media are *not* the source, as so often supposed, but rather the providers of their *selective interpretation* taken from the originating sources. Those sources intend that their messages will have effects and, as we have seen, take measures, with varying degrees of certainty and efficiency, to optimize their intended outcomes. There is, therefore, *something of a gamble about communication via the media*, and **it is the elimination of this hazard that drives media relations practice**.

The desired outcomes vary, however, in the ***levels of change***, whether in attitudes, perceptions or behaviours, that they seek. For instance, in MPR it is likely that a communication will intend that the recipient *acts purposefully* *in response*, probably by buying something. But that may not be always the case. Often, for instance, 'mere' *making known* is intended, as in publicity. And frequently communication is designed to communicate *shared values*. In other words, the effect sought is **mental and emotional agreement**, the purpose being to gain or renew commitments that may of themselves, in the short-run result, require only the most minimal adjustments.

This shared-values approach is widely used in advertising, where the receiver is driven to discontent until he or she has acquired the missing product or service that completes the three-cornered picture presented: the product or service, the shared values and the purchaser. In public relations shared values are often communicated in the context of *memberships*, whether commercial or social, educational or cultural, religious or political, the *primary* purpose being 'bonding' rather than expenditure. Such messages benefit from universally felt human need of companionship, fellowship, association and faith, of identification with a purpose or cause, of belonging, unity of purpose.

Nor is communication composed simply of words, pictures and sounds alone. There is much *signalling* in communication, both interpersonally and in corporate and cultural contexts. That is why so much care and attention is given to corporate identity signs and symbols, colours and typographies. For how the sender intends these to be perceived may differ from how the receiver regards them after decoding, and the intervention of the media further exposes the communication to the risk of interpretation that is at variance with what the sender intends.

11.4 online media

The development in electronic media continues apace, but, to adapt a famous remark, reports of the death of traditional media have been exaggerated. The use and abuse of the new media is controversial, as we shall see, but without doubt they have brought many potential efficiencies.

The cracking pace and enthusiastic hype of the 1990s has given way to greater realism among the '**new media industry**'. One disappointed US online manager of a newspaper in San Francisco offered six explanations for why early expectations of creating 'some darn good online newspapers' had not been met, among them: 'Journalism, as defined by highbrow traditionalists and communications school professors, no longer seems to carry the weight it once did' (*The Guardian*, 31 January 2000). However, there is plenty of evidence that quality journalism most certainly *does* attract readers to the electronic text, but whether they still value it when they have to *pay* for it is in doubt. There are successful free sites but paid-for access meets customer resistance.

EXAMPLE

Slate, the 'trail-blazing internet magazine' started by Microsoft and now published by the *Washington Post*, has approaching 10 million readers every month. Its editor-in-chief, who is also a columnist for the *Financial Times*, is a 'cyberspace zealot' who says all the evidence tells him that in 2006 'America's "political conversation" finally and decisively' moved from traditional media to the web 'with far-reaching implications for the industry as a whole. He says: "Anyone who really wants to participate in that conversation has to have a presence on the web now – not necessarily a blog, but they have to have a website or write for an online publication. Within half an hour of posting a piece [on *Slate*], I get a direct, often hostile and personal, response from readers."

'He says: "That's part of what I think has been so frustrating for the columnists on the New York Times … who are online but are behind a 'pay-wall' – you have to be a subscriber to the paper or subscribe separately to the website before you can get them. That effectively cuts them out of the political conversation… Online you can't be scooped. If you are scooped, it's no one's fault but your own… If you talk to anyone in American newspapers today, I would say that this year it's gone from deep worry to panic. They are very worried about their future… people in college today don't read [newspapers]. They may read the content of the newspapers in digital form, but they don't actually buy the paper."'

An 'iPod-style hand-held device' is predicted that 'will enable readers to download newspapers – and indeed, books – on the move. "When this thing arrives it's going to transform books, newspapers and magazines and, if they figure it out in time, it's not necessarily going to harm them in the way the iPod has made things very hard for the music industry, partly because they don't have to repeat those mistakes and partly because it has the potential to increase their reach and audience, as well as offer, potentially, some very lucrative advertising opportunities."'

(*The Guardian*, 27 November 2006)

Many *specialist* publications are including electronic access without extra charge within their annual subscriptions. Publishers of business-to-business (B2B) titles

> say they are now in a much better position to make it pay: 'there has been a realization and recognition of fundamentals again. What is it that motivates a reader to read, what is the must-have information and what are the things people really do value in the working life' … market-specific news appears to be a key element… The key question is whether readers will buy… 'There is a lot of stuff in trade magazines that historically people like to think of as must-have content. But it might actually turn out to be "nice to have" or even "not that bothered about having".' (*The Guardian*, 9 December 2002).

Some people obtain their news and information solely online, and presumably their numbers will increase with time. They usually have a *strong predisposition* to the new media already, perhaps because they work in the sector. This is reflected in the experience of MPR specialists, who find those products that have a closer relevance to the new electronic media, such as computer consoles and games and mobile telephone messaging, are more likely to achieve the greater flow of **website visits** and resultant response.

Video streaming is also being used extensively and this is capable of sophisticated evaluation. Other activities include **web conferencing** and '**online chat**', '**viral marketing**', placing e-mail attachments that are sufficiently entertaining to induce receivers to forward them to friends, family and work colleagues, and, above all else, **e-mailing**, whether in text, audio or audio-video formats. Some public relations people endeavour to participate in **chat rooms** that are known to be frequented by their primary publics, as a means to *anticipating and countering criticisms*, although this may prove to be time-consuming and relatively impractical. Some use '**blogging**', although disclosure of tendentious journalism via this means has proved damaging and caused great resentment among bloggers, who see practitioners as unwelcome intruders who are trying to 'hijack the conversation' and cannot 'buy buzz'.

'The real strength of e-PR as a tool has been its ability to launch products and build awareness, rather than manage issues. Marketers are increasingly looking to the Internet as a powerful tool.' However, 'E-PR is not a part of Internet marketing; it is a type of Internet marketing. That is to say that it provides a way of viewing the whole online marketing process, from promoting your site through to the way you sell your products and services. The Internet is about interactivity and information, which provide the foundation for all e-PR activity' (Haig, 2000).

While public relations people may use the web for a variety of communication purposes, clearly it is e-mail that is of primary interest to them, reflecting the overwhelming general preference. 'E-mail is being used increasingly by business managers to communicate quickly with employees and colleagues. Furthermore, you can send online newsletters via e-mail to different target audiences.' But then 'E-mail and Web-based discussion groups are also a big e-PR concern. It is important to monitor these online groups in order to prevent misinformation spreading about your business, and to keep an eye on what people are saying about you and your competition.'

So great is the flow of e-mail, and mobile phone, or cell phone, text messaging, that it has inspired a new term, '**spam**', because it is all proving to be too much. It is estimated that about 40 per cent of all e-mails are now unsolicited, and unwanted text messages are particularly intrusive. Spam is a nuisance for both Internet users and service providers. Additionally, soon it will be possible to send a single text message to thousands of handsets, so worsening the problem.

The European (EU) Telecommunications Data Protection Directive that took effect in October 2003 requires that all commercial e-mail must include an address to which a recipient may send a request to cease such communication. All such Council Directives are 'binding as to "the results to be achieved" but ... have to be enacted by national procedures within a time limit. Legal rights can be created even if a particular country fails to meet the deadline' (Smith, 1995).

The UK government and many other EU member states wanted this 'opt-out' provision instead of the original 'opt-in' proposal, similar to the US legislation, that was proposed by the EU. Then the UK government produced legislative proposals that had at their core a requirement that the senders of unsolicited e-mail and text messages must *first* obtain the permission of their intended receivers. Meanwhile, the UK's Advertising Standards Authority decided bulk e-mailing and text messaging must be clearly marked 'unsolicited' or not be sent without *prior* permission of the intended recipients. All of this confirms that there is a real problem, which requires a global response.

11.5 the relationship between public relations and the media

The UK media comprises over 4,400 titles, of which about half are newspapers and consumer magazines and the balance are trade and technical publications. Throughout the EU the print media includes in aggregate an estimated 7,500 titles, about 500 on average in each country. These estimates (Stewart-Hunt, 2003) suggest that *over one third* of the EU print media is located in the UK. Given this concentration, there is extensive media relations activity; some public relations people are in contact with journalists, one way or the other, throughout the working day, and the busy interaction continues over weekends.

It is, generally, an uneasy relationship, supposedly distinguished by a pronounced asymmetry, based on the widely accepted notion that public relations people need journalists but journalists do not need public relations people. In consequence the public relations side persistently refuses, usually, to say a bad word about the media, much less countenance a scintilla of criticism against a journalist, not in public anyway. And the journalistic side persistently insists, usually, in excoriating everyone who works in public relations, or may even ever have done so, at every public and private opportunity.

This, however, is for the most part a *charade*, largely played out for third-party consumption. In reality the relationship is much more symmetrical. For public relations people now have the Internet, by which they may communicate *without mediation* of journalists, a significant and increasingly substantial addition to their various unmediated tools. And journalists have a *lot less time and opportunity* to originate material themselves and *much greater pressures* to consider 'ready-baked' offerings that can be swiftly transformed into tempting nourishment for their customers. Various estimates suggest high use of public relations-sourced material by journalists; sometimes very high, in the order of 60–80 per cent of all items that finally appear.

There is an **interdependency** here that must not bear mention. 'Journalists are complicit in the in-take of PR material. They seek the material, use it to fill expanding editorial space and benefit from any audience or reader increases', observes Moloney (2000), who offers two related explanations for 'this contradictory mixture of hostility and complicity'.

Firstly, he considers journalists to be 'too weak as a professional group', owing to a 'marketisation' of their 'institutions', too few jobs and lesser distinction between editorial, advertising, promotion and circulation (sales). It is certainly the case that new technologies have greatly impacted on print production, resulting in ever more available space to fill, while, owing to intensified competition for advertising and readers, there are even fewer resources with which to fill the space. In consequence the media have opened their editorial pages to commercially sourced inputs on a scale that was unimaginable but 20 years ago. 'Media placement' has long since ceased to be for the public relations practitioner the arduous and painstaking endurance trial of yesteryear.

The second explanation is that the journalists are the 'news managers', those who, they claim, objectively decide what goes in the space when there is too little 'hard' news to fill it. 'Now they are more likely to accept [PR material]. Journalists have increased their reliance on secondary sources (including PR), especially when these sources produce copy in a pre-prepared, journalistic form. Journalists thus rely more on official and company spokespeople as primary definers of events. This reliance gives the sources the ability to co-operate or obstruct depending upon the favourability of journalists' copy.'

Journalists have always been the final arbiters of what appears, and probably, being only human, they have often indulged their preferences and prejudices in doing so. Undoubtedly their dependence on outsider contributors, in whatever shape or form, has most definitely increased, and they have always, very sensibly, tended to prefer inputs that better understood and met their requirements. That public relations people are the *primary* definers of events, however, is very doubtful, although they might strive to be so. Clearly, in matters politic and in reporting corporate 'hard' news such as annual results, that *may* be so, but it is difficult to see the multitude of MPR events in quite such an awesome light. And, yes, the public relations contributor does indeed seek to exert influence on what appears, much as most other people do when they are in contact with the media.

That journalists routinely pass judgment on public relations people, in public, *as if their audiences are as fascinated with PR as clearly they are*, may be in part at least attributable to the long-standing prejudices held within the **media schools**. The comments of an unidentified media department head at a London university is likely to be typical: 'I would be surprised if one per cent of each intake got jobs in a mainstream media outlet. A few might get into PR.' This person 'spoke on condition of anonymity' (Silver, 2002).

Theaker (2001c) observed 'signs that antagonism between journalists and PR people is not as widespread as commonly held. Several [journalists responding to her survey] quoted local councils, police and health authorities, housing associations and utilities as providing good service. One journalist mentioned a leisure company which were "masters at forcing us to do stories".' Although we are not told *why* or *how*. The general tone of her respondents is condescending: their tips are of the typically banal and trite variety that many journalists still use in their endeavour to patronize public relations people, often just before applying for jobs with them.

This uneasy relationship, conceived with built-in tension, nevertheless has its more subtle dimensions. For example, consider these:

▸ 'Journalists often have advance notice of which companies and organizations are going to do badly. Experience frequently shows that rot in an organization begins on the public relations side, with slow, inadequate and especially defensive responses. Maybe stockbrokers should employ freelances [writers] as scouts' (*Writers' News*, June 2001).

- '"For every story I've broken [originated], there are 20 I've stopped," he [a leading UK publicist] boasts' (*The Times*, 23 September 2002).
- 'Family firms may exist in all sectors of industry ... but in the stuff of popular legend, businesses outside the traditional women's fields of hair and beauty, public relations or child minding are predominantly father/son concerns' (*The Guardian*, 9 June 2003).
- 'It is hardly a secret among less idealistic PROs that journalists regard themselves as gatekeepers barring access to the truth, rather than facilitators on the path to enlightenment' (*PR Week*, 4 October 2002).

CHECKLIST

- ☐ The media have three basic duties: to inform, educate and entertain.
- ☐ Collectively, they are the main source of information, and are said thereby to exert power, for 'knowledge is power'.
- ☐ The media provide the venues of the modern public sphere, where people 'meet' to consider current affairs and topics.
- ☐ They create the framework, or reference-point, for forming private worldviews.
- ☐ They are the main means to projecting images for gain.
- ☐ Public relations practitioners, by supplying the media without charge, are partly responsible for broadcasting and print output standards and values.
- ☐ The use of infomercials, product placement, advertising features, advertorials and other PR-generated devices may corrode editorial values.
- ☐ Uses and gratifications theory states that the media may be used: (1) for entertainment, (2) to find interesting items, (3) for diversion, (4) in substitution for social relationships and (5) to check on personal identity and values.
- ☐ Key elements of mass communication are (1) how and with what effect messages are received and (2) agenda setting, by which the media filter and alter messages to match their interpretation of their receivers' worldviews.
- ☐ For McQuail the media operate in two dimensions: (1) seeking either to achieve social change or reflect current conditions; (2) emphasizing either culture and ideas or materialist forces and factors. Accordingly media relations strategy may be: (1) campaigning and focused or reserved and broader; (2) concerned more with the social content and effect or with the technical means of communication.

CASE STUDY

WHEN THE e-MAILING HAS TO STOP

The incidence of unsolicited e-mail soared in the 12 months to December 2001, according to a survey of 119 UK newspaper and magazine journalists. Almost 20 per cent reported a 100 per cent or more increase. 'Over a quarter of unsolicited e-mails received by journalists are from public relations practitioners and 75 per cent of respondents believed that there should be a formal e-mail code of conduct to govern the way in which public relations practitioners use e-mail' (Mason, 2002). Furthermore, 'only 50 per cent of respondents had received any form of training in the use of computers and e-mail'.

The survey focused on the impact of unsolicited e-mail on communications between UK print journalists and public relations practitioners. Similar studies of both print journalists and broadcasters had been conducted annually in the USA since 1994 by Middleberg and Ross. Their most recent study, in 2000, had stated that the preferred method for communicating with unknown sources was e-mail, placed by 32 per cent of respondents ahead of telephone, face-to-face, post and facsimile. Questions in the study relating to computer-aided reporting, or e-mail, were replicated in the British research, in order to compare and contrast US/UK attitudes, allowing for the US e-mail take-up levels being at least five years ahead, 'in an attempt to predict how British newspapers and magazines might react to their increasing in-box overload in the future.'

The 119 respondents who agreed to participate comprised 52 per cent of the random sample of 228 selected publications. Among respondents, 38 per cent were from trade and technical titles, 53 per cent from consumer publications, three per cent from daily newspapers and six per cent from weekly titles. All had noticed a significant increase, and 40 per cent reported an increase in excess of 50 per cent.

Principal complaints related to the receipt of large picture file attachments that take a long time to download, untargeted e-mails and incompatibility of differing operating systems. Some respondents indicated preference for faxes and post. Comments included '...information in an e-mail has less impact and is less likely to be retained in the mind ...' and '... posted press releases could have more impact and were more likely to have a longer "shelf life".'

'In comparing the findings of this study with those of the Middleberg Ross Cyberspace research, it seems that UK journalists could perhaps be approaching the point reached by their American counterparts five years earlier in 1997. Many British journalists report in-box traffic increase of up to 100 per cent and a large percentage (30 per cent) of those surveyed never open unsolicited e-mails. ... In 1997 Middleberg/Ross report that US journalists turned their backs on e-mail and reverted to sourcing many of their stories either through telephone, fax, face-to-face or postal communications.'

QUESTIONS

1 Should television news be 'slanted to a particular point of view', like newspapers?
2 What responsibility should public relations bear for 'the sterility of popular culture'?
3 Why might the media be used as 'a check on personal identity and values'?
4 Might journalism no longer seem to 'carry the weight it once did' and if so why?
5 Why might 'rot in an organization begin on the PR side'?

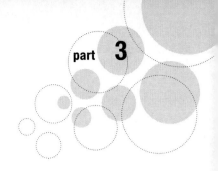

part **3**

global public relations

The development of public relations internationally – global public relations linkages – practice growth factors – cultural differences – beyond the clichés and slogans – non-governmental organizations – the European Union

12.1 the development of public relations internationally

The development of public relations outside the USA and the UK began to accelerate from the middle of the last century. The first talk of organizing public relations practice internationally occurred in November 1949, when a group comprising four British and two Dutch public relations men conceived of a 'para-national society' to raise practice standards and improve quality and efficiency. This led to a second meeting in March 1950, attended by PR people from the UK, the Netherlands, France, Norway and the USA, under the auspices of the Royal Netherlands International Trade Fair and the Public Relations Society of Holland (Black, 1989).

At that meeting a provisional committee was established, with the purpose of promoting international exchange of information and co-operation. This met regularly in England, occasionally observed by people from Australia, Belgium, Canada, Finland, Italy and Switzerland, and led to the establishment of the **International Public Relations Association** (IPRA) in 1955. The list of countries represented is a useful indication of where the paid practice of public relations was taking root around the world in those formative years.

IPRA adopted a formal **code of conduct** in 1961, comprising practice guidelines for members, and, in 1965, **an international code of ethics** for public relations practice, the 'Code of Athens'. The **United Nations** formally recognized IPRA 'on a consultative basis to the Economic and Social Council' in 1964 and later it was also recognized by Unesco as a non-governmental organization (NGO) in the 'mutual information category of relationship'. Over the years IPRA, whose membership comprises senior practitioners, has issued a succession of influential papers, including a 'gold paper' at each of its triennial world congresses.

In 1997 the association published a survey of eight countries in relation to the effects of *globalization* on corporate communication. The countries studied were Australia, Brazil, Japan, Singapore, South Africa, Switzerland, the UK and the USA. 'There was unanimous agreement that companies would need improved communications in the global field' (Theaker, 2001d).

The spread of public relations practice around the world has been accompanied by a **slower development of related research**, which has been undertaken primarily in north America and Western Europe. Corporate communication research was 'still in its infancy', according to van Riel (1995), who somewhat defensively declared 'I take the view that it is necessary to keep research progressing at full speed, yet never to lose sight of the connection with practice'. He cited a number of European academic writers whose work had been published in the previous 20 years. In the UK great emphasis has been placed on the work of various American scholars.

12.2 global public relations linkages

Several regional associations of national public relations bodies have been long established. These include the **Inter-American Confederation of Public Relations Associations** (FIARP), which stimulated development throughout Latin America, and CERP, whose members cover the whole of Europe. In 1986 the consultants formed their own discrete organization, the **International Communications Consultancy Organization**, whose membership comprises corporate membership associations in 24 countries, with the aim of working towards 'quality, efficient PR consultancy practice across borders', including harmonization. (ICCO website, 29 May 2002). It too has a professional code, the 'Rome Charter'. In 2000 the desire to collaborate internationally gave birth to yet another body, the **Global Alliance for Public Relations and Communications Management**. Although this was formally inaugurated in Chicago, it too was conceived in London, at a series of meetings the previous year.

The Global Alliance brings together over 20 national and international associations and has been established in response to the influence of global trends and issues; it aims through co-operation 'to strengthen the influence of the public relations industry among our constituents around the world'. In addition to the usual purposes, this new organization 'enhances networking opportunities for professionals and serves as a vehicle for examining ethical standards, universal accreditation options, and other initiatives to strengthen the profession around the world' (Alliance website, 26 May 2002).

The membership of the Global Alliance provides another indication of where public relations practice is well established. Member associations are in:

▸ The Americas (Canada, USA, Mexico, Puerto Rico),
▸ Europe (IPRA, CERP and several national associations),
▸ India,
▸ Asia (Australia, New Zealand, Philippines), and

> Africa (an association covering southern Africa and an association in Kenya).

The *urge to merge* has served to continually produce ever-larger firms, as has occurred in accountancy and some other occupations; in public relations some 10–12 global consultancy service providers are in the top echelon, genuinely capable of delivering around the world from start to finish through offices and practitioners in local markets.

12.3 practice growth factors

The growth of public relations practice around the world is driven by several key factors. Probably *the* most powerful factor is **industrialization**, with all its accompanying implications and consequences. As the developed 'first world' countries steadily replace their manufacturing activities with supposedly 'cleaner' knowledge-based occupations and trades, countries in the 'second world' are industrializing rapidly, energetically serving their growing domestic markets and supplying markets hitherto the domain of first world providers. This process looks destined, climate conditions permitting, to steadily roll out across the planet, so that in the future we shall see growing numbers of third world developing countries also industrializing. With it comes a phenomenal increase in world trade (three quarters of the world's nations are now members of the World Trade Organization), environmental impact, rebalancing of political power between regions and countries, mutuality of interests and intensification of economic rivalry. This is not a smooth transition – why should one ever expect it to be? – but the overall picture is clear enough.

The second, closely linked, factor is **globalization**. Porter (1980) eloquently describes the process by which companies gradually morph into behemoths that stride the globe. They start out tentatively enough, seeking to do business internationally, by one means or another, and as they prosper they slip into qualifying as truly international businesses, until they eventually 'go global', that is to say, they compete 'on a worldwide, co-ordinated basis ... in many national markets. ... The sources of global advantage stem broadly from four causes: conventional comparative advantage, economies of scale or learning curves extending beyond the scale or cumulative volume achievable in individual national markets, advantages from product differentiation, and the public-good character of market information and technology'.

Next up is the rapid enhancement of **communication and transportation technologies**. This may seem like the blindingly obvious, but it should not be minimized: the physical and psychological 'shrinking' of the world is heavily dependent on the spread of Internet access, growth in physical accessibility to hitherto remote places and 'taming' of wild and rugged hinterlands. All of which permits dissemination of ideas and information, observation and familiarization with differing customs, lifestyles and practices, and so on. The surge in the facilitation of communication may well prove to be, in retrospect, *the* single greatest factor from a public relations perspective.

Closely tied with this is the advent of **multiculturalism**, resulting from the dramatically greater movement of people around the globe, many such migrants resettling far from their homelands, in search of greater prosperity. The surge of peoples in all directions, notably south to north, east to west, from ex-colonies to former colonial countries, indicates a turbulence hitherto unimaginable. Starck and Kruckeberg (2001) illustrate how this is changing the USA: 'Previously homogeneous small towns in America's hinterlands are becoming rapidly diverse as multiculturalism invades even the most insular U.S. communities, but requisite corresponding harmony, tolerance, and cultural literacy remain elusive.'

Democratization is also an important factor, because political systems strongly influence social structures and societal environments. Gradually the world is becoming formally described as democratic, which *implies* that people are being allowed by their political masters to express their views and exert influence on how the ruling elites perform, supposedly, on their collective behalf. By the start of this century there were 119 electoral democracies, occupied in aggregate by an estimated 58 per cent of the world's population; that's up from nil a century before. Such democratization intensifies and deepens civic and social pluralism.

Not everyone, however, is sanguine about democracy's prospects. Some consider it threatened by globalization: that global companies are, or can be, more powerful than nation states, and they exert that superiority to their advantage over the democratic will of those peoples. That they are relatively few in number is itself thought sinister, an elite bent upon creating a 'world corporate order' that is gradually taking over important governmental tasks yet report only to their owners, not electors.

Related to this is **politics**. There have been significant changes in recent years. These have been followed by a slower rate of acclimatization; for instance, as the dramatic collapse of the Soviet Union has given way to a period of 'transition' that by stages has brought several countries into membership of the democratically configured EU. In Eastern Europe national public relations membership bodies have been formed; as also, in 1991, in China, which, together with Russia and India, is a vast country experiencing political change driven by economic imperatives. Prevalent political ideologies impact directly on economics, and vice versa, the two together largely determining the character and rate of development.

12.4 cultural differences

Coping with **cultural nuances** is fundamental to global practice. Unfortunately, practitioners do not always recognize this; particularly susceptible are those that suppose *most* people speak their language and more or less live by *their* norms. They don't: cultures *coexist*, but *proximity* is no assurance of similarity. There are, still, some 6,000 languages being spoken, for instance, over 300 of them in London alone, according to Transport for London. 'So in the key communications area of languages, the public relations practitioner has much to consider when venturing abroad... Even between countries supposedly speaking the same language ... it is necessary to ascertain the correct choice of words is made, both to ensure clarity of meaning and to avoid the possibility of giving offence' (Black and Davis, 2002).

Just what *is* culture? Sriramesh and Vercic (2003) cite a 19th-century definition (Taylor, 1871): 'that complex whole which includes knowledge, belief, art, morals, custom, and any other capabilities and habits acquired by man as a member of society'. That is certainly comprehensive, except, of course that it applies to all humankind. We know what we mean by 'culture', but its component parts may prove elusive to enumerate. Four **determinants of culture** were identified by Kaplan and Manners (1972), reported by Sriramesh and Vercic:

▸ *Technoeconomics* (technical and economic conditions);
▸ *Social structure* (institutions, class distinctions, etc.);
▸ *Ideology* ('values, norms, worldviews, knowledge, philosophies, and religious principles'); and
▸ *Personality* (individual traits, 'based especially on the child-rearing practices of that society as well as acculturation [cultural mixture] in school and the workplace').

These determinants act powerfully to create a distinctive culture that people adopt and perpetuate, perhaps without much conscience effort, at home, in the workplace, wherever they frequent.

Hofstede identified **five dimensions of culture**:

▸ *Power distance*: the distance between the individual and where power lies; and *social mobility*: 'the ease [or otherwise] with which members of lower strata can achieve a higher status in society'
▸ *Collectivism–individualism*: the degree to which individualism is valued, compared with the group and 'collectivity'
▸ *Masculinity–femininity*: the degree to which gender determines status and role
▸ *Uncertainty avoidance*: the degree of capacity to handle ambiguity
▸ *Long-term orientation*: 'the tendency where a collectivity values long-term commitments and traditions' – this dimension was originally called Confucian dynamism.

All of these have particular resonance for practitioners: generally, the stronger the individualism the greater the self-orientation; in many countries women now well outnumber men in practice (hence references to the 'feminization' of public relations); some practitioners place uncertainty avoidance at the very top of their concerns; the degree of social flexibility sets many agendas for the 'do-able'; short-termism is a constant that needs vigilant supervision, to make sure the benefits keep outweighing the disadvantages.

These dimensions have been variously related to the four types of public relations practice, in efforts to optimize the scope for two-way symmetrical communication in a variety of economic, political, social and other contextual factors. Of these probably that which would be uppermost for most practitioners is the **current state of the mass media** in a given country or market. There are **three primary factors** to consider (Sriramesh (1999), cited by Sriramesh and Vercic, 2003):

> **Ownership,** therefore control, and therefore determination of editorial slant. Throughout the world the media is in surprisingly few hands, whether governments or companies. In developed countries it is predominantly the 'capitalistic entrepreneur' who owns the media, and 'the need to sell news as a commodity is naturally strong in such an environment, leading to interesting choices in coverage'. In developing countries media may be privately owned, but government and politicians are seldom far away: media 'are strictly monitored and controlled through overt and covert means'. Significantly, 'editorial freedom is directly proportional to the level of economic development of a country. It is the lack of resources and infrastructure that have limited editorial freedom in developing countries'.

> **Outreach,** the extent to which the media disseminates information and *who* is receiving it. Illiteracy and poverty restrict this outreach to the better-educated and more affluent people, which can be only a small percentage of the population (even though accounting for a much higher proportion of spend, directly and indirectly). There is a 'symbiotic relationship' between economic growth and television, but in many countries the radio is the principal medium. The limited development of modern mass media may necessitate using traditional tools, travelling around and using visual symbols more than print. 'In India, for example, many public information campaigns have used folk media such as docudrama, dances, skits, and plays in rural areas' (Sriramesh, 1992, cited in Sriramesh and Vercic, 2003).

> **Access,** the extent to which people can use the media to disseminate their messages. 'A savvy international public relations practitioner will recognize that just as an organization's access to the media is critical, so is the extent to which the media are accessible to the organization's opponents, principally activists'. This 'activism' is a dynamic factor that can be not only threatening to the organization but also opportunistic, for both sides, because symmetrical communication usually has to follow, and most pressure groups, after their initial attack, soon settle down into trying to develop mutually useful dialogue, because that is what they are really interested in, hoping to eventually in some dimension gain thereby.

The public relations consequences of limited media outreach were well described by Jefkins, who had extensive experience of training Nigerians in public relations. He pointed to the disparities in that country's state of educational progress during those years. On the one hand, there were some dozen universities and many technical colleges, secondary and private schools, and many Nigerians were being educated in Western universities, but on the other, universal primary education had not been introduced until 1977. This had commercial consequences: for instance, with labelling of products. 'It is not enough to print the label and instruction in the local language since the majority of people will not be able to read. Cartoon-type instructions are necessary, although rare' (Jefkins and Yadin, 1998). Similarly, weights and measures 'are incomprehensible to people who do not weigh anything nor use rulers or tape measures. This has been a problem with products such as powdered baby milk, many buyers having no means of measuring or sterilization.'

Sensitivity to cultural differences is probably *more necessary* in public relations than in any other occupation. Whereas such differences routinely close to hand may be more readily understood, they are likely to provide far greater challenges when encountered abroad. And sensitivity has to be accompanied by a determination to *adapt* as necessary to meet local circumstances. The growing tendency to look across from one whole continent to another and suppose that 'the other' is homogeneous has to be resisted. **Making generalized assumptions about other cultures can be the death of communication**, and an understandable reluctance to recognize heterogeneity because it spells 'more effort' is a serious hazard; thoroughly researching and understanding differing cultures is *fundamental* to international public relations practice.

Any desire in the practitioner for a *uniformity* in communication soon has to come against this 'heterogeneity of the context of the environment in which the organization operates', which leads to recognition that 'it is not always desirable nor practical to stimulate "uniformity" in overall communication policy' (van Riel, 1995). This is *particularly* so given the **reputational significance** of the signals that the organizations emits and the 'rational and (apparently) irrational ways in which members of the target groups select signals from those put out by the organization'. These considerations provide a counterbalance to the, often, extravagant claims for the Internet. The very *ease of use* does not eliminate the very real differences that exist around the world. 'Geographical limitations are all but eliminated when you are online' (Haig, 2000) sounds seductive, but does not quite tell the full story.

Jekfins wrote scathingly of the business outsiders' misperceptions about the developing world. 'Foreigners rarely understand the communication problems. They sit in London, New York or Geneva, and plan marketing schemes as if they were selling to a mass market in an industrial society.' However, he observed that many people in developing countries might have little faith in home-produced products, *preferring* foreign-made. This preference is not confined to the developing countries, as witness the popularity of German motor cars, but he thought that in the developing countries, given the circumstances, 'A PR task may well be to foster pride in home production.'

12.5 beyond the clichés and slogans

Generalizations abound in consideration of international communication. Whole races of people are readily labelled, personal experience is happily extrapolated, inferences are drawn from slim evidence and lingering doubts are soon made *fact*. And in the pursuit of *effectiveness* much wise counsel is offered.

Think global, act local is the cliché of choice. Segment, segment, segment, cross-refer and cross-refer again. Public relations knows no frontiers. Communicate away the world's differences. Stretch the hand of friendship across continents. Speak the right language. Unite in common understanding. And so on. It is as if distance not so much makes the heart grow fonder as the head more woolly.

The reality of international public relations is that the ground rules are much the same, **but the conditions have changed**:

▸ *Unfamiliar* environments have to be scanned with the *utmost* care and attention to detail
▸ *Each* public has to be scrutinized to the *n*th degree
▸ The drive for *control* has to be intensified
▸ *Consistency* has to be maintained under often challenging conditions
▸ Measurement and evaluation has to reflect the *exact* specifics of each circumstance.

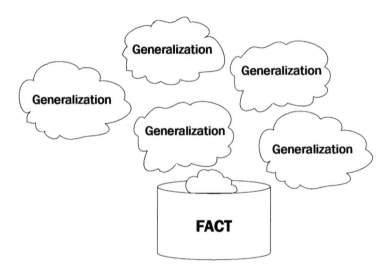

figure **12.1   generalizations made 'facts'**

12.6 non-governmental organizations

The people who appear to excel at international public relations are the NGOs, which are often referred to as advocacy groups or 'watchdogs', although there are many to whom such appellations do not readily apply. They vary greatly in size, origins and duration. Their purposes are correspondingly many and varied, from, for instance, regulating the use of the high seas to harrying corporate transgressors to distributing food and medicines.

They 'have become the new sophisticated communicators and perceived instigators of change in the global marketplace' (Wootliff and Deri, 2001). 'Some [NGOs] are pro-industry; others more cautious. Still others can find no redeeming qualities at all in multinational corporations or global free trade.' 'Business people tend to be at least as suspicious of the NGOs as they are of the media' (Lambert, 2002). 'But this year they have been starting to talk about ideas for working alongside them in various forms of partnership.'

EXAMPLE

What happened to the US sportswear manufacturer Nike both illustrates NGO communication effectiveness and explains business wariness of them. Early in 1996 CBS television broadcast a 'stunning exposé' of working conditions in factories in China, Indonesia and Vietnam that were supplying the company. The wages paid were less than the local minima, conditions were appalling and there was physical abuse. The damage changed Nike's carefully cultivated youth brand image from 'urban cool' to rapacious exploiter of poorer peoples; the company sought to defend itself by rebutting the allegations (*The Times*, 23 September 2002).

Then a leaked confidential report, from management consultants who had been inspecting a factory in Vietnam for Nike, did more damage. The revelations, in *The New York Times* in November 1997, led to a trenchant hail of international criticism of Nike, on both the business and sports pages, and an NGO called Working Assets Citizen Action generated 33,000 letters of complaint addressed to Nike's CEO, 'urging him to pay workers a living wage and to implement a comprehensive third party monitoring system'. Other NGOs, such as Global Exchange and Vietnam Labor Watch, joined in, together with student groups, demanding that universities 'doing business with Nike' put pressure on the company to achieve higher standards. There was a telling documentary broadcast; sales fell and the share price suffered accordingly (Wootliff and Deri, 2001).

In April 1998 a prominent environmental activist and anti-corporate campaigner sued Nike under California's Unfair Competition and False Advertising Law in relation to its public relations defence. He accused Nike of making false claims about its labour record. He argued that as these claims had commercial intent and impact, they amounted to 'unfair business practice'. Soon after Nike pledged to end child labour in its suppliers' factories, to enforce US standards there and, probably most tellingly, to allow NGOs to participate in monitoring its Asian factories. 'The company also publicly stated that the conditions in its factories needed to be drastically improved.'

Nor has the damage been limited to the company. Public relations practice has been held to account for the accuracy of its statements. The California Supreme Court found that statements made by businesses were not protected by the American constitution's guarantee of free speech. 'California is the fifth-largest market in the world... The ruling also applies to charities, non-governmental organizations, possibly political groupings and even journalists,' according to a Harvard law professor. 'The decision [allows] any California citizen to drag a business into court and bring it to its knees unless it persuades a jury that everything it said was error-free and omitted nothing' (*The Times*, 23 September 2002).

The impact of NGOs on international public relations practice probably cannot be fully calculated because their influence extends to the most mundane day-to-day decisions, such as consumer choice of food. On *credibility* the NGOs score remarkably well. In a 2000 survey, by public relations consultants Edelman Worldwide, of some 1,300 plus 'thought leaders' in Australia, France, Germany, the UK and the USA (Wootliff and Deri, 2001) NGOs were more trusted than government, business and the media on:

> • '*The big issues* such as the environment' – by over half of the sample
> • *Human rights* – by almost 60 per cent of the sample
> • *Health* – by over half of the sample.

When it came to 'who is more "trusted to do the right thing"':

> • In the USA business scored well clear of the others, at 44 per cent
> • In Australia the NGOs were strong winners at 53 per cent
> • In Europe the NGOs came top again, on 48 per cent.

For the purpose of the survey, thought leaders were defined as men and women aged 35–64 who are college graduated, registered to vote and have an annual $75,000 plus 'household income'.

The researchers advance some explanations for why they consider NGOs are 'winning':

> • Effective use of the power of images, particularly in broadcast and on the Internet
> • Speaking directly to consumers and appealing to their emotions
> • Focusing on a clear agenda with a call to action
> • Building coalitions, with companies, other NGOs and consumers
> • Being seen as selfless crusaders.

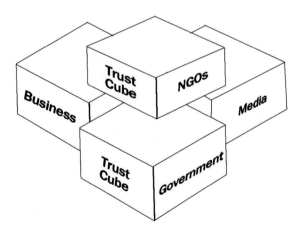

figure **12.2**   **varying levels of trust in NGOs, government, business and the media**

By contrast, Wootliff and Deri say that companies, government and the media have 'a myriad of agendas and audiences'; business is poor at creating coalitions and often organizations lack external support; and 'businesses might be perceived as supporting corporate greed'.

12.7 the European Union

An increasingly important dimension in international public relations practice is the growth of regional alliances and groupings *between nations*, of which the **European Union** (EU) is probably creating the greatest interest, owing to its expansion to embrace most countries in the whole continent of Europe and the development of its constitutional structures in order to cope with this. The EU is now very much part of the politics of EU member states; in the case of the UK, the **European Commission** (bureaucracy), **Council of Ministers** and **European Parliament** take their place alongside other components of 'the system' (Miller, 1998, cited by Theaker, 2001e), a complex web that binds civil service departments, special advisers, committees, task forces, bodies and regulators, and the 'cabinets' that advise European commissioners (ministers).

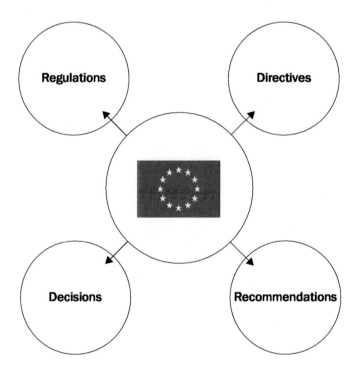

figure **12.3**   **the four main forms of European Union legislation**

Directives are but one of four main forms of **EU legislation**; they also include:

- *Recommendations*, which amount to guidance for national legislation
- *Regulations* and certain decisions that are binding as soon as they are published in the *Official Journal*
- *Decisions*, which are directives that apply only to certain countries or companies.

'A final element in this complex political scene is the large number of Union documents produced. These are of varying status and require the most discriminating monitoring. In an average year some 7,000 pieces of draft or final legislation emerge.' The emphasis is on consultation and compromise, according to Smith (1995), another prominent UK lobbyist, 'with a marked preference for lobbies organized at a Union rather than a purely national level.' Where differences occur between the Council of Ministers and Parliament, reconciliation of views is sought by the Commission, 'acting as honest broker and guardian of the treaties – the outcome of this process is known as a Common Position.' Perhaps not surprisingly, 'Lobbyists and public relations people form a key part of the emergent European political elite' (Miller and Schlesinger, 2001).

CHECKLIST

- ☐ Major factors have promoted the spread of public relations practice throughout the world, the creation of international linkages between membership bodies and the emergence of global consultancies.
- ☐ Sensitivity to language and cultural differences is probably more necessary in public relations practice than in any other occupation.
- ☐ In international public relations practice, the ground rules are much the same but the conditions have changed.
- ☐ Non-governmental organizations (NGOs), alias 'advocacy groups' or 'watchdogs', excel at international public relations; their influence extends even to such mundane matters as consumer choice of food.
- ☐ NGOs offer instructive examples in skilled communication, with their: (1) effective use of images, (2) direct appeal to consumers, (3) clear focus and calls to action, (4) creation of coalitions and (5) projection of selfless goodwill.
- ☐ Regional alliances and groupings between nations are increasingly important to practice.
- ☐ In the developing countries there are major impediments, including inaccessible media, geographical and climatic hindrances, inadequate transport, illiteracy and multiple ethnic, linguistic and dialectical differences.
- ☐ Practice there is mainly concerned with public information and educating markets, often involving primary instruction and ancillary explanation and demonstration.

CASE STUDY

COMMUNICATING FOR SUSTAINABLE DEVELOPMENT

Shell Philippines Exploration BV decided from the outset to integrate economic, social and environmental factors into the development of the Malampaya deepwater natural gas project in the Philippines. The basic challenge was to maintain the rich biodiversity while creating a gas industry that will provide 30 per cent of the country's energy requirement, reduce dependency on imported fuel and generate $8–10 billions over two decades in government revenues.

The company consulted with both national agencies and local communities to 'promote a partnership approach based on open dialogue and co-operation.' Social and environmental impact studies were undertaken and a 'social management process' was designed, to develop health, education and employment programmes for local communities, supported by 'strategic partnerships' with 'NGOs and institutions experienced in community mobilization and capacity-building.'

This combination of local dialogue and partnership programmes was judged to be the key to gaining local acceptance of the project and making it a success. 'Early wins' were achieved in new education and health provision, employment and conservation of indigenous flora and fauna. The healthcare advance was obtained through Shell sharing its emergency medical facilities with local people; employment was stimulated through a partnership with the Pilipinas Shell Foundation aimed at stimulating local enterprise.

Recognizing that maintenance of positive relationships with stakeholders will be key to the long-term success of the project, Shell has also established a Sustainable Development Council in the Philippines, to identify issues requiring attention, and is pursuing on-going dialogue and partnership-building both locally and nationally.

Meanwhile in India, Tata Steel is similarly concerned to develop economic, social and environmental conditions, through an ambitious programme that began with 32 villages in 1979 (DTI website, 9.3.03). The company is Asia's first, and India's largest, integrated private sector steel company. It has a long history of CSR initiatives. Through the Tata Steel Rural Development Society (TSRDS), the company is addressing a wide range of issues in over 700 villages local to its diverse operations in the states of Jharkhand and Orissa.

Priority is given to assisting the poorest and most underdeveloped and under privileged areas of the region. Here training is being provided to villagers on methods of multiple crop farming, water management, re-forestation, poultry and animal husbandry. Rapid progress has been achieved and many of the programmes have developed into self-sustaining schemes managed by local communities.

TSRDS also has a number of projects designed to bring about improvements that may be managed by local people trained for the purpose. These relate to education, medicine and sanitation; family planning; the supply of drinking water and irrigation; agriculture, animal husbandry and afforestation; vocational training, rural industries, entrepreneurship and handicrafts.

The Indian Chamber of Commerce and Industry has awarded the Society three times for its outstanding achievements in rural development and it has also been publicly recognized for its service to the severely disabled. Tata Steel is often cited as an example to other companies, nationally and internationally, and through the work of TSRDS it benefits from reduced dependency on it by local communities that have achieved self-sustainable health, education and other schemes.

QUESTIONS

1 What recent political changes may have stimulated the development of public relations and with what likely substantial consequences?

2 Why could sensitivity to cultural differences be 'probably more necessary in public relations than in any other occupation'?
3 What are the likely public relations implications of 'Think global, act local'?
4 When might a 'Common Position' fall victim to communication, and why?
5 What type of public relations is likely to be most appropriate in the developing world and why might that differ from practice in the developed countries?

the occupation of public relations

Size and structure – the person specification – integrated services – image and reputation of public relations – self-regulation – education and training

13.1 size and structure

Just how many people are employed in public relations worldwide is subject to conjecture. It is clear, though, that public relations is widely practiced. For Sriramesh (Sriramesh and Vercic, 2003) the 'significant spurt in global communication' has placed PR people 'at the forefront of managing the relationships among people of varied nations and cultures on behalf of organizations of all types' and 'saddled' public relations educators 'with the awesome responsibility of helping educate future professionals'. This implies burgeoning growth in public relations practice, but how to quantify it?

The well-rounded published estimates of numbers employed suffer from insufficient distinction between those who are practitioners, those who are their support staff and those who are their dedicated specialist suppliers. The picture is further complicated by the varying structures of the occupation in different countries: here the consultancies outnumber the in-house departments; there it is the other way around. Here there are more public relations people employed in the public sector than in the private sector; there it is, again, vice versa. Here is a sizeable voluntary sector employing PR; there a small voluntary sector relies on volunteers to do PR work. And what about the multinational organizations: their proliferation has created many more public relations jobs, sometimes introducing PR to countries where hitherto it has been unknown.

The presence of established individual or corporate membership public relations organizations might be indicative of the scale of practice in that country, but that may be misleading. Seldom do such organizations' members comprise more than a percentage of all practitioners or their firms, and the percentage may be quite modest. The commercial pressures that encourage membership vary from country to country, depending upon local factors such as demand and competition levels. In some countries there is public relations practice, but no representative body or no specialist publication, elsewhere there may be governmental stimulus to or containment of growth in public relations practice. In Italy, for example, public sector communication is formally recognized as a strategic task and every element of the public sector must have three communication departments, for politics, media and public information; in Portugal, a limit is placed on the number of students permitted, although demand for places is several times greater; in Brazil, every practitioner must be a public relations graduate and formally licensed to practise.

Here are some *indicative* figures for several countries in Europe: at the higher end – Austria 100,000; Italy 70,000; the Netherlands 55,000; the UK 50,000; Germany 20,000; France 17,000; at the lower end – Hungary 6,000; Sweden 4,200; Portugal 3,000; Norway 2,500; Greece 1,500; Croatia 1,500. The Swedish Public Relations Association is the second largest such body in Europe (after the UK). But all such figures have to be viewed with caution, not least because public relations is not necessarily a full-time practice, many occupations include a substantial element of public relations but are *not specified as being PR*, and, as has been mentioned, a potentially *confusing array of differing titles* are used to describe the occupation: this latter point applies in many countries.

So it is necessary to recognize that figures may be arrived at by including people who are 'working "in some way" [in PR]' (Moloney, 2000). Added to which, there are a welter of jobs, starting with those of chief executives, that include a *significant element* of public relations. When *they* are included it would be realistic to suppose that there are many more people engaged, either for a living or as *part* of their occupation, in recognizable public relations activities. And to them has to be added the many people who undertake PR on a voluntary basis or their own behalf, in itself a growing trend.

13.2 the person specification

In addition to other marketing communications – advertising, direct marketing, sales promotion and direct sales – public relations is related, by varying degrees, to a *number* of other occupations, owing to either *the nature* of its activities or *its effects.* Marketing consultancy is the most obvious, but the list also includes

▸ Management consultancy,
▸ The law,
▸ Politics,
▸ Diplomacy,
▸ Journalism, and
▸ Broadcasting.

To a lesser extent, there are connections also with occupations that include photography, creative writing, theatre production and sports promotion.

Given this, it might be imagined that the public relations person, certainly the generalist, is at risk of being a 'jack of all trades but master of none'. The early writers did little to counter any such supposition and the qualities they specified were numerous.

EXAMPLE

'To sum up, one needs honesty, integrity, character, intelligence, imagination, ability to write, to speak in public, administrative capacity, a wide general knowledge and a very high ethical standard. Sympathy, understanding, leadership, sound judgement, ideas and courage' (Lloyd, 1963). 'This may sound rather like a religious cult, or some esoteric philosophy, but do not be disheartened.'

More recently the requirements have grown.

EXAMPLE

'Students need an understanding of psychology so that they understand motivation and persuasion; a better background in political science for the understanding of how government functions so that it can be made more responsive to societal needs; an understanding of anthropology so that they understand change and how it takes place and the importance of cultural adaptation; and of sociology so that they are able to more accurately evaluate societal trends and human interaction.' And they also need 'common sense, curiosity, objectivity, logic and clear thinking [which are] perhaps the most important assets of a successful public relations practitioner'.
(Black, 1989)

It *may* be that public relations people meet all of these requirements and many more, but the *greater* probability is that they meet *some* of them very well. So, for instance:

- A public affairs specialist may have a background in law,
- An internationalist in diplomacy,
- A publicist in journalism or sports agency,
- The consumer specialist might have come from elsewhere in marketing and
- A person working in public information may have transferred from the civil service or administration in a major public service.

There are some generally agreed *core skills* needed, regardless of the specific practice circumstances. In no particular order, they include the ability to:

- Listen, and to hear, and to assimilate information
- Write, cogently, to order, in a variety of styles to meet a range of requirements
- Interrelate with people at all social and power levels as circumstances require
- Think and plan with discipline and resource, particularly under pressure.

The third of these is often described as 'knowing how to deal with people' or 'getting on with people', but that might be equally said to be the requirement of the hotel receptionist or any one of many other customer-interface jobs. In public relations it implies *persuasive* skills, either overt or covert. Practitioners deal in impressions, and their encounters are conditioned accordingly. They aim to 'get the best' out of the situation, like most other people, but, unlike most other people, they are rather more accomplished at it.

13.3 integrated services

The formation of large international and global marketing services groups that bring together all marketing communication, including public relations, advertising, direct marketing, sales promotion, design, media buying and Internet, facilitates a complete 'turn-key' service from a single source and enhances prospects for achieving IMC. In the UK and elsewhere, there has been a decline in marketers' reliance on advertising and a corresponding increase in using a broader combination of promotion tools; from advertising typically accounting for around two-thirds of expenditure to it taking about one-third, the balance being spread between the others. Public relations, direct marketing, sales promotion and Internet marketing have all noticeably benefited from this trend.

This integrated approach, however, is not without practical difficulties, since it is not only differing disciplines that are being welded together under one roof.

> One plus one has to equal more than two. For the London office of Weber Shandwick [public relations consultancy, part of the Interpublic Group], this issue is particularly pertinent because the new outfit has nine separate units. But referring clients to sister practices isn't straightforward. Managers generally earn their bonuses by maximizing revenue for their own unit, so it's often in their interests to hang on to business, even if it would be better handled by a sister practice, or even another agency in the group. (*Financial Times*, 12 March 2002)

It appears that confidence about *personal rewards* and sharing clients with *known colleagues* is the key to making these large combines work.

13.4 image and reputation of public relations

Without doubt public relations practitioners do have problems with their collective image and reputation. Why is it that public relations may, as often it does, attract such approbium once its practice begins to develop significantly? Practitioners are well aware: some are in denial, Moloney (2000) thinks they are the senior practitioners, while others simply think it of no real consequence, at least to them. 'These conviction PR people [senior practitioners] are not faced down by low reputation; they reject the stereotypes of film and fiction ... However [with the majority of practitioners] reaction to low reputation is usually shrugged off.'

Not everyone dismisses it, though; some offer explanations, typically on a strictly non-attributable basis. For example, a senior consultant in New Zealand, on practitioner status there: 'I think generally they are perceived as being purveyors of snake oil and hokum. It is partly the glass and glitz ... in terms of corporate launches ... and also public relations is very much associated with some of the more distressing or more unpopular government policies ... I think public relations as a whole has become discredited and identified with those things in the popular mind' (Leitch, 1994, quoted by Motion and Leitch, 2003).

It is surely deeply ironic that the occupational group most concerned with the fostering and maintaining of sound reputation can have such a very poor one in many countries. This is by no means universal, though. In those countries where practice is well developed, the image and reputation of public relations is *variable* and by no means universally poor. For instance, public relations is a respected occupation in Austria, Germany and the Netherlands; in Norway it is intrinsic to formal government information policy; in Italy it has legal status in the public sector. However: 'In many countries it is even "not done" to talk about public relations (especially the northern, the north-western and Central European countries)' (van Ruler and Vercic, 2004). There is likely to be a correlation between the extent of this avoidance of the term and the local severity and scale of criticism published by journalists.

It seems reasonable to assume that *all* practitioners regret the circumstances, wish very much that they were collectively held in higher regard (which would probably further raise their earnings, which, in any event, are well into the middle range for similar occupations), hope that their various bodies can do more to relieve the situation and prefer meanwhile to concentrate on the job in hand, doing it both effectively and creditably. They may reason that in an increasingly questioning and critical environment there is a degree of inevitability about this, particularly for any activity that is at the *forefront of cultural change and influence.*

13.5 self-regulation

Professional bodies and trade associations generally suffer from, sometimes severe, criticism by those they seek to represent, and those in public relations are no exception, but that does not excuse any perceived inadequacies in their performance. One sure test is the number of people who are entitled to join but *prefer not to do so.* Those who opt to remain outside membership present problems for those who seek to represent them, in their attempts to gain greater control and thereby **enforce their ethical codes**. The member who is found wanting may be ejected, but, if the market *pays little regard to that membership,* this sanction represents no hazard.

This is a worldwide problem for public relations. In the USA, for instance, a former president of the PRSA resigned his membership to avoid enquiry into alleged breaking of the ethics code. In the UK there have been similar cases, famously including one involving purchasing editorial. Motion and Leitch (2003) cite a very public case in New Zealand involving the Deputy Prime Minister: the practitioner had filmed him without permission while he gave evidence at a judicial enquiry he had instigated into large scale tax avoidance by leading companies. In these and similar cases the member simply quits, thereby avoiding an enquiry into allegations against him or her, and continues practising regardless. For so long as practitioners can make a living without having to observe the relevant codes, these are vulnerable to being disregarded. Such abuses are fuel for the critics of public relations as a whole.

So self-regulation is difficult, however well intentioned. And in most countries there is no formal bar to practice such as a state-sponsored certification, on the grounds that public relations practitioners do not place people at risk in consequence of incompetence, comparable to, for instance, accountancy, law and medicine. There is, after all, a battery of legislation that applies to different aspects of practice. By not having *all* practitioners or *all* consultancies in membership, all types of membership bodies have a problem in asserting their credential to be *wholly* representative, and this again makes it more difficult for them to promote public relations as effectively as some of their members may wish.

These problems may be abated gradually through the growing web of supranational bodies and the onward growth of public relations practice around the world. Practitioners who remain outside the various bodies may come by stages to recognize that observance of the *broad intent*, if not the letter, of the codes, which heavily overlap, is *within their interests*, since an **orderly market** for their labour and services is mutually beneficial to all practitioners.

13.6 education and training

By some accounts public relations is a 'graduate profession', by which it is meant that only university graduates need apply. There is undoubtedly **the search for status** underlying this assertion, the supposition being that since learned professions have long since come to insist on graduate-only intake, public relations may be aligned with them, or repositioned, by following suit.

In **higher education** public relations is now widely taught, noticeably in the USA. Similarly, throughout Europe and elsewhere, there is a growth in public relations education at this level. In consequence, there is a growing incidence of recruitment directly from the universities and colleges, as is common in other occupations. However, many experienced practitioners came into public relations via other routes and brought with them their knowledge and skills gained there, which their new employers, and in turn, in most cases, their clients, deemed both relevant and of value. This admixture of background skills, experience, understanding and contacts continues to be recognized outside academia as the *sinew* of public relations, what gives it relevance and depth, the surer feel for contemporary thinking, purposeful outlook and effectiveness.

In addition to public relations-specific undergraduate and graduate programmes, public relations is widely taught, often as a third year option, across a widening range of other degree courses, notably in business, marketing, law and journalism studies. The widespread presence of public relations taught at this level over the past 20 years does not appear, however, to have much changed *the nature of demand* for public relations expertise, except perhaps to add **greater expectation**, in *some* quarters, of those levels of tactical skill and resources expected of graduates. Graduate practitioners benefit from knowing about the theory and from acquiring the various personal disciplines necessary for gaining an advanced specialist education, but in the event of any subsequent mismatch between theory and practice the latter often tends to prevail.

For their part, some academics endeavour to resist pressures from practitioner bodies to turn academic study into what they perceive to be job training, and they complain of friction between themselves and practitioners. For instance, 'some of the material has ... been presented at conferences – with varying responses, some of which have been quite hostile. While this has not always been a pleasant experience, we firmly believe, journalistically, that if people appear not to want you to say something, then there is all the more reason to say it' (L'Etang and Pieczka, 1996).

At the **further education** level, there are numerous practice-based diplomas, some postgraduate. These are delivered through day and evening courses, at college and within the workplace, and by distance learning. The diploma qualifications are steadily acquiring material value for those who hold them, but a surprisingly large proportion of public relations practitioners appear to continue to rely upon qualification by experience, usually based on a degree and/or qualification from another area, such as law, management, political science, sociology, psychology and anthropology. Many practitioners who are reluctant to engage in further study tend to emphasize that practice is 'about having plenty of common sense', which is a substantial understatement, as they well know. The broad range of knowledge and skills required contradicts this simplification.

For all practitioners there is also **continuous professional development** (CPD) to provide the means to obtain information and knowledge of contemporary issues and conditions of practice-based relevance. There are three categories of such schemes in the UK:

▸ Some are *statutory*, and if not adhered to members lose their right to work in that occupation: this draconian approach applies, for example, to medical doctors
▸ Some are run by *chartered* bodies and, although CPD is not a legal requirement, members must comply in order to retain their individual chartered status
▸ And others are *voluntary* schemes, where it is hoped that members will want the status appellation on offer in exchange for doing CPD.

It is unlikely that any prudent practitioner would wish *not* to pursue some form of CPD, and many do so anyway, without the need of schemes that offer formal inducements. The problems that arise with CPD schemes are more likely to relate to exactly *what* does or does not qualify: firstly, promoters specify the number of hours they want to be spent on this or that activity, say reading or attending lectures, but these allocations can be over-prescriptive for the individual if his or her needs are not similarly balanced; secondly, the choice of 'qualifying events' and other content can be at variance with what the individual requires. Despite these potential deficiencies, non-statutory CPD schemes serve an excellent overall purpose of emphasizing the importance of 'lifelong learning' in a relatively structured and relevant manner outside the routine of daily practice.

CHECKLIST

- ☐ Many more people are likely to be engaged, for a living or as part of their occupation, in recognizable public relations activities than is indicated by the published estimates, which in any case are subject to qualification.
- ☐ Many more people undertake public relations on a voluntary basis or on their own behalf.
- ☐ Core PR skills are the ability to: (1) listen, hear and assimilate; (2) write cogently to order in various styles; (3) interrelate at all social and power levels; and (4) think and plan with discipline and resource, particularly under pressure.
- ☐ The larger marketing services groups that include public relations, formed to offer total integration of services to clients, depend upon managers having confidence about their personal reward prospects and sharing clients with known colleagues.
- ☐ The emergence of highly specialized public relations practices that serve very small niche markets is likely to continue and probably accelerate.
- ☐ Practice self-regulation, however well intentioned, may be weak where a substantial number of practitioners are not in institute or association membership and far from all employers and clients insist on either one or both.
- ☐ There is a growing number of undergraduate and graduate degree courses in public relations internationally.
- ☐ UK graduate entry to practice may be via a public relations degree, a degree in a related subject that includes an element of public relations, or a degree in a relevant field (without a PR element).
- ☐ Mature entry to public relations may be via a variety of other occupations such as journalism.
- ☐ Formal training and qualification in public relations may include one or more of numerous public relations diplomas.
- ☐ Practitioner members of public relations bodies are encouraged to gain formal recognition of their continuous practice development (CPD), by fulfilling on-going training specifications.

CASE STUDY

RAISING DESIGN PROVISION FOR BLIND PEOPLE

When the UK charity Action for Blind People launched the country's first ever hotel designed and built for use by blind and partially sighted people, it embarked upon a media relations campaign with the central objective to further demonstrate and encourage the adoption of best practice in adapting public space for use by people who are visually impaired.

The charity already operated three other leisure hotels around the UK, all converted for use by blind and partially sighted visitors, but the £4 million Russell Hotel overlooking the seafront public gardens at the south coast resort of Bognor Regis was the first to be purpose built. The new hotel was a joint venture with another charity, the Guide Dogs for the Blind Association, which also contributed funding for the redevelopment and expansion.

The opening of this new hotel in 2002 provided a valuable opportunity to press the case for best practice with specialist professional and technical magazines read by opinion formers, including specifiers such as architects. It also provided the means to give a valuable boost to awareness of this niche player among hotels through the travel and tourism pages of the national press and to launch the charity's hotels business regionally, through the regional media.

A core message to be communicated was that blind and partially sighted people expect hotel facilities that, in the words of the architect, 'really aren't that different from what you would expect in any hotel'. So the 40 new bedrooms have all the latest features and superior discrete bathrooms, the catering is to a high standard and available in a choice of locations and there is a heated indoor swimming pool and an instructor-attended gymnasium.

The differences are subtle and may not be that noticeable to most fully sighted people. They include, for example, enlarged corridors and bedrooms, big enough to also accommodate guide dogs, textured carpets that guide visitors to reception and plenty of handrails. These design features have been implanted so carefully that they complement the attractive interior designs. In addition, staff members are specially trained to understand the specific needs of their guests and there are also voluntary sighted guides to assist.

Consumer research had provided the architects with many pointers to requirements and left them convinced that if these can be met in a hotel they can be satisfied also in the design of any other facility or amenity for people with a range of disabilities. The strength of demand indicates that there are niche market opportunities for owners and developers who invest in quality adaptation. Occupancy levels in the chain are typically 75–90 per cent throughout the year, well above hotel industry norms, and capacity reservations for Christmas are reached a year or more in advance.

Armed with such a strong story, Action for Blind People secured valuable coverage for the opening in three national daily newspapers and heavy media reporting in London and the southeast of England, on television and radio and in the press. A few local newspapers in the midlands also reported on the new hotel.

But the most prized coverage came more discreetly, from most of the specialist press read by opinion formers. These titles deal with architecture, design, interior design, catering, leisure, the voluntary sector and the visually impaired. Often with relatively small circulations, such publications carried weight where it was wanted, prompting positive and prompt feedback requests for more information from new contacts, such as hotel owners, property developers, public authorities and their various advisers and representatives.

These specialist newspapers and magazines, often also published electronically, account for around half of the UK's entire 4400 or so publications. They provide the means, as occurred here, for public relations to demonstrate three of its prime strengths: explain complex arguments and issues; educate markets; and communicate with opinion formers, who, incidentally, may not be that readily identifiable by other means.

Like many other charities, Action for Blind People is no stranger to success in media relations, counted in terms of favourability and quantity, and it also aims for outcomes that satisfy underlying objectives based on its core purposes. The corporate mission is to inspire change and create opportunities to enable blind and partially sighted people to have equal voice and equal choice. To that end it provides housing, information and employment development services through five centres and three supported employment factories, in addition to its specialist hotels business.

The charity had no campaign budget for this project, other than staff time. The return includes substantially strengthened prospects for securing wider adoption of best practice and generation of possibilities for furthering the hotels business. And the media coverage has persisted, through national reporting under leisure, travel and tourism, where lead times extend over months; each item provides valuable ongoing support for little if any additional effort.

QUESTIONS

1 Why might public relations people be licensed to practice?
2 What might be the 'perfect' academic or vocational background for a non-PR graduate practitioner, and why?
3 Why might public relations consultancy remain permanently fragmented, and how?
4 Why might senior practitioners deny that PR is held in low repute, and with what possible consequences?
5 Why might CPD be no laughing matter?

futures

The Internet – media law – editorial standards – globalization – practice development

14.1 the Internet

The 'global village' may very well describe the Internet, but Marshall McLuhan memorably coined the term when thinking of television, which he regarded not as a visual but an 'aural and tactile' medium that was 'thrusting the new television generation back into what he termed a "tribal" frame of mind' (Wolfe, 2000). McLuhan gained recognition as a world authority following his establishment of an extracurricular seminar on popular culture at the University of Toronto, where he taught English literature, and the publication of his first book, *The Mechanical Bride* (1951). More than that, the name of Marshall McLuhan entered into popular folklore, synonymous with modern communication, but he died in 1980, aged 69, over a decade before the advent of the Internet.

Not that McLuhan got there first. Pierre Teilhard de Chardin (1881–1955) (usually referred to as Teilhard, pronounced TAY-yar), who died in 1955, had the 'stunning prescience' to conceive of mankind being united through technological advance 'by a single "nervous system for humanity," a "living membrane," a single "stupendous thinking machine," a unified consciousness that would cover the earth like "a thinking skin".'

Both men, by their differing language, had foretold the Internet, which is that web or skin that connects humanity, potentially shrinking the earth to a scale of apparent familiarity and certainty that would have confounded previous generations. It is an advance that ranks with some of the greatest historic developments, including the invention of printing, which also revolutionized communication. But in the 16th century, as now with the Web, only relatively few people benefited.

It took centuries for the advantages of printing to reach most people, and still there is substantial illiteracy in the world: there are some people in the advanced countries that cannot read and write. So, how long is it likely to take for the Internet to truly 'cover' the earth, even given our much faster modern timescales? And will everyone necessarily *want* access; much less gain it? On the assumption that the value of the Internet is beyond question, may there be developing a new '**information poor**', a form of *disadvantaged underclass*? A 1999 report by the UN Development Programme thought so. It pointed out that:

▶ 80 per cent of the language used was English, although less than 10 per cent of the world spoke it, and
▶ At that time a personal computer cost the equal of a month's salary in the USA but eight years' average income in Bangladesh.

The report identified a ***direct correlation* between differing levels of income, education and Internet access**. 'When people in these two worlds [those with and those without access] live and compete side by side, the advantage of being connected will overpower the marginal and impoverished, cutting off their voices and concerns from the global conversation.' In other words, ***not* to be using the Internet is *to be marginalized*.** That is quite a threat, and measures to foster universal access without reference to personal circumstances must surely meet with general approval, most particularly from public relations practitioners. But, as with all media, what about *content*? What is it that 'information poor' people are at risk of missing, and *could they live without it*? What knowledge and conversation are they being cut out of? In short, is the Internet equal to the aspirations held out for it? Can a 'single seamless Web' deliver against the promise? 'The simple truth is that the Web, the Internet, does one thing. It speeds up the retrieval and dissemination of information. ... That one thing the Internet does, and only that. All the rest is Digibabble' (Wolfe, 2000).

A key feature of the Internet, from a public relations perspective, is that it facilitates ***direct, unmediated, communication***, and most future public relations effort doubtless will focus on developing ever more innovative ways of achieving this. It is also a **very cost-effective channel**, not only for sending messages out but *receiving them back as well*: the Internet is a democratizing tool that tests organizational claims to wanting *genuine* two-way symmetrical dialogue. In other words, **for the organization it can be a great leveller**.

One prominent UK public relations consultant probably spoke for many when he complained of the Internet: 'Give a bunch of paranoiacs access to cyberspace and their imagined grievances become "fact" in the twinkling of a megahertz. ... The reputation managers of the future will need to understand more about activist psychology, to be fast and perceptive in their early monitoring of the internet – and know how to exploit it. They must understand that "perception is reality" and will need to learn new, more subtle psychologies to regain public confidence' (*Financial Times*, 2 October 2001).

The widely-held assumption that the Internet is some place where normal conventions and rules of conduct do not apply is likely to be formally challenged more frequently.

A recent decision in the Australian high court established that **those publishing material on the Internet could face legal liability anywhere in the world**. Joseph Gutnick, an Australian, brought a libel action against Dow Jones concerning allegations of money laundering and tax evasion published in its *Barron's* magazine. The magazine was published in hard copy in the USA, but in Australia, where Gutnick chose to sue, it was available only on the Internet.

Dow Jones, an American company, sought to obtain a hearing in the USA, not only for greater convenience but because US law is far more favourable to defendants in libel actions. It argued that there had been no publication in Australia because the Internet server was in New Jersey, USA, and the magazine was almost entirely directed at an American readership. It also argued that 'it would be potentially catastrophic if an Internet publisher were to be held to publish material wherever it could be received, since it could be held liable according to the laws of any country'; being aware of every country's laws was impractical (Tench, 2002).

But to no avail. 'Defamation at its heart is about damage to reputation. Since the reputation of Gutnick was damaged wherever the defamatory material was received ... an action could be brought in any such place... a special ad hoc exemption could not be invented for one technology.' And as to Australia not being a sensible place for the hearing, it was likely that the subject matter would have a predominantly Australian element. The decision is not binding elsewhere, but is 'likely to be seen as highly persuasive' throughout the Commonwealth.

There is a further element to this: the 'developing law' whereby *a defence of qualified privilege* may be available to a publisher in a libel action, 'even where the allegations complained of are wrong, if [the publisher] behaved responsibly in publishing them'. In a separate earlier case, a Spanish news agency succeeded with qualified privilege in England, partly because back home it would have had that defence available to it against any action for defamation brought in Spain. The law of the defendant's country was imported into the law of the English court.

So on the one hand the claimant can say that the matter in question *is* published, thanks to the Internet, as if it had been handed out in hard copy on the local streets, and no matter where the computer is located from whence it came. On the other hand, the publisher may say having to know and understand the law everywhere is impractical and unreasonable. Public relations practitioners will need to follow these developments closely.

Similarly, the law is likely to continue evolving with regard to **issues of privacy**: throughout the world such matters are seldom *not* being aired in public, particularly in and about countries with poor human rights records. In Europe, the Convention on Human Rights' article eight provides a right to respect for private life, while article 10 gives rights to free expression. Questions therefore arise as to which should prevail in any given set of circumstances. The European Court of Human Rights has adopted a 'generous approach' to deciding what private information can or cannot be published. The test, according to a 2005 decision to grant an injunction preventing publication of parts of a biography, appears to be: is there a *strong public interest justification* for publishing this or that snippet of private information? This case was influenced by two important cases in 2004, both concerning well-known people in the public eye. In the second, the European Court held that frequent publication of photos of Princess Caroline of Monaco taken *in public places* was an infringement. Furthermore: 'unless a report relating to the detail of a public figure's private life contributes to a public or political debate its publication is unlikely to be justified' (Evans, 2006).

Similarly, questions about the *transferability of a right to commercial confidentiality* are likely to continue unabated, presently owing to the long-running case based on the wedding of actors Michael Douglas and Catherine Zeta-Jones, who granted *OK!* magazine the exclusive right to take and publish photographs of their New York hotel happy event. Rival *Hello* magazine managed to obtain, and then publish, photographs too, thus 'spoiling' the exclusive: does *OK!* have an enforceable commercial confidence claim against *Hello?* Significantly, if it *does*, 'this could be used to argue for the creation of an image right, of value not just to the celebrity but also to a third party'. This area of law also needs watching by practitioners, most particularly by those that have routine dealings with 'public figures', in all their many guises, celebrated or otherwise.

14.2 editorial standards

The lead presenter of the BBC's main breakfast-time radio news and current affairs programme in the UK survived in post following an outburst in which he championed **editorial standards**, complaining that the BBC had substituted entertainment for news, gimmickry for facts, emotionalism for direct reporting. Soft, cosy journalism intruded everywhere because it was assumed that the listener preferred news pre-digested rather than delivered straight. 'If we all spent half as much time worrying about writing good, simple English free of linguistic pomposities, jargon and journalese as we do messing about with the latest wizardry, the viewer would be better served.' To which he might have added the irritating laboured over-use of currently fashionable words and the easy repetition of clichés.

There is a widespread public perception that in both television and radio news *unadulterated information* is at a premium and that much of what is presented comes through a mist or hue of emotional interpretation. Viewers and listeners who can remember when 'news was news' resent this 'lowest common denominator spoon-feeding' approach and research indicates a substantial fall in audiences for television and radio news. The people quitting are reckoned to be generally the better educated and wealthier. This may not much concern politicians, who deal in numbers: they usually count people in their millions first before attending to their opinions. But it should concern public relations practitioners, particularly those that are alternatively known as **'spin doctors'**, for the broadcast media are fundamental to their communication programmes.

News and current affairs coverage in *newspapers* has for long been suspect, in the view of the more thoughtful. Now that many newspapers provide news 'with attitude' designed to most closely match their markets, public relations must take the *fullest account* of these differences of interpretation, editorial preferences and underlying policies. These include ageism, an important consideration for the practitioner: the glorification of youth in order to attract younger readers, because advertisers demand them, can, and does, alienate older people and drive many of them away, including the wealthy. The media may well start rediscovering 'the oldies', and segmenting them even more finely into discrete audiences, as life expectancy steadily improves everywhere.

What seems to be sure amidst this turmoil of change is that most newspapers the world over are intent on positioning themselves in relation to their target markets, much as if they were *any other type of product*, and that has **consequences for news and current affairs**, which has to *fit their positioning policies*. Since news is largely about politics in some shape or form, this is a reality that all spin doctors, in particular, also have to fully take into account. They need to address the subtleties of editorial worldview that result in, for example, a recent French headline: 'We are all Americans now'. This trend is likely to *intensify* as markets for readers and advertisers become increasingly *competitive and fragmented*.

Perhaps not surprisingly, therefore, 'news' is often not news at all but propaganda, and of that there is currently no shortage. The *greatest* casualty of propaganda, it may be argued, is not truth but **trust**: without that, how readily *can* viewers, listeners and readers **believe the veracity of the news**? This too has implications for public relations practice *as a whole*. This debasement of the news and current affairs coinage can *contaminate other areas of media*, as well as reducing the **credibility**, and therefore **value**, of the media as **communication intermediaries** between a public relations source and its public. It is likely to hasten the greater use by public relations practitioners of all *direct channels* of communication, such as the Internet, and a *corresponding reduction* in use of the mass media for relaying 'serious' content.

14.3 globalization

Historically, as we have seen, public relations, in North America and in Europe, has been at least as much about **notions of democracy** as about marketing, so much so that there is 'the public relations obsession with democracy' (L'Etang, 1996) and 'a nervous preoccupation with the perils of democracy that has chaperoned the growth of corporate public relations for nearly a century' (Ewen, 1996). The PR links between democracy and commerce are strong. Since the early 1990s public relations has played a full part in the development of 'McWorld', which 'celebrates market ideology with its commitment to the privatization of all things public and the commercialization of all things private. Consequently it insists on total freedom from government interference in the global economic sector (laissez-faire)' (Barber, 2001).

And McWorld has not been obtaining a universally good press. Every time political leaders gather in numbers, 100,000 or more protestors, the 'children of McWorld', turn up to demonstrate and seek as much media coverage as they can contrive. 'They understand ... that globalization's existing architecture breeds anarchy, nihilism and violence.' Globalization's 'freedom from interference – the rule of private power over public goods – is another name for anarchy. And terror is merely one of the contagious diseases that anarchy spawns.' A major economic consequence of this is that people in the developed countries benefit from free markets in capital, labour and goods, while those in the developing countries are 'largely unprotected'.

In this globalized world, communication is instantaneous and the importance of geographical location is thereby reduced. So, it is argued, the **'market paradigm'** has within it the means to spawn economic abundance and misery *with equal facility*, through 'what sociologists call a "collective consciousness"' that is shared by all the principal players, the senior managers of the multinational and global companies, their investors, brokers, analysts, bankers and so forth (*Financial Times*, 10 November 2001). When a few members of that community feel bullish or depressed *it can rapidly become infectious.* In other words, a tidal wave of sentiment sweeps across all who are informed.

The financial markets of the world, notably those in New York, London and Tokyo, watch each other very closely, continually making adjustments accordingly. Companies and *other types of organizations are at it too*, observing each other and individually trying to decide what future actions are likely to be in their best interests. However, 'the aggregate results of many individually rational decisions are often far from rational for all the agents considered as a group'. For instance, universal cost-cutting reduces aggregate demand for the output of the cost-cutters, thereby increasing the risk of recession. Globalization *of communication*, needed for this new market-driven world, brings public relations back to its democracy-orientated roots *even as it takes a more central and critical role in commerce.* For 'the process of globalization has transferred so much decision-making power to individuals and companies that the collective irrationality of their separate decisions may prove much harder to counter through government action than in the past'.

Where does that leave the public relations 'obsession with democracy'? Some practitioners regard themselves as the consciences of their employing organizations. That implies a **mediation** role for public relations, one that is gaining recognition among administrators, civil servants and managers of other organizational functions. Those for whom dialogue and rhetoric are central to their occupation should be ideally suited to the task of reconciliation, compromise and normalization of relationships, provided, of course, that they command the necessary respect. In the coming years it is likely that ever more practitioners will find themselves much of the time trying to reconcile differences between those they represent, typically their employers, and those publics who challenge them, acting as the go-betweens, working to secure mutually beneficial solutions that both parties can live with. '**Activism**' is on the increase, and it will continue to grow as competition intensifies in a multitude of dimensions: practitioners will need to take an increasingly holistic view of the politico-economic ebb-and-flow of McWorld. They should not fear activism so much as be prepared for it, always remembering that publics formed around contentious issues are just as likely to be *for* something as *against* it.

14.4 practice development

There are several key strands that are likely to greatly influence the future content of public relations practice.

Tugging at the strings of both democratization and globalization is **culture**; or, more precisely, the multitude of cultural differences and nuances referred to in Chapter 12. In this supposedly multicultural world, in which strenuous efforts are made to homogenize peoples, to serve a variety of interests, there are growing signs of cultural fight-back: many people rejoice in the differences, and growing numbers of them are trying to find ways of perpetuating, even increasing, these sometimes rather subtle variations. How well, or otherwise, practitioners manage to handle this is likely to have a substantial impact on their collective futures. New PR functions and ways of tackling differing situations, some quite novel, are evolving, and, although much public relations practice is undertaken in an organizational context, increasingly public relations is accessible to and undertaken by *any* group of people or *any* person: *that* is a trend too.

Next up is **trust**, that delicate plant that needs such careful nurturing. Practitioners know the ingredients of trust; it's the practicalities involved in building and maintaining it that are often so very testing; and have to be hard worked at, based on accurate readings of sometimes opaque situations. Grunig *et al.* (2002) define trust as being 'one party's level of confidence in and willingness to open oneself to the other party', which is certainly the acid test where the relationship is thought by one or both parties to call for it (it may not). They identify three dimensions of trust, 'a complicated concept': integrity, dependability and competence. These cut both ways, of course, applicable to both sender and receiver. Trust, it is often said, has to be *earned*; it is probably as frequently remarked that trust is in short supply in materially advanced societies. Practitioners will need to successfully address this growing problem more wholeheartedly in the coming years, because growing awareness, knowledge and communication often render people *less* trusting, and widespread *distrust* can regress progress and exacerbate otherwise solvable problems.

Trust facilitates and underpins **relationships**. The familiar exchange relationships of marketing are not necessarily enough for relationship management purposes; just having feedback, better though it is than none, may not satisfy either side. What may be needed goes further, to become a 'communal relationship', where

> both parties provide benefits to the other because they are concerned for the welfare of the other – even when they get nothing in return. The role of public relations [practitioners] is to convince management that it also needs communal relationships with publics such as employees, the community, and the media. Public relations professionals add value to an organization when they develop communal relationships with all publics affected by organizational behaviors – not just those who give the organization something in return. Communal relationships are important if organizations are to be socially responsible and to add value to society as well as to client organizations.

These deeper relationships must have certain characteristics, in descending order of importance: *mutual control*, the extent to which each side can agree on 'who has rightful power to influence one another' and has 'some degree of control over the other'; *trust*; *commitment*, because the effort is deemed worthwhile; and *satisfaction*, thanks to positive expectations being 'reinforced'. These qualities set the two-way symmetrical practice model in context; gritty reality intrudes, both sides facing each other as relative equals based not on some ideal scenario but practical dynamics. These high quality relationships are likely to become increasingly the aim of practice, but achieving them requires much more than mere 'lip service' to a worthy-sounding concept.

Ethics are becoming increasingly critical to how public relations practice is likely to develop further. That is because practitioners 'will need to change from one of merely wielding self-serving influence, crafting communications, and researching publics. Ethical practice for the field of public relations will require practitioners to be facilitators of dialogue and listeners as much as speakers. Strong leadership will be needed from high-profile organizations that exemplify best practices in opening their own practices and decision-making to public criticism' (Day *et al.*, 2001). On that latter point, they may not have much of a choice. And as for the modern fashion among some practitioners to prefer 'doing the talk' instead of leaving that to those they represent, undoubtedly more listening by them is going to be increasingly desirable, not to say absolutely necessary.

The ethical practice standards, so relentlessly criticized, will improve, albeit gradually, reflecting the pace of advance in the recognized status of practitioners. Ethical practice has to be *demonstrably* evident for sustaining any credible claims to be the conscience or 'ethics officer' of any organization, group or, for that matter, person. It is unlikely that any practitioner will opt for *either* the deontological, rulebook, path, favoured by the membership bodies, *or* the teleological, consequences, route – because all practice has consequences for someone, be that a public or society as a whole. For most, it is not an either/or choice; as mentioned in Chapter 6, they tend to refer to theories drawn on both, often relying quite heavily on the fundamentals instilled during childhood.

The larger challenge is likely to be in deciding how to deal with *differing* ethical standards encountered *internationally*. There is a multitude of public relations practice codes, promulgated around the globe, and several writers have argued for a *universal* ethics code that would provide some firm, common unequivocal standard that publics may expect practitioners everywhere to abide by. Draft codes have been proffered, presumably by way of illustration only, and existing codes have been criticized, the inference being that they insufficiently address two-way symmetrical communication. Kruckeberg, according to Taylor (2001), assigns practitioners the 'task of serving as cultural and ethical interpreters for corporations in the future of globalization', for which doubtless one single code might be very handy. Although, reported by Day *et al.* (2001), he thought this single ethics code would have to be 'slightly tempered to adjust to the moral taste of each country'. And there's the rub: for moral and social standards vary, as do business practices. Accordingly, 'one should keep intact the ethical guidelines that one considers to be important'. Clearly, practitioners are going to have to address these ethical dilemmas increasingly over the coming years, in their daily practice quite as much as in solemn council, but a modus operandi that satisfies everyone seems highly improbable.

Crises and **change** together comprise another key strand. *Crises* are, ironically, rather good for practitioners; they tend to raise their status among members of the dominant coalition, often quite rapidly. The heat of battle can be another great leveller; it is the moment when calm heads and clear thinking are needed, and the public relations practitioner may be one of the few who is able to claim convincingly to have both. This probably owes more than a little to careful planning and forethought, perhaps also to reliance on some well-nurtured relationships. That crises, of all varieties, are on the increase, and this can be expected to continue, is therefore a feature of life not entirely to be disheartened about, from a practitioner's perspective, although crises in relationships are an obvious exception. In any event, crises management, in all its guises, now plays a large part in practice, and will continue to do so.

EXAMPLE

London is to have a vast new football stadium, but the foreign contractors building the scheme are a year late and £400m over budget. 'Mission impossible?' asked *The Guardian* of the completion of London's new Wembley Stadium, under the page heading Crisis Management. 'Unlike marketing a fizzy pop brand or chocolate bar, the challenge of working on Wembley is not about getting the press coverage. "Wembley can get you a headline, whether it's good or bad, just because it's Wembley," says Gregory [marketing and commercial director of Wembley Stadium]. When you are marketing an FMCG [fast-moving consumer goods] product, the aim is just to get people to buy it, but for Wembley it is about making the fans buy in to the idea of the national stadium. As such, the task so far has been more about PR – getting journalists and stakeholders on board – than about creating nifty advertising campaigns to raise awareness.'

Success with selling 'hospitality packages' had created 'another PR job – passing the message to football fans that the new stadium was not all about big business buying up all the good seats and ripping out the soul of what many fans see as the "Home of Football"... Strategy-wise, he [Gregory] says, they have always focused on being honest and realistic with the messages going out, be they to fans, the media or the Club Wembley seat-holders, who had paid up with the expectation of being at the first cup final at the stadium [which in May 2006 had to be held elsewhere]'.

(*The Guardian*, 22 January 2007)

Crises can be, often are, generated by *change*, and coping with change is the principal preoccupation of many practitioners. Much turbulence, as discussed in Chapter 4, is a condition of life, and practitioners can thrive on it, provided it comes in what they consider to be manageable quantities. In reality, *they* are the source of much of it, because they are themselves *agents of change*. This is reflected in how the practice of public relations itself evolves: 'As in the United States, Russia, and China, wherever public relations is practiced, it most likely will go through the following stages: an initial wave of media manipulation, a more substantial stage of public information, a readjustment period as the practice takes root, and a final stage of sustained growth' (McElreath *et al.*, 2001).

Because crises are in abundance, many of them 'unknown unknowns' owing to natural disasters or ever more interactions between people and their organizations, the public relations practitioner is obliged to identify with increased vigilance and effort any opportunities to anticipate, minimize or avoid crises. A proven avoidance method is to adopt the 'communitarian' outlook, allocating more time to striving for quality relationships, not only with the neighbours, although CCI, which, in its limited community relations origins, has not always had as much attention as it deserved, but also in the wider sense as well. Corporate effort at this is guided by the concept of corporate social responsibility, CSR, but increasingly practitioners are likely to recognize even deeper reasons and greater urgency for wanting to build more relationships worth having with more publics, quicker.

A final key strand is **media access**, which was identified in Chapter 12, together with ownership and outreach, as one of the three primary factors to be borne in mind when considering the current state of local media development. There are several pertinent aspects, including:

- Many of the more developed parts of the world are inhabited by the most **media-literate** generation ever, and that understanding of the media will continue to grow exponentially.
- Increasingly, people at large are participating in **creating media content**; witness the rise of 'reality' television and the growth in media buying of amateur video 'footage' of events: both are relatively inexpensive and plentiful.
- The growth in Internet '**blogging**' and the appetite for **cyberspace conversation** that promises an alternative view of 'reality'; a feeling of empowerment against authority, commerce, 'dark forces'.

Practitioners are not alone in having to think about the likely future course of these developments, but how they choose to *relate* to them could well influence strongly the future direction of much else connected to their practice.

All these strands – culture, trust, relationships, ethics, crises, change and media access – are shaping the nature of practice of public relations, and will do so in the foreseeable future. Practitioners are good at coping, and they have enviable reserves of energy and resilience, but they are beset by detractors, notably journalists, some with hostile agendas, many with laboriously well-rehearsed objections. They are often pilloried for allegedly unethical behaviour and low morals by vested interests that know full well such deficiencies are widespread among many other occupations, where often they go largely unnoticed. Much of what PR people do is determined, sometimes dictated, by their employers and clients, yet the so-called 'dirty tricks' are held to be entirely of their own making. In short, the poor reputation of public relations is less than *entirely* self-earned; to a substantial degree it is 'planted' by a variety of interests, which practitioners appear to have continuing difficulty in countering.

There is much talk of graduation by the public relations function from 'doing' less to 'thinking' more, from technical performance to strategic calculation. Clearly this is well under way, and a world desperately in need of professional communicators beckons, surely in itself sufficient encouragement to sustain the weary traveller, tired of being assigned mostly 'low-end' tasks and cast in roles that invariably underestimate the scope and potential of this maturing discipline. There are some compelling, and increasingly obvious, reasons for public relations to be taken seriously and for the function to be admitted to the 'dominant coalition' of organizational managers: not least because not a little public relations practice, across all its dimensions, might be regarded *dispassionately* as being positively beneficial to all society.

CHECKLIST

- ☐ Internet news content is likely to become one of substantial and increasing relevance to public relations, especially once major publications become only available electronically.
- ☐ The Internet facilitates direct, unmediated communication; ever more innovative PR techniques are likely to be developed in order to optimize this benefit.
- ☐ The Internet is a democratizing tool that tests organizational claims to wanting genuine two-way dialogue, being a very cost-effective channel to use. Public relations will educate its masters about this new reality and seek ways to benefit from it.
- ☐ Increasingly those who publish on the Internet will face the risk of legal liability anywhere in the world, since defamatory material is now held to be published, and therefore actionable, wherever it is receivable. This will rein in the informality of the net and affect the content and presentation of public relations messages.
- ☐ Of particular relevance to practitioners is the developing law on qualified privilege in libel, privacy under human rights legislation and the exercise of a right of commercial confidentiality in the media.

- Poor editorial standards, news 'with attitude' and segmentation and targeting of media markets affect media credibility and status as communication intermediaries, and increases the need for news and current affairs to be made to fit the subtleties of editorial bias.
- Propaganda, presented as news and current affairs, can contaminate other areas of the media and reduce the credibility and value of the media to practitioners. Its growing incidence is likely to hasten their greater use of all direct channels and lessen dependence upon the media for relaying 'serious' content.
- As public relations continues to help develop McWorld, it may use its global communication skills to play a pivotal role in seeking reconciliation between the 'market paradigm' and democracy, in which it has a deeply embedded historic interest.
- Future development of practice will be heavily influenced by how practitioners deal with issues relating to culture, trust, relationships, ethics, crises, change and media access.

QUESTIONS

1 Why might the Internet be a great leveller and a great unleveller?
2 Why might ageism in editorial policy be an asset or an obstacle to communication?
3 What may be the results of changing news and current affairs reporting standards?
4 What are the communication implications of the 'collective consciousness'?
5 When might public relations be a powerful force for society as a whole, and how?

references

Barber, B.R. (2001) 'Ballots versus Bullets', *Financial Times* (20 October)

Bentele, G. (2004) 'New Perspectives of Public Relations in Europe', in van Ruler, B. and Vercic, D. (eds) *Public Relations and Communication Management in Europe*, Mouton de Gruyter

Bernays, E.L. (1928) *Propaganda*, Liveright

Bernays, E.L. (1955) *Engineering of Consent*, Liveright

Bernays, E.L. (1961) *Crystallizing Public Opinion*, Liveright

Black, S. (1989) *Introduction to Public Relations*, Modino Press

Black, S. and Davis, A. (2002) *Public Relations*, 3rd edn, Old Bailey Press

Bland, M. (1995) 'Strategic Crisis Management', in Hart, N.A. (ed.) *Strategic Public Relations*, Macmillan

Bowman, P. and Ellis, N. (1977) *Manual of Public Relations*, 2nd edn, Heinemann

Burkart, R. (2004) 'Consensus-orientated Public Relations (COPR): A Concept for Planning and Evaluation of Public Relations', in van Ruler, B. and Vercic, D. (eds) *Public Relations and Communication Management in Europe*, Mouton de Gruyter

Campbell, A., Devine, M. and Young, D. (1990) *A Sense of Mission*, Economist Books

Cartwright, R. (2001) *Mastering the Business Environment*, Palgrave Macmillan

Chen, I. and Culbertson, H.M. (2003) 'Public Relations in Mainland China: An Adolescent With Growing Pains', in Sriramesh, K. and Vercic, D. (eds) *The Global Public Relations Handbook*, Lawrence Erlbaum

Curtin, P.A. and Boynton, L.A. (2001) 'Ethics in Public Relations: Theory and Practice', in Heath, R.L. (ed.) *Handbook of Public Relations*, Sage Publications

Cutlip, S.M., Center, A.H. and Broom, G.M. (1985) *Effective Public Relations*, 6th edn, Prentice Hall

Davenport, T.H. and Beck, J.C. (2001) *The Attention Economy*, Harvard Business School Press

Day, K.D., Dong, Q. and Robins, C. (2001) 'Public Relations Ethics: An Overview and Discussion of Issues for the 21st Century', in Heath, R.L. (ed.) *Handbook of Public Relations*, Sage Publications

de Bono, E. (1978) *Opportunities*, Associated Business Programmes

DeSanto, B. and Petherbridge, J. (2002) 'BBC in America', in Moss, D. and DeSanto, B. (eds) *Public Relations Cases – International Perspectives*, Routledge

Doyle, P. (2000) *Value-Based Marketing*, Wiley

Dozier, L.D. (2002) 'Oklahoma City and Kerr-McGee – Managing Internal Communication During an External Crisis', in Moss, D. and DeSanto, B. (eds) *Public Relations Cases – International Perspectives*, Routledge

Drucker, P.F. (1980) *Managing in Turbulent Times*, Heinemann

Ehling, W.P. (1992) 'Estimating the value of Public Relations', in Grunig, J.E. (ed.) *Excellence in Public Relations*, Lawrence Erlbaum

Ehling, W.P., White, J. and Grunig, J.E. (1992) 'Public Relations and Marketing Practices', in Grunig, J.E. (ed.) *Excellence in Public Relations*, Lawrence Erlbaum

Evans, C. (2006) 'Appeals test scope of privacy', *The Guardian* (4 December)

Ewen, S. (1996) *PR! A Social History of Spin*, Basic Books

Fawkes, J. (2001) 'What is Public Relations?', in Theaker, A. (ed.) *The Public Relations Handbook*, Routledge

Fifield, P. (1992) *Marketing Strategy*, Butterworth-Heinemann

Goubert, P., tr. Ultee, M. (1991) *The Course of French History*, Routledge

Grunig, J. (2001) 'Two-Way Symmetrical Public Relations – Past, Present, and Future', in Heath, R.L. (ed.) *Handbook of Public Relations*, Sage Publications

Grunig, J.E. and Grunig L.A. (1992) 'Models of Public Relations and Communication', in Grunig, J.E. (ed.), *Excellence in Public Relations*, Lawrence Erlbaum

Grunig, J.E. and Hunt, T. (1984) *Managing Public Relations*, Holt, Rinehart and Winston

Grunig, J.E. and Repper, F.C. (1992) 'Strategic Management, Publics, and Issues', in Grunig, J.E. (ed.) *Excellence in Public Relations*, Lawrence Erlbaum

Grunig, J.E. and White, J. (1992) 'The Effect of Worldviews on Public Relations Theory and Practice', in Grunig, J.E. (ed.) *Excellence in Public Relations*, Lawrence Erlbaum

Grunig, L.A. (1992) 'Power in the Public Relations Department', in Grunig, J.E. (ed.) *Excellence in Public Relations*, Lawrence Erlbaum

Grunig, L.A., Grunig J.E. and Dozier, D.M. (2002) *Excellent Public Relations and Effective Organizations – A Study of Communication Management in Three Countries*, Lawrence Erlbaum

Grunig, L.A., Grunig, J.E. and Ehling, W.P. (1992) 'What is an Effective Organization?', in Grunig, J.E. (ed.) *Excellence in Public Relations*, Lawrence Erlbaum

Haig, M. (2000) *e-pr The Essential Guide to Public Relations on the Internet*, Kogan Page

Handy, C. (1989) *The Age of Unreason*, Century Hutchinson

Hansen-Horn, T. (2001) 'Labor and Public Relations: The Unwritten Roles', in Heath, R.L. (ed.) *Handbook of Public Relations*, Sage Publications

Harrison, S. (2000) *Public Relations: An Introduction*, 2nd edn, Thomson Learning

Hart, N.A. (1995) 'Marketing Communications', in Hart, N.A. (ed.) *Strategic Public Relations*, Palgrave Macmillan

Heath, R.L. (1992) 'The Wrangle in the Marketplace: A Rhetorical Perspective of Public Relations', in Toth, E.L. and Heath, RL. (eds) *Rhetorical and Critical Approaches to Public Relations*, Lawrence Erlbaum

Heath, R.L. (2001a) 'A Rhetorical Enactment Rationale for Public Relations', in Heath, R.L. (ed.) *Handbook of Public Relations*, Sage Publications

Heath, R.L. (2001b) (ed.) *Handbook of Public Relations*, Sage Publications

Henderson, T. and Williams, J. (2002) 'Shell: Managing a Corporate Reputation Globally', in Moss, D. and DeSanto, B. (eds) *Public Relations Cases – InternationalPerspectives*, Routledge

Hiebert, R.E. (1966) *Courtier to the Crowd*, Iowa State University Press

Holmstrom, S. (2004) 'The Reflective Paradigm of Public Relations', in van Ruler, B. and Vercic, D. (eds) *Public Relations and Communication Management in Europe*, Mouton de Gruyter

Hutton, W. (2007) *The Writing on the Wall*, Little, Brown

Ind, N. (1995) 'The Practice of Corporate Identity', in Hart, N.A. (ed.) *Strategic Public Relations*, Palgrave Macmillan

Inoue, T. (2003) 'An Overview of Public Relations in Japan and the Self-Correction Concept', in Sriramesh, K. and Vercic, D. (eds) *The Global Public Relations Handbook*, Lawrence Erlbaum

Jefkins, F. and Yadin, D. (1998) *Public Relations*, 5th edn, FT/Prentice Hall

Johnson, G. and Scholes, K. (1999) *Exploring Corporate Strategy*, Prentice Hall

Kidder, R. and Bloom, S. (2001) 'Ethical Fitness in Today's Business Environment', in Moon, C. and Bonny, C. (eds) *Business Ethics*, Economist Books

Kitchen, P.J. (1997a) 'The Evolution of Public Relations: Principles and Practice', in Kitchen, P.J. (ed.) *Public Relations: Principles and Practice*, Thomson

Kitchen, P.J. (1997b) 'The Interaction between Public Relations and Marketing', in Kitchen, P.J. (ed.) *Public Relations: Principles and Practice*, Thomson

Kitchen. P.J. and Papasolomou, I. (1997) 'The Emergence of Marketing PR', in Kitchen, P.J. (ed.) *Public Relations: Principles and Practice*, Thomson

Kotler, P. (1991) *Marketing Management*, 7th edn, Prentice Hall

Kunczik, M. (2003) 'Transnational Public Relations by Foreign Governments', in Sriramesh, K. and Vercic, D. (eds) *The Global Public Relations Handbook*, Lawrence Erlbaum

Lambert, R. (2002) *The Lambert Challenge*, Business in the Community

Lancaster, G. and Massingham, L. (1988) *Essentials of Marketing*, McGraw-Hill

L'Etang, J. (1996) 'Public Relations as Diplomacy', in L'Etang, J. and Pieczka, M. (eds) *Critical Perspectives in Public Relations*, International Thomson

L'Etang, J. and Pieczka, M. (1996) 'Introduction', in L'Etang, J. and Pieczka, M. (eds) *Critical Perspectives in Public Relations*, International Thomson

Lloyd, H. (1963) *Public Relations*, The English Universities Press

Mason, L (2002), unpublished Public Relations masters dissertation

McCorkell, G. (1997) *Direct and Database Marketing*, Kogan Page

McDonald, M.H.B. (1989) *Marketing Plans*, 2nd edn, Heinemann

McElreath, M., Chen, N., Azarova, L. and Shadrova, V. (2001) 'The Development of Public Relations in China, Russia and the United States', in Heath, R.L. (ed.) *Handbook of Public Relations*, Sage Publications

McNair, B. (1996) 'Performance in Politics and the Politics of Performance', in L'Etang, J. and Pieczka, M. (eds) *Critical Perspectives in Public Relations*, International Thomson

Miller, D. and Schlesinger, P. (2001) 'The Changing Shape of Public Relations in the European Union', in Heath, R.L. (ed.) *Handbook of Public Relations*, Sage Publications

Moloney, K. (2000) *Rethinking Public Relations – The Spin and the Substance*, Routledge

Moss Kanter, R. (1984) *The Change Masters*, Allen & Unwin

Motion, J and Leitch, S. (2003) 'New Zealand Perspectives on Public Relations', in Sriramesh, K. and Vercic, D. (eds) *The Global Public Relations Handbook*, Lawrence Erlbaum

Newman, W. (1995) 'Community Relations', in Hart, N.A. (ed.) *Strategic Public Relations*, Palgrave Macmillan

Oliver, S. (2001) *Public Relations Strategy*, Kogan Page

Pearson, R. (1992) 'Perspectives on Public Relations History', in Toth, E.L. and Heath, R.L. (eds) *Rhetorical and Critical Approaches to Public Relations*, Lawrence Erlbaum

Peters, T. (1987) *Thriving on Chaos*, Alfred A. Knopf

Pieczka, M. (1996) 'Paradigms, Systems Theory and Public Relations', in L'Etang, J. and Pieczka, M. (eds) *Critical Perspectives in Public Relations*, International Thomson

Porter, M.E. (1980) *Competitive Strategy*, Free Press

Portway, S. (1995) 'Corporate Social Responsibility: The Case for Active Stakeholder Relationship Management', in Hart, N.A. (ed.) *Strategic Public Relations*, Palgrave Macmillan

Quirke, B. (1995) 'Internal Communication', in Hart, N.A. (ed.) *Strategic Public Relations*, Palgrave Macmillan

Raupp, J. (2004) 'The Public Sphere as Central Concept of Public Relations', in van Ruler, B. and Vercic, D. (eds) *Public Relations and Communication Management in Europe*, Mouton de Gruyter

Regester, M. and Larkin, J. (1997) 'Issue and Crisis Management: Fail-safe Procedures', in Kitchen, P.J. (ed.) *Public Relations: Principles and Practice*, International Thomson

Shaw, C. (2002) 'TV News with Attitude', *The Times* (29 November)

Silver, J. (2002) 'Newcastle? It's a city in Scotland', *The Times* (5 July)

Smith, D. (1995) 'Parliamentary and European Union Relations', in Hart, N.A. (ed.) *Strategic Public Relations*, Palgrave Macmillan

Smith, P.R. (1999) *Great Answers to Tough Marketing Questions*, Kogan Page

Somerville, I. (2001) 'Public Relations, Politics and the Media', in Theaker, A. (ed.) *The Public Relations Handbook*, Routledge

Sriramesh, K. and Vercic, D. (2003) 'A Theoretical Framework for Global Public Relations Research and Practice', in Sriramesh, K. and Vercic, D. (eds) *The Global Public Relations Handbook*, Lawrence Erlbaum.

Starck, K. and Kruckeberg, D. (2001) 'Public Relations and Community: A Reconstructed Theory Revisited', in Heath, R.L. (ed.) *Handbook of Public Relations*, Sage Publications

Stewart-Hunt, C. (2003) conversation with author (5 March)

Stone, N. (1995) *The Management and Practice of Public Relations*, Palgrave Macmillan

Taylor, M. (2001) 'International Public Relations: Opportunities and Challenges for the 21st Century', in Heath, R.L. (ed.) *Handbook of Public Relations*, Sage Publications

Tench, D. (2002) 'Long arm of the Internet – Web Publishers Face Worldwide Legal Liability', *The Guardian* (16 December)

Theaker, A. (2001a) 'Corporate Community Involvement', in Theaker, A. (ed.) *The Public Relations Handbook*, Routledge

Theaker, A. (2001b) 'Research and Evaluation – PR grows up?', in Theaker, A. (ed.) *The Public Relations Handbook*, Routledge

Theaker, A. (2001c) 'Media Relations', in Theaker, A. (ed.) *The Public Relations Handbook*, Routledge

Theaker, A. (2001d) 'Future Challenges for PR', in Theaker, A. (ed.) *The Public Relations Handbook*, Routledge

Theaker, A. (2001e) 'Public Affairs and Issues Management', in Theaker, A. (ed.) *The Public Relations Handbook*, Routledge

van Riel, C.B.M. (1995) *Principles of Corporate Communication*, Prentice Hall

van Ruler, B. (2003) 'Public Relations in the Polder: The Case of the Netherlands', in Sriramesh, K. and Vercic, D. (eds) *The Global Public Relations Handbook*, Lawrence Erlbaum

van Ruler, B. and Vercic, D. (2004) 'Overview of Public Relations and Communication Management in Europe', in van Ruler, B. and Vercic, D. (eds) *Public Relations and Communication Management in Europe*, Mouton de Gruyter

Varey, R. (1997a) 'External Public Relations Activities', in Kitchen, P.J. (ed.) *Public Relations: Principles and Practice*, International Thomson

Varey, R. (1997b) 'Public Relations: The external publics context', in Kitchen, P.J. (ed.) *Public Relations: Principles and Practice*, International Thomson

White, J. (1991) *How to Understand and Manage Public Relations – A Jargon-Free Guide to Public Relations Management*, Business Books (Random Century)

White, J. and Dozier, D.M. (1992) 'Public Relations and Management Decision Making', in Grunig, J.E. (ed.) *Excellence in Public Relations*, Lawrence Erlbaum

White, J. and Mazur, L. (1995) *Strategic Communications Management – Making Public Relations Work*, Addison-Wesley

Wolfe, T. (2000) 'Digibabble, Fairy Dust, and the Human Anthill', in Wolfe, T. (ed.) *Hooking Up*, Random House

Wootliff, J. and Deri, C. 'NGOs: The New Super Brands', *Corporate Reputation Review* (Summer 2001)

index

NEWBURY COLLEGE LRC